TOWARD
A
REASONABLE
SOCIETY

TOWARD
A
REASONABLE
SOCIETY

The Values of Industrial Civilization

BY C. E. AYRES

UNIVERSITY OF TEXAS PRESS
AUSTIN AND LONDON

International Standard Book Number 0-292-78026-5
Library of Congress Catalog Card Number 61-12911 7-2-79
Copyright © 1961 by C. E. Ayres
Printed in the United States of America

First Paperback Printing, 1978

ACKNOWLEDGMENTS

TWO CHAPTERS OF THIS BOOK have appeared in slightly different form in the pages of *The Southwest Review,* and one in the pages of *The Texas Quarterly;* I am grateful to the editors of these publications for permission to reprint these sections.

For many years my colleagues in the Department of Economics of The University of Texas have been extraordinarily tolerant of my extra-territorial gropings, and the Administration of the University has granted me "research leave" to complete work on a certain portion of this book—for all of which I am extremely grateful.

I wish to thank Mrs. Margaret Petmecky, of Austin, Texas, for the patience and skill with which she transformed my scrambled manuscript into a beautiful typescript.

My greatest debt, not only for the writing of this book but for everything I have accomplished, is too deep to be absolved by any words.

C.E.A.

CONTENTS

TOWARD
A
REASONABLE
SOCIETY

PART ONE

INTRODUCTION

IN A SENSE I AM WRITING THIS BOOK for my own satisfaction. But the concern which has prompted it is shared, in one way or another, by all thoughtful people. Is industrial society at a dead end, or rushing down a steep place into oblivion, as so many people seem to fear? Committed as we are to the life of reason, are we therefore, as both scientists and theologians seem to think, spiritually crippled? Is it true that the modern mind, nourished on science, is therefore spiritually sterile? Are all our efforts to improve our lot short-circuited by the impossibility of knowing in what direction improvement lies? My answer to these questions is No, and I am writing this book to try to justify that answer.

The moral confusion and vacuity of our age is not a consequence merely of easy living, or of loss of nerve induced by the Soviet challenge and the horror of nuclear war. The seat of the trouble lies deeper than that. We talk glibly of the possibility of civilization's being wiped out by a nuclear holocaust, but our real fear is that it may not be worth saving. Our misgivings arise not from the uncertainties of the future but from the moral sterility of the present. This is clearly evidenced by the anxiety with which in recent years we have been seeking to restate and reaffirm our national purpose. Obviously anyone who has to inquire the way has already lost it.

This moral confusion by which we are now plagued is a consequence of the forces by which modern civilization has been shaped. Ours is a secular civilization. Very gradually it has become so over a period of several centuries during which science and technology together have reshaped not only the physical setting of our lives but our mental furniture as well: our whole conception of the universe and of ourselves. Our sense of values has not escaped this process, and here at least the result has been disastrous.

5

Our ancestors believed their values—all their convictions with regard to what is good and what is bad, what is right and what is wrong—to be absolute, unchanging, and eternal. They held this belief, as all human societies have always done, because they believed that all values derive from a Higher Power. But with the advancement of knowledge it became obvious that the values so held by various peoples differ widely. Thus the modern mind has been forced to the conclusion that values are absolute only for the peoples who hold them. That is to say, all values are relative.

Such is the moral vacuum into which we seem to have been projected by the irresistible momentum of science and technology.

But there is a hidden assumption here, the assumption that only two possibilities are conceivable. We must assume either that values are absolute, as simple peoples naively suppose, or that they are relative to the various societies in which they prevail. But are these the only possibilities? Is it not possible that values derive their meaning and their sanction not only from tribal deities, and not merely from parochial beliefs, but—at least in considerable part—from the human adventure itself, from the quest for knowledge and ever more knowledge, and from the never-ending struggle to harness the forces of nature to human use? Are there not in all societies two sets of values, sacred and profane, so to speak; and is it not the former which differ so widely from people to people, whereas the latter are the same for all?

Perhaps this is the point at which I should confess that what has occasioned the writing of this book is not compassion for suffering humanity so much as the excitement of discovery. Moreover, as so often happens, the discovery has been made in economics, quite a different area from the one in which it now seems applicable and significant.

As a student of economics I have long been in revolt against the dogma of the classical tradition. According to the Grand Tradition of Adam Smith, Ricardo, Malthus, James and John Stuart Mill, Stanley Jevons, Alfred Marshall, and all their many and distinguished collaborators and associates, all the vast congeries of activities by which mankind gets its living are organized and directed by the market, by the price system. No one directs these activities. There is no pattern, no master plan. But, in the immortal words of Adam Smith, all men are led by the "guiding hand" of self-interest to make what is for each his most appropriate contribution to "an end which is no part of his intention," that is, the common good. As everyone knows, the classic formulation of this amazing theory by Adam Smith was a (well deserved) attack on the "mercantilist system" of chartered monopolies. But it was also, and most significantly, "An Inquiry into the Nature and Causes of the Wealth of Nations," which was increasing so rapidly even in the eighteenth century as to challenge explanation; and as everyone also knows, this "simple and obvious" theory, as Adam Smith described it, attributes the whole of the vast transformation which European society was even then undergoing to what is now called "the profit motive."

But can we really attribute the whole of this vast process to the activities of merchants? How then shall we explain the existence of merchants? Does a society invent, discover, or devise all sorts of products in order to have something to exchange? Or is it the discovery or invention of a variety of products that prompts people to exchange; and if so, what is it that prompts people to discover and invent? I do not mean to suggest that these are the only questions which are raised in restless minds by the market theory of the economy, but only that it is questions such as these which, once they are raised, direct our thoughts to the process, whatever it is, of which modern science and technology are (or as I would prefer to say, is) the supreme manifestation.

Modern science and modern technology are of course inseparable, and, no less obviously, modern science is built on the foundation of ancient science and technology, modern technology on the foundation of ancient technology and science. What the circumstances were that led to a scientific-technological "explosion" in the modern Western world is a question that need not be pursued at this particular point. What is essential is the continuity of the process by which tools and know-how have developed through the ages. All peoples have participated in this process. For various reasons some have been more "creative" than others. But all have been tool users, and all have been possessed of some modicum of the knowledge that is inseparable from the use of tools.

Furthermore, we have learned to identify early cultures by the degree of sophistication of their tools. Thus we speak of the culture of the Old Stone Age, that of the New Stone Age, the Age of Bronze, and then of Iron. Moreover, no one argues that the tools of the Old Stone Age may have been better than those of the Bronze Age. Some anthropologists protest against the use of the word "primitive" to describe either early or extant cultures, arguing that the people we stigmatize as primitive may be as happy as we, or even happier. They may be kind, gentle, and in character altogether admirable. So they may. But as regards their tools and their knowledge of materials and of the forces and processes of nature, nobody mistakes or questions the meaning of the term "primitive."

In short, we have here a process in which all peoples have participated, which has the same meaning for all, and which therefore constitutes a standard of valuation for all. Everyone knows what *better* and *worse* mean with reference to tools, and all peoples judge such "betterness" and "worseness" by the same standard. These values are the same for all.

It may be argued that although these may indeed be values, they are not moral values. They are merely judgments of efficiency. This is a very important matter which will therefore be discussed at length in later chapters. But let me say this now. We should not misunderstand efficiency. It is sometimes said that dictatorship is more efficient than democracy, but that democracy is "better." But in such a statement the meaning of efficiency must be sharply limited. Otherwise the statement is a flat contradiction in terms. We might say that the Supreme Soviet of the U.S.S.R. is "more efficient" than the Congress of the U.S.A., meaning only that it does whatever it does in a hurry and adjourns *sine die,* whereas our Congress argues interminably and often seems to adjourn eventually without having got anything done. But this is of course a very narrow conception of efficiency. Suppose it could be shown that a certain kind, gentle, and altogether amiable people were in process of starving to death, or being eaten one at a time by prowling cannibals, and that the causes of their decline were inseparable from these admirable qualities. Would we then without qualification judge those qualities so admirable? Unless democracy is more efficient than other systems in the long run when all the chips are down, it is not only doomed—it is a sad mistake and altogether

8

bad. Democracy is better than other systems for one reason only: in the long run (which is the only thing that counts) it is more efficient. Why this is so is the crux of the matter, and will therefore be discussed at some length later. At this point I wish only to register the conviction that operational values *are* moral values, embracing as they do all human interests and all walks of life.

It is true that operational values—those which occur in the context of science and technology—are not absolute, since they are by definition confined to human experience. But is this a fault? The supposition that values transcend human experience is a manifestation of the animism which suffuses the tribal legends and beliefs of all peoples. That is, it imputes human qualities to the nonhuman universe. But such suppositions and the values which are supposed to go along with them are relative to the societies which hold them. The real issue is not whether values transcend human experience. We know that supposedly absolute values not only do not transcend human experience; they do not even transcend the beliefs of the peoples who imagine them. The real issue is whether that is all—whether there is any standard of value which has the same meaning for all peoples. That is the question to which our present knowledge of the unbroken continuity of what we now call science and technology throughout the life process of mankind now gives an affirmative answer.

The present book is the result of a long-growing realization that such is the case—that the inherent dynamism of the technological process has more than economic significance. It is the answer, or the source from which we can seek answers, to the enigmas by which mankind is perpetually haunted.

PART TWO

CHAPTER II

REASON AND UNREASON

I

INDUSTRIAL SOCIETY IS THE MOST SUCCESSFUL way of life mankind has ever known. Quite literally, we have never "had it so good." People eat better, sleep better, live in more comfortable dwellings, get around more and in far greater comfort, keep in better repair, and—notwithstanding all the manifold dangers of the industrial way of life—live longer than men have ever done before.

Nor is ours a barren physical existence. People are better informed than ever before. Not only do they listen to radio and watch television; they read more books, see more pictures, and hear more music than has any previous generation. We are now living in a golden age of scientific enlightenment and artistic achievement.

There is no question about any of this, since the facts are obvious to all. Nevertheless it is highly unfashionable to say so. For there are fashions in ideas, no less than in clothes, cars, pictures, and music; and today it is the intellectual fashion to regard industrial man as all dressed up with nowhere to go.

There are reasons for this, of course, as there are for all fashions. Fashions are set by fashion designers, and in the case of ideas the designers are scholars and intellectuals: the people who write books and the people who read books. These people are not frivolous. They are both sincere and knowledgeable. But knowledge is never complete. We advance step by step, and our perspectives change from step to step. It was once the fashion to suppose that the earth is flat, and as a matter of fact at the time this supposition was generally held people had very good reasons for thinking so. On the supposition that the earth is round it seemed reasonable to suppose that if one walked, or rode a horse, far enough one would begin to go downhill; indeed, the water of the oceans would

13

obviously run down such a hill; and since neither actually occurred, the only reasonable inference seemed to be that the earth is flat. In short, this idea prevailed before anything was known about gravitation.

The intellectual fashions of the twentieth century are not fundamentally different. It is generally supposed by twentieth-century scholars and their readers that values derive from, or reflect, the irrational sentiments with which all of us are imbued in infancy and childhood and to which we are held throughout life by our susceptibility to community approval and disapproval. Conversely, it is supposed that values and scientific knowledge have nothing to do with each other; that science is morally sterile, or "value-free" (*wertfrei*: it is much more convincing in German); and that all the technological apparatus of modern life is "in itself" neither good nor bad but only a sort of neutral grey. It is as though one could not say that food is good without knowing who is eating it and whether he is a sinner or a saint.

As was the case with the flat-earth theory, there are reasons for the prevalence of such ideas. In the chapters that follow I shall try to show how these ideas have flowed from very important and relatively recent discoveries. Indeed, within certain definite limits they are true, just as the flatness of the earth is true within the limits of ordinary townsite surveying.

But the important thing about limits is to recognize them and to go beyond them. In the last few generations we have been learning a great deal about the importance of sentiments and attitudes and community traditions in all human life. But we have also begun to learn something of the forces and processes that have brought about in Western civilization a vast scientific-technological revolution that is now spreading throughout the world. As we are beginning to see, the force that has produced this vast upheaval is a continuation of the effort in which mankind has always been engaged: the effort, as we often say, to control the environment. That is a bad way of saying it, not only because it is grandiose (we never "control" the forces of nature but only manipulate them), but chiefly because it suggests that man and nature are divisible, whereas the obvious fact is that man is a part of nature. It would be much better to say, as the great British archeologist

Verne Gordon-Childe did in the title of one of his books: man makes himself. But even here the important word is "makes." Doing-and-knowing, science-and-technology, is the real life process of mankind. This is the process from which modern industrial civilization has resulted, and it is the process in terms of which men have always judged things good and bad, and actions right and wrong.

Science and technology are not *wertfrei*. On the contrary, this life process is the matrix from which all genuine values—as distinguished from sentimental fancies—derive their meaning. It is quite true, as philosophers and moralists have always said, that values, ideals, and aspirations have meaning and take effect only if they transcend the puny lives of the individual men and women who adhere to them. But this does not mean that such transcendence must be supernatural. The life process of mankind transcends the individual existence of every man and woman. There is no more final answer to anyone who, caught in a fateful conflict between duty and immediate self-interest, cries out, "Why should I do this?" than the answer, "Because you are a man; because if mankind generally did otherwise, there would be no human race."

Precisely this, indeed, is Kant's "categorical imperative": so act that your every act is consistent with the life process of mankind. The universe may be supremely indifferent to the fate of the human race, if indeed it means anything to impute a human attitude, indifference, to the universe at large. Human values do not derive from the universe at large. They are not quite as extensive as all that. Nor do they derive only from the sentiments and superstitions of particular tribes. They are vastly more extensive than that. Genuine values derive from the life process of mankind, a process to which every man is committed by virtue of already being a man.

This is the process to which we owe industrial society, and we can therefore say with certainty and precision that the industrial way of life is good—and not only good: the best that man has ever known. This is true not only of the affluence which the industrial revolution has brought. Ours is also the most reasonable society mankind has ever known; for the revolution in doing has also been a revolution in knowing. We have more knowledge, and knowledge counts for more today, than has been true of any previous generation or society. Superstition still persists. Irrational attitudes and sentiments persist. But we are beginning to know them for what they are, and we are beginning to see that no society has ever been wholly irrational; and this is a further step toward a reasonable society.

2

Thus the message of this book is a simple one, so simple that it is almost universally rejected. It is that the major decisions of life and society are made by the same process by which one decides what to eat for breakfast—that is, by a simple calculation of cause and effect.

In calling this process a simple one I do not mean that it may not be extremely complex. Obviously important decisions are recognized as such because a great deal is involved. My point is rather that there is nothing mysterious or occult about even the weightiest decision. What is involved is the same sort of thing, however many times multiplied, that is involved in deciding what to eat for breakfast.

We relinquish the sense of mystery only with the greatest reluctance. When I was a small boy I had a playmate who lived across the street. He breakfasted on coffee and doughnuts. This seemed to me a most attractive way to start the day, most especially perhaps because it was forbidden to me. In spite of all our pleading we children were never allowed to drink coffee or tea, and although we sometimes had doughnuts as a great treat, that never happened at breakfast, the *pièce de résistance* of which was always oatmeal or a similar cooked cereal. The reason for this decision, so we were told, was that coffee and doughnuts are "bad" for small children, whereas oatmeal (though admittedly not very palatable) is "good." Thus even at breakfast we found ourselves in the presence of a Great Mystery.

Trivial as it is, this incident illustrates a common human failing that contributes to the perpetuation of our sense of mystery. How much easier and nicer it is to terminate a disagreement about a picture or a poem by saying, "Well, I like it," than it would be to enter into an extended discussion the effect of which might well be to expose our neighbor's ignorance! To do my mother justice, I am quite sure that she had none but dietary considerations in mind when she forbade us to breakfast on doughnuts and coffee. But it would have been impossible for her to go into an extended analysis of comparative dietetics without making it quite clear to us children that our neighbors were ignorant fools, and this for many reasons she thought it better not to do. Hence she terminated the argument with a dogmatic "good" and "bad."

Far more important, of course, is the sense of mystery we all inherit from our aboriginal past. How persistent it is! Even in this age of scientific enlightenment and even among the best educated people it lingers in the form of "unanswerable questions." Why are we here? What is the meaning of it all? Whither are we going? It is because such questions as these are almost universally supposed to lie at the back of the major decisions of life and society that most people reject obvious and simple explanations.

But why do we ask such questions? Where do they come from? Not from any actual situation by which any individual or any community is confronted! In actual fact, as we all know, major decisions are indeed made by the same process by which we decide what to eat for breakfast. The key word of this proposition is process. Breakfast is neither the beginning nor the end of human existence, and neither is any decision by which anybody is ever confronted. All decisions are made in situations which occur in the midst of life. They are part of a process which is already going on and will continue in some fashion whatever the decision. A breakfast is always an incident in the life of a person of a certain age and state of health. Always that person is engaged in a certain occupation which makes certain demands, and always what is "good" for such a person in such a situation he determines, as do all of us—more or less wisely, to be sure—on the basis of the incident in question and the setting in which it occurs; and all this is true of all decisions.

I am not saying that this is how we should make decisions. This is how we do make decisions, and have always done so. This is what "good" and "bad" do mean. Such meanings always have reference to an on-going process, the life process of mankind: a process that has already been going on for an indefinitely long time when the situation in question arises and one that will continue thereafter and will be affected by the decision that is made.

This process is real, and in this sense mystery questions such as "Is life worth while?" are unreal and meaningless. As a matter of logic they belong in the same class as the famous conundrum about the irresistible force and the immovable obstacle. No such collision ever occurs or could conceivably do so. Margaret Fuller is said to have declared that she accepted the universe, and Thomas Carlyle is said to have remarked, "Egad, she'd better!" But in fact no one is ever called upon to decide whether to accept the universe or not, and no one is ever called upon to decide whether the existence of the human species is "a good thing" or not. No one could possibly do so, since the term "good" has clear and definite meaning only with reference to the on-going life process of mankind.

Why, then, do we ask such questions? Why do such enigmas haunt us? As I have already suggested, the answer is that we inherit them from our superstitious past. Even after we have left behind all specific and recognizable superstitions we continue to suffer from an aching void. We feel that we must have something to "take their place." It is quite true that knowledge can never take the place of superstition. Why should it? And what, after all, is the role of superstition? This is an interesting and important question which therefore I shall try to explore in a later chapter. At this point, however, the bare fact must suffice.

3

As we now know, all the cultures of all the peoples of the world have been riddled with fantasies, and these fantasies have had a very great emotional impact upon the peoples who have entertained them. Tribal beliefs and tribal codes of behavior have always gone together. Thus all human beings have always been emotionally conditioned to observe various taboos and obey various commandments. The blush of shame and smirk of self-satisfaction begin in infancy and continue throughout life as responses to our elders' "Naughty! Naughty!" or their pat on the head.

Since these experiences are common to all mankind, reflective people have always been aware of them to some extent. But our knowledge has been vastly increased within the past two or three generations by systematic investigation, especially in the fields of anthropology and psychiatry. Whereas the practices of "heathen" peoples used to be regarded as fantastic and "beastly" aberrations of "human nature," recent investigation has established the functional significance even of the oddest beliefs and most repulsive ceremonies. In every case fuller knowledge of the culture in question shows that the whole life system of the people under investigation depends on the scrupulous observance of the practice in question. For example, an African tribe makes a practice of filing the front teeth of their young men to a sharp point. This is an extremely painful and (to us) disfiguring operation which (so far as we can see) serves no useful purpose. But to the people of this tribe, only by this practice can young men qualify to take their places in society as adults, and only this practice can establish the unity of the tribe.

Meantime we have learned from the pioneers of modern psychiatry that emotional responses which are established in early childhood—even in infancy—often stay with us throughout life. Thus a child may be conditioned to endure pain without flinching, and so prepared for the eventual filing of his teeth, while at the same time he may be conditioned to regard any man whose teeth are unfiled with fear and even horror. Or he may be conditioned to regard women as his natural servitors, hewers of wood and drawers of water, by nature lacking those higher powers of ratiocination by which men are ennobled.

Moreover, both sets of scholars have recognized the bearing of their discoveries on each other. Anthropologists have recognized the significance of emotional conditioning for the transmission of cultural practices from generation to generation, and many of them have therefore made a point of studying psychiatry; and from the first the pioneers of modern psychiatry—and most notably the greatest pioneer of all, Sigmund Freud—have seen the clear manifestations of psychopathology in the myths and rituals of ancient cultures. Clearly these two lines of investigation support and amplify each other.

Thus we can take it as scientifically established that the sense of mystery to which I have referred derives from our cultural past. It persists by a sort of cultural inertia, being "internalized" through the process of emotional conditioning to which each individual is inevitably subjected. That it is still going on is a matter of common observation. We no longer file the teeth of adolescent boys. But any young man who had never used a razor or submitted to the barber's shears would have a hard time "adjusting" to the requirements of "civilized" society—that is, to the conventions now prevalent.

The question is: What does this mean? Granted that irrationality persists, does this mean that it must do so—that otherwise human life, or organized society (which is the same thing), is impossible? Strangely enough, this is the conclusion to which mid-twentieth–century social science has somehow or other come. Nobody has proved that man, or society, is essentially irrational. Indeed, that would be impossible, since such is not the case. Instead, our ultimate irrationality has come to be taken for granted. Carried along by several more or less distinct but converging currents, contemporary social theorists have drifted into a sort of anti-intellectualism.

Not only is this a false position; it is one of very great danger to the whole of Western culture, as I shall try to show a little later. Indeed, it is this danger which motivates this book. But in order to understand this extraordinary situation it is necessary to see how the social thinking of our time has drifted in such a direction.

4

One anti-intellectual current has seemed to flow from the very idea of values. In the effort to understand the beliefs and practices and social systems of peoples seemingly very different from ourselves, investigators have begun, as I have already suggested, by recognizing the functional significance of even the weirdest beliefs and most revolting practices. But if these "culture traits" perform a function it is obvious that they have value for the people concerned. This is true because such is the meaning of value.

To be sure, if this anthropological inquiry had begun with the effort to understand the nature and meaning of value its drift would have been in quite a different direction. Whatever value we assign to the things we eat for breakfast is so assigned because of the cause-and-effect dietary significance of our various foods and drinks. Proceeding from this point, then, we would almost inevitably make a distinction between the genuine values which derive their meaning from clear and certain knowledge of demonstrated cause-and-effect processes and the pseudo values which derive their meaning from the fantasies of superstition. Granted that all superstitions are fantasies in which imagined causes have imaginary effects: the values which derive their meaning from such processes must be clearly different from those which derive from clear and certain knowledge. This difference is not that of supposedly "primitive" and supposedly "enlightened" peoples. Some clear and certain knowledge is possessed by every people, and—alas!—some superstition continues to prevail among even the most enlightened people. The difference is between the genuine knowledge and the real values of any people and the fancied values and the fantasies of that same people.

Anthropological inquiry, however, did not proceed in this direction. Beginning with the effort to understand ideas and practices very different from our own (or at least from those of our own scientists), it led to the recognition of values which likewise are very different from our own. Moreover, it was at once apparent that such values exist in systems. As a matter of fact, all values do. Dietary values mesh with those of hygiene in general, and so with knowledge in general; and the validity of modern knowledge, and so of the values that flow from it, derives from its continuity with the investigatory efforts of mankind from the discovery by dawn man (the earliest man) that stones are harder than heads. But, I repeat, anthropological investigation did not proceed in this direction. From the recognition that values exist in systems it was an obvious and seemingly inevitable step to think of values-as-such as existing in community-limited systems. Thus the Tlingit Indians of Alaska have one set of values, the Zuni Indians of New Mexico have another, and modern Western civilization has still another, and that is all there is to it.

Thus the meaning of value, as it seemed to emerge from anthropological investigation, seemed to lead to a conclusion which nobody has established by any sort of demonstration—one that is only suggested by the accident of proceeding in this direction—namely, that values—all values—are irrational emanations of the social practices which happen to prevail among the people whose values they are.

All this seems to mean that the anthropologists (and contemporary social scientists generally; for to do the anthropologists justice, their ideas have won general acceptance) are just as superstitious as the people they investigate. But such an inference would overlook the major premise of culture. A simple people does as it does and values what it values because it believes the Great Manitou has so ordained. Anthropologists do not so believe. But they know that all peoples believe as they do and value what they do because their cultures so ordain. Thus knowledge of the process by which all men are shaped by culture forms another current which contributes to the drift toward irrationality. Here too the obvious fact that scientific knowledge is a cultural heritage, no less than superstition, is likewise overlooked, or disregarded. That, seemingly, is not what is at issue. What is at issue is (pseudo) value systems and the fashion in which the members of every community are indoctrinated—a process which does indeed go on and one with which it is easy to become obsessed to the exclusion of everything else.

Another current that sets in the same direction is that of emotionality. All decisions are accompanied by some sort and degree of emotional intensity. On any given morning the choice of breakfast foods may not arouse strong passions. But that is true only if the issues are trivial and the consequences momentary. If what is involved is a policy affecting all breakfasts, as was the case in the incident I have cited, the situation engenders the whole gamut of feelings: indignation, affection, anger, shame, and contrition.

Actions that involve irrational values are peculiarly fraught with emotion. This is true because in the nature of the case the value suppositions in question have been established by a process of emotional conditioning. There is nothing emotionally disturbing about the sound, or even the literal meaning, of naughty four-letter words. (In every case there are synonyms and circumlocutions which may be used even in polite society.) We are disturbed when such words are uttered (in polite society) only because they are taboo and because the taboo has been emotionally "internalized" from early childhood onward.

This circumstance seems to identify the essential meaning of value with irrationally induced emotion, especially if one begins with the emotion and then proceeds backward, so to speak, to the identification of value. Thus the strong emotions, which are unquestionably present in the irrational taboo-behavior of all peoples, contribute to the general drift toward irrationalism.

Another current that comes from quite a different source also contributes to this drift. Scientists quite commonly dissociate the whole area of their investigations from the realm of values. Why they do so is an important and complicated matter to which therefore I shall return later on. At this point all that needs be noted is how they do so, and this can be explained quite simply. Here again the vital issue is one of direction. If we begin with rationality and proceed to identify science as an extension and systematization of the rational, experimental, and demonstrative behavior in which all mankind participates and has always done so, then it is clear that all rational decisions, and the values they define, are quasi-scientific and that science is the refinement and systematization of that universal and continuous process. But if we begin with science, defined as the sum of the sciences of mathematics, astronomy, physics, chemistry, geology, zoology, and all the rest, together with all their subdivisions and hyphenations (biochemistry, geophysics, and the like), then it is quite evident that there is no science that tells us what to do with our lives. Having leafed through the scientific treatises in vain for any mention of human values, we seem to be forced to the conclusion that science has nothing to do with values.

This seems to confirm the teaching of the anthropologists and their social-science colleagues. They are scientists too, of course. But their investigations likewise do not give rise to any value judgments. On the contrary, what they seem to discover about value judgments is that such "judgments" (the word itself seems on this showing to be a misnomer) are essentially irrational and derive only from social conventions.

5

This is an essentially false position and one that is of very great danger to the whole of Western civilization, as should be evident to every thoughtful person. For it means that Western civilization has no case. If values are defined only by the conventions of the societies in which they prevail, then there can be no general, or transcultural, standard by which the conventions of any one society can be judged better than another. This is a dictum to which a substantial number—perhaps a majority—of present-day social scientists explicitly subscribe. But if such is the case, then there is no ground whatever save only that of sheer partisanship on which it can be convincingly maintained that free, democratic society and the liberal culture of the Western peoples is any better or worthier of perpetuation than such dictatorships as those of Hitler and Stalin (not to mention their living representatives) or, for that matter, the "idyllic existence" of Polynesian islanders.

Not only that: such moral agnosticism provides no basis whatever for any possible improvement. For on this basis what can improvement mean? Only that each generation rewrites history on the basis of its own prejudices! This is indeed a familiar cynicism, and one that is quite in line with current thinking.

So is the economic doctrine known as *laissez faire*. For several generations the thinking of the Western peoples—especially the English-speaking peoples—has been dominated by a set of ideas now commonly known as "classical liberalism." In origin and application these ideas are primarily economic. They arose at a time when rapid economic growth was the most conspicuous feature of Western life and they are peculiarly appropriate to what is still predominantly a commercial society. That is why they still occupy a central place in the thinking of the Western peoples.

The economic revolution of modern times was of technological origin. That is, its root cause was a long series of inventions and discoveries which began well back in medieval times and developed with cumulative effect. One obvious effect was (and is) the growing prevalence of trade. The advantages of technological specialization are possible only if the various specialists exchange their products. Thus to anybody who reflects upon this process with a mind innocent of doctrinal convictions it seems obvious that it was the technological process that brought about the commercialization of Western society.

But for a variety of reasons the opposite has seemed to be the case. Thus Adam Smith declared in the opening pages of *The Wealth of Nations* that it was exchange which brought about "the division of labor," and all the rest of that great treatise was in effect an explanation of how "enlightened self-interest," by prompting every buyer and seller to drive the best bargain he can, operates to the best advantage of the whole community.

In the six generations that have passed since the time of Adam Smith this doctrine has come to be held by the community at large with an intensity of conviction that approaches religious faith. This is due not only to the persuasive powers of Adam Smith and the series of great writers who followed him. After all, the free trade for which they spoke was certainly better than the "unnatural restraints" of the preceding age of mercantilism. But more than to anything else the policy of letting the market take its course owes its hold over the modern mind to the industrial revolution. By the time of Adam Smith the technological process had acquired a momentum which nothing could have stopped. Power-driven machinery had already made its appearance; railways and steamships were just around the corner; electrical communication was on the way; and the machine age was already upon us. And since the sole existing explanation of this prodigious development was that of Adam Smith and his successors, it is not surprising that their theory should have enjoyed considerable prestige, or that it should do so still.

But now we find ourselves in a dilemma. The scale of our industrial operations has now grown so large that conscious deliberate regulation of some sort has been forced upon us in steadily increasing degree. The "restraints" we impose on the movements of airplanes may be "unnatural," but the alternative is catastrophic. It is all very well to argue that government is not responsible for business failures; when bank failures become epidemic, even the most conservative government is stirred to action. But what action? In the perpetual running argument between "free competition" (that is, letting the market take its course) and "economic planning," free competition enjoys one great advantage, and economic planning, however necessary, suffers from a crippling disadvantage.

However great our need for guidance may be, intelligent guidance is impossible if knowledge of good and bad is impossible. That is why even staunch advocates of economic planning commonly acknowledge that no "general" planning is possible. Seemingly "free competition" makes no such demand, since on that basis no one need know what is for the best. Actually, however, the supposition that the "decisions" of the market are for the best was based on certain theological beliefs which enjoyed wide currency among the intellectual elite of the eighteenth century. According to this doctrine it was supposed that man had been endowed with a full complement of senses, sentiments, and predilections such that by following his "natural" predilections he would be led "by an invisible hand" (Adam Smith's most celebrated phrase) "to promote an end that is no part of his intention," to wit, the general welfare.

Certainly the irresistible onward march of the scientific-industrial revolution was no part of anybody's intention. But one of its developments was Darwinism, which of course made mincemeat of eighteenth-century theology. No longer is it possible to suppose that in buying cheap and selling dear man is giving effect to the original plan of an all-wise Creator. If "the general welfare" has only the meaning that is given it by the traditions and beliefs of a particular community, one can still argue (as opponents of economic planning do) that no deliberate plan can possibly do better. But no one can argue that the traditions and beliefs of any one community are any better than those of any other.

It is in this fashion that modern Western society, and especially modern Western scholarship, has got itself into a thoroughly false position. I emphasize the role of scholarship because that is where the responsibility lies. What makes this state of mind dangerous is its prevalence throughout the community. But it owes its prevalence to the extraordinary plausibility that has been built into it by a long succession of extremely able thinkers. Not one in a thousand of those who glorify "free competition," or "free enterprise," and oppose all economic and social "tinkering," has any clear idea of what he is glorifying or why it is glorious. For the community at large it is sufficient that the great scholars who together constitute the grand tradition of classical political economy have established the meaning of these slogans. Such is the responsibility of scholarship!

6

In a sense, therefore, the present book represents an act of rebellion: rebellion against the grand tradition of classical political economy and modern economics. But the rebellion is not against the consequences of these ideas; it is against the ideas themselves. We must be very careful about this. The fact that the consequences of any given set of ideas are unpleasant does not establish their unsoundness, nor even point in that direction, though it may cause us to turn back and subject them to re-examination. In the present instance, however, it was the ideas themselves which ignited the first sparks of doubt.

What I first began to doubt was whether the configurations of the market have the meaning that classical theory imputes to them. An eminent contemporary economist has declared that all economic planning must be either "for competition" or "against competition." I cite this declaration because it seems to me to betray complete misunderstanding of the ideas and motives of dissenting economists. To question whether all marriages are made in heaven is not to argue "against" marriage; and to question whether the operations of the market—that is, the whole apparatus of buying and selling—mean what they have been traditionally alleged to mean is not to argue against buying and selling. Of course, if sexual attraction does not necessarily betoken the intervention of heaven, that fact does imply that other considerations may perhaps be canvassed advantageously. By the same token, if the adjustments effected by the market are not necessarily heavenly, then even while they continue (as sexual attraction does) we may find it advantageous to canvass other forms of economic and social adjustment. But it is the meanings that inspire the doubts.

The first glimmerings of doubt were insinuated into my mind during my apprentice-teaching days by a very remarkable personality: Walton Hamilton. I had been "properly" brought up, as most undergraduates still are; and as Professor Hamilton discoursed to Amherst freshmen about "social and economic institutions" (in his once-celebrated course, "S&EI," in the conduct of which I was his assistant) I began to wonder when he was going to get around to unfolding to these freshmen such basic ideas as "marginal utility." Finally I mustered up my courage to ask him, and through the forty-four years that have since elapsed I have never forgotten the gleam of amusement in his eyes as he replied, "I'd do so at once if only I understood them myself!" Like Henny-Penny, I felt the heavens falling, for already I had conceived a tremendous admiration for the mental processes of this extraordinary young professor. Could it be that all the elaborate analytical apparatus of marginal analysis was actually without meaning?

It could. As Professor Hamilton showed me, that was exactly what Veblen had been saying for some time. Critics of "orthodox price theory," and most especially Veblen, have often been reproached for not having anything to put in its place—that is, for not coming up with an alternative theory of how the economy is regulated by the price system. This is a little like reproaching a religious skeptic for not having anything to "take the place" of the Holy Trinity. The whole point to the Veblenian criticism of the classical tradition is that the economy is not regulated by the price system. It is regulated by the institutional structure of Western society, of which the market is at most only a manifestation. That is why, ever since Hamilton first used the term, this way of thinking has been generally known as "institutionalism."

It is true, however, that Veblen was a disconcertingly elliptical writer. Some of his most important insights lie buried beneath great heaps of ironic rhetoric. Thus scholars have only recently become aware that despite his ironic denials a theory of value had been implicit in all his work ever since his doctoral dissertation on Kant's *Critique of Judgment.* In my own case this realization came years later, and only after I had obtained from other sources what had seemed to be an essential missing link in the institutionalist chain of reasoning.

For if Adam Smith's "propensity to truck, barter, and exchange" cannot be depended upon to guide us toward the general welfare, something else must indeed be found to take the place it never filled. If society is to progress, there must be some means of knowing in what direction progress lies. Or rather, if human society has been progressing all along—if our present way of life is truly superior to that of *Pithecanthropus erectus*—that must mean that, whether scholars recognize it or not, mankind has all along had some way of knowing, clearly and consistently, what is good and what is not.

It was from John Dewey that I first learned what that way of knowing is. It is what Dewey called the "instrumental" process. This, as Dewey clearly realized, is identical with what Veblen was calling the "technological" process. Both of these great pioneers recognized this process as (in Veblen's words) "the life process" of mankind, a process that runs in unbroken continuity through the activities of all societies and has the same meaning for all, so that a good charitable bequest, or a good peace treaty, or a good system of regulation of the flights of airplanes, is good in exactly the same sense that a cave man's striking stone was good: good in the sense of bringing home the bacon.

We do have the means of knowing good from bad, exactly as we have the means of knowing truth from error. This does not mean that we do not make mistakes. But it does mean that we can eventually recognize a mistake and go about correcting it. We can do so because this continuous instrumental-technological process itself provides the standard of judgment both of truth and error and of good and bad. That is what I mean by saying that we draft a constitution by the same mental processes by which we decide what to eat for breakfast. There are very great differences of complexity and importance, but there is no essential difference of kind.

7

While acknowledging the influence of Veblen and Dewey, I am torn by conflicting impulses. If I do not admit my indebtedness I imply that I alone have dreamed up everything I propose to say; and if I do, I imply that everything I have to say has already been said—and probably much better—by my teachers. But neither of these propositions is true without qualification. No one is utterly original, not even the greatest pioneers. Indeed, it stands to reason that the work of such pioneers as Veblen and Dewey is important precisely because it is a manifestation of significant currents of thought, and those currents are significant not because of the great names that have been associated with them but rather because the ideas they have borne along have by the logic of events gradually come to permeate our culture. In recent years both Veblen and Dewey have been widely repudiated, almost altogether for reasons that are irrelevant to their real contributions, while at the same time their most significant ideas have become the idiom in terms of which the present generation thinks.

At the same time it is true of ideas as it is of rivers that as they flow down the watershed of history they spread and form new contours on a broader landscape. Nothing that Veblen did is more significant or more characteristic than his recognition of technology, or workmanship, as a dynamic force or of institutions as a limiting factor in the process of economic and social development. Yet with all his insistence on the dynamism of the technological (or, as Dewey called it, instrumental) process Veblen never spelled out the details of that process in such a way as to show why it is dynamic and how it grows. Thus I feel that my exposition of the role of tools, and the physical availability of tools for combination into new and more potent tools, serves to make one of his central ideas a little more intelligible. Moreover, Dewey's recognition of this process as the matrix of all standards of judgment of real values makes an understanding of how the process unfolds all the more important.

As regards the institutional process (or ceremonialism, as Veblen often called it) much the same is true. Veblen expended some of his choicest irony on what he called the "archaism" of this aspect of culture, and yet he never bothered to spell out why the process of institutionalization is past-binding. By showing how the different features of this process fit together and reinforce each other and how each necessarily derives its meaning and its grip from the past I have tried to make its inhibitory character somewhat more intelligible.

I have also pointed out, somewhat more explicitly than either of these masters did, that tribal beliefs, and the institutional and ceremonial practices in which they are objectified, are simulacra of scientific knowledge and technological skills. That is, what Veblen calls "ceremonial adequacy" is an imitation of technological adequacy. The tribal medicine man purports to be altering the course of events in imitation of the tool activities by which technicians really do alter the course of events. Recognizing this makes possible a clear differentiation of technological reality from ceremonial fantasy, and so of real values from fancies, or pseudo values.

Of all the speculations in which I have indulged perhaps the most daring (or reckless) is my conjectural explanation of the origin of myth-making, ritualism, and institutionalized conventions generally. But we must face it somehow! How did this extraordinary bifurcation of human mentality and culture come about? Why should our species, endowed as it is with capabilities of brain and hand far beyond those of any other creature, be subject in such amazing degree to self-stultification?

I believe that the work of recent decades on what has come to be known as the symbolic process has been hovering on the verge of a satisfactory resolution of this profound enigma. But it has been held back by an excess of what has passed as broadmindedness. Just as the anthropologists, in their zeal for doing justice to erstwhile savages, have in effect put us all in that category, so the students of symbolism have been so eager to make sense of occult symbolism that they have in effect validated it. But the fact remains that some symbolism has operational validity and some does not; and if we firmly recognize this basic truth, the relationship between the two orders of symbols then becomes unmistakably clear, and the enigma is resolved.

In somewhat the same spirit I have also tackled another immemorial enigma: that of the evidentiality of feelings. We are all creatures of emotion. All our significant experiences are fraught with emotion. Is that why they are significant? Are we guided by our feelings? Quite commonly we feel that such is the case, and for that reason the feeling-theory of value has cropped up generation after generation in one form or another. It is of course the foundation of the modern culture-limited theory of value: that all values are established (internalized) by a process of community emotional conditioning.

If such tribal values are false values, this means that the testimony of our feelings is unreliable. But we never feel so sure of anything as of our feelings. How can this be? By way of resolving this enigma I offer a theory of emotional feedback the upshot of which is that an emotion is self-intensifying by a process that bypasses its origin. Thus our feelings are focussed on their ostensible object (of value or disvalue), leaving us entirely unaware of the conditioning process. In sum, feelings are a tremendously important part of our make-up. Life would be dull indeed without them. But they tell us nothing. On the contrary, we tell them.

8

All this raises a truly fateful question. Can society ever be wholly reasonable? Properly speaking, this is not a question of a life devoid of feeling. Neither is it a question of "mind" having "mastery" over the emotions. What we call "mind"—that is, the activity of perceiving and conceiving, which is to say knowing—always has mastery over the feelings. Always we feel what we have learned to feel. The important question is what sort of learning and knowing it is to which our feelings have been conditioned to respond. Thus the question should be phrased: Can genuine knowledge ever wholly supplant superstition, and can real values ever wholly supplant tribally perpetuated fancies?

In one sense there is no answer to such a question. It is like asking what happens at the end of an endless process. But if we put the question in terms of process and ask whether life can be more rational than it is at present, the answer obviously is, Yes. All our experience points in the affirmative direction. The more knowledge we have, the less we are exposed to the wiles of superstition; and the whole experience of mankind has been that of gradually broadening knowledge. The same is true of values. The more we know, the better able we are to make valid judgments as to what is good and what is bad.

Mankind has always known that health and strength are good, and that food conduces to health and strength and so is good too. But we know a great deal more about foods today than any previous generation has ever known. We know that people who have ample supplies of food may nevertheless suffer and die if they lack certain particular foods. Some of these deficiency diseases have been known as such for centuries. This is true of scurvy. Others, such as pellagra, were so identified only a few decades ago; and for all such deficiencies it is only in recent years that the controlling vitamins have been identified, and then synthesized, and so made available in pure form in large quantities. Not only is this good; it is better than mere food.

The same sort of knowledge identifies the so-called "higher" values. Throughout the ages men have judged freedom more valuable even than food. This judgment is based on two sets of facts. For one thing, a human being may receive an ample supply of food in circumstances analogous to those of a domestic animal. Nourishment does not necessarily lead to freedom. The second and decisive fact is that deprivation of freedom does affect all the activities in which one may (or may not) engage. It is coextensive with life itself.

So it is with all the higher values. As I have said, we relinquish the sense of mystery only with the greatest reluctance. Such reluctance is greatest where the higher values are concerned. This is due in part to the hold of tradition, fortified as it is by emotional feedback. But it is also due to ignorance, and especially to ignorance of which we are largely unaware, such as prevails quite generally even at the present time in the region of the fine arts. A connoisseur of painting has just published a book with the suggestive title, *I Like What I Know*. So do we all! But most people, unaware of the immensity of their own ignorance, insist rather that they know what they like, and find it easier to attribute differences of "taste" to mysterious differences of native "endowment" than to face up to their own delinquencies, especially since they have no idea how their knowledge can be increased.

Indeed, it is only within recent generations that such knowledge has become generally accessible. In ancient times it took the wisdom of Socrates, or Plato, to see that justice is a *sine qua non* of the Republic. Today, however, the nature and necessities of social organization in all its aspects are the object of extensive and resolute investigation, and as a consequence "we" know far more than earlier generations did about the operational significance of the higher values, just as we know far more about The Art *in* Painting—to quote another title by another eminent connoisseur.

To be sure, the "we" who know are not the entire community, or even a majority of all the people. We ought rather to say that such knowledge exists, is a community possession, so to speak, accessible to anybody who seeks access to it. Thus "we know" how to calculate the occurrence of eclipses of the sun, although only a relative few have ever done so. In this case the only difficulty is that of acquiring the necessary mathematical and astronomical skills, whereas in the case of value judgments the obstacles are those of tradition and emotion. Thus with regard to the taking of human life no great fund of knowledge or subtlety of reasoning is required for anybody to see that the termination of a human life is a momentous matter, since it terminates all the activities in which the subject has ever been engaged and so affects, more or less catastrophically, all those in whose affairs he has ever been involved. As everyone can see, death is the most completely irreversible incident in life, and this is true quite independently of all suppositions with regard to the sacredness of human life. Indeed, not only is this simple truth entirely adequate as the basis for a value judgment; it has always been the foundation-fact upon which all suppositions with regard to the sacredness of life have been erected.

It is for this reason that I plan to devote the later chapters of this book to a discussion of such values as freedom and equality, security, abundance, and excellence. This naturalistic, instrumental, technological theory of value is not "mere" theory. As I have already said and will continue to repeat, it is not a theory of how value judgments ought to be made. It is an account of how we do, now and always, actually evaluate the things we value. These are values to the preciousness of which we all subscribe, as in one way or another men have always done. We feel them to be the most precious heritage of our civilization, and so they are! But they are so not because of our feelings, nor by virtue of inheritance. On the contrary, we have inherited these values because we have inherited civilization—because they are logical corollaries of the way of life to which mankind committed itself hundreds of thousands of years ago. Like Plato's justice, they define the conditions on which alone this way can be successfully pursued.

Moreover, the farther we advance, the more clearly we can see the path. We call our way of life "industrial." But as such it is a continuation of the technological life process by which all the achievements of mankind have been won. Such being the case, it stands to reason that the scientific-industrial revolution, by which all our "ordinary" powers have been multiplied, should also bring a fuller realization of all the higher values; and, as I said at the beginning, the truth is that it has. Notwithstanding all the hazards to which our increased powers have exposed us, we are now living in a golden age; and we owe it all—our freedom, our comforts, and the flowering of our culture—to the basic civilizing process from which all good things derive.

As we are just beginning to understand, it is all one process: science and freedom; technology and beauty. Indeed, as I shall try to show in a closing chapter, after eons of thinking in terms of substances and beings, we are just beginning to think in terms of process; and so doing, we stand on the threshold of a new civilization. That is the significance of the industrial way of life.

PART THREE

CHAPTER III

THE RISE OF MORAL AGNOSTICISM

I

FOR SEVERAL CENTURIES WESTERN CIVILIZATION has been undergoing a process of secularization. As we have learned more and more about the world we live in, and have learned to do more and more with it, otherworldly considerations have dropped farther and farther into the background of our everyday life. But they have by no means disappeared. On the contrary, they still continue to supply the language and perhaps the inspiration of all our common purposes and higher aspirations, to which in turn our everyday activities are commonly thought to owe their meaning. Thus the Western peoples find themselves living in a divided world, one that is half-secular and half-sacred. Or, to put it another way, our civilization is impaled on the horns of a dilemma, one of which is the irresistible forward surge of science and technology, the other the stubborn persistence of traditions which are the direct antithesis of science and technology.

With regard to the role of science and technology I need say very little at this point, since it is the most conspicuous fact of modern life. I link science with technology because that linkage contains and elicits the essential meaning of both; and for the same reason I call the scientific-technological way of thinking "secularism" rather than "mechanism" or "materialism." Indeed, it might save needless misunderstanding to give a moment's consideration to these words and their implications.

In such a connection as this, the whole meaning of the word *secular* is that of the antonym to *sacred*. It has no further semantic overtones, as do so many other words that are sometimes used in this connection. Thus the word *profane* is likewise an antonym to *sacred;* but it also conveys unpleasant and even scandalous suggestions which are absent from *secularism.* So also the trouble with words like *materialism* and *mechanism* is that they characterize the opposite to sacred in terms to which most scientists would now object. Thus the term *mechanical* might be thought to exclude the chemical and electrical, not to mention the organic and even the cultural. By suggestion at least it has the effect of limiting the meaning under consideration to the revolving wheels and clashing gears with which mechanics deal. Similarly the term *material* carries the suggestion of a particular range of substances which are conceived as being in the most literal sense like the earth on which we stand. Thus the materialist is in effect identified as an "earthist," and so relegated to a position that is both undignified and indefensible. For reasons such as these most scientists now avoid identifying themselves as either materialists or mechanists. But no one could deny that science is secular.

The term *natural* also is the antonym of *supernatural*, and therefore of the occult and the sacred. Indeed, this is the word which has been longest and most widely used for this very purpose. It is in this spirit that we speak of the natural universe, meaning the universe as it appears to human eyes and ears and to all the delicate and cunning instruments with which men have learned to supplement their senses. In the same spirit men whom we now identify as scientists used to refer to their discipline as "natural philosophy." But in recent years the "natural sciences" have come to be so designated in distinction from the social sciences and sometimes even to distinguish physics, chemistry, astronomy, and geology from the biological sciences. Meantime, as we know to our sorrow, the partisans of all sorts of social practices and propensities have sought to establish the validity and permanence of their concerns by declaring them to be "natural" and so in effect invoking for them "the authority of Nature," with the result that *Nature*, spelled with the capital letter, has come to have a metaphysical significance that is redolent of supernaturalism—the very meaning we are now seeking to avoid. Usage being what it is, we cannot altogether avoid the word *natural* and its related forms. But in using it we can still hope to avoid confusion by generous application of the word *secular*, the significance of which is unmistakable.

The dilemma with which Western civilization has been confronted in consequence of the scientific-technological revolution of recent centuries was perhaps inevitable. As a strictly secular process, the growth of science and technology was bound to occur at the expense of traditional beliefs and the way of life of which those beliefs were an expression. Moreover, the community was bound to cling tenaciously to its time-honored way of life and to the beliefs that sanctified it. All communities do so. Nevertheless the severity of the disturbance has been greatly intensified by an ideological paradox to which the intellectual leadership of the twentieth century has fallen victim.

2

One of the strangest paradoxes of modern Western civilization is the prevalence of moral agnosticism among the intellectual elite. At this moment, when knowledge of the world and of man has reached levels which even a few generations ago no one would have believed possible, and when supernaturalism is at a greater discount than ever before in the entire history of mankind, those who are best informed have somehow persuaded themselves that good and evil lie beyond the scope of scientific knowledge and beyond the grasp of trained intelligence. This is thought to be the case because good and evil, right and wrong, are matters of value, and because it is now generally supposed that science deals only with facts, never with values. At this moment when more than ever before the whole community looks to the trained intelligence of scientists and scholars for leadership, astronomers and anthropologists, chemists and economists, anatomists and sociologists, all seem to be agreed that science tells us only *how* to do whatever our tribal traditions and group loyalties may impel us to do. Never does it tell us *what* to do.

The essence of this notion is that "knowing" and "valuing" are two separate and distinct activities. Supposedly the former is wholly a function of intellect, whereas the latter is predominantly emotional. Thus it is said that science is wholly "descriptive" or "analytical." Its findings can be stated only in the indicative or subjunctive moods, never in the imperative. The earth turns on its axis and describes an elliptical orbit around the sun. Food nourishes the body. Poison causes death. Such propositions can also be stated conditionally: "If you eat that poisonous mushroom, it will kill you." But scientific knowledge never justifies anybody in saying, "Don't eat that mushroom!" For such an imperative assumes the "normative" (or, to use another expression that is a great favorite among contemporary scholars, "value-loaded") judgment, that living is good and death is bad. Such judgments, so it is said, express "attitudes" with which (in one form or another) all of us are deeply indoctrinated. Such attitudes can have no other source, for they are matters of emotional conviction or belief rather than of factual knowledge. Thus it is argued that notwithstanding all our scientific knowledge and all the wondrous skills to which it has given rise (and vice versa), in making any decision with regard to what we shall undertake to do we are ultimately dependent upon tribally indoctrinated attitudes and beliefs. In studying the phenomena of life and death the scientist draws freely upon the vast store of previously accumulated knowledge; but the only thing that deters him from vivisecting his laboratory colleagues is a hangover of childish squeamishness and fear of the police.

In a sense, of course, this pestilence of moral agnosticism bears witness to the persistence of immemorial tradition. But this is true only in a very general sense. The intellectual posture of twentieth-century scholars and scientists is not a case of ordinary social atavism. It has an explicitly intellectual pattern and is a consequence of three distinct, though not wholly unrelated, intellectual situations.

3

One of these, the oldest and perhaps the most significant, is the situation in which the pioneers of the great secular revolution have found themselves ever since the dawn of modern times. Every major discovery has been contrary to prevailing belief, and every major invention has been at odds with the prevailing way of life. But the progress of science and technology has always been a piecemeal affair. Consequently there has never been a time when any particular innovation has necessarily challenged the whole traditional scheme of thought and way of life. Opposition there certainly has been. We must never forget that even so innocuous a discipline as astronomy now seems to be was once the scene of violent struggle. Even the Hindu-Arabic numerals were once denounced as devices of heathen and infidels which good Christians should eschew. But they came into use nevertheless; and since the heavens failed to fall, it could be argued pretty convincingly that such innovations are not contrary to the main body of tradition.

Most significantly, the scientists themselves so argued. This betokens no insincerity on their part. Scientists are people, and as people they share the beliefs and sentiments of the community. It was not revolutionary zeal that led them to discover the moons of Jupiter or the law of falling bodies. Quite typically they were just as much surprised as everybody else by what they saw when they peered through a large tube with lenses mounted at each end. They did not thereupon abandon all the idols of the tribe. Bacon himself did not do so. They did as the community was doing: they accepted the heliocentric theory of planetary motion and otherwise comported themselves with propriety in that station in life to which they felt they had been called.

But in doing so they set a pattern that is now a source of great embarrassment. It is a pattern of compartmentalization. In effect, the community has been induced to accept and prize science and technology on the understanding that scientists and technicians will stay in their shops and laboratories, respect the opinions of others, especially in matters of faith and morals, and leave all decisions to the duly constituted authorities. Needless to say, no convention or contract to any such effect has ever been formulated, nor has this compartmentalization resulted in any sharp division of the community. Rather the scientists themselves, and to some extent the entire population, have become accustomed to leading double lives. For scientists are of course also parents, homeowners, careerists, citizens, political partisans, and (predominantly) church members; and as such they share the sentiments and beliefs of their nonscientist relatives, friends, neighbors, and fellow communicants. Meantime virtually every member of the community at large, whatever his sentiments and prejudices may be, has learned to recognize the truth of an immense body of scientific knowledge and the efficacy of a tremendous complex of technical operations.

This compartmentalization, which, as I have indicated, has its origin in practice and has become the standard practice of our community, is now quite generally regarded as being itself a scientific axiom. No one has ever proved that the process by which parents arrive at a decision is inherently and necessarily different from the process by which scientists formulate a hypothesis.

In deprecating this compartmentalization of the modern mind I wish to avoid exaggeration. It may be true that such a scientific-technological revolution as the last five centuries have witnessed could have come about in no other way. If the political and ecclesiastical authorities of feudal Europe had somehow been able to realize what was going to happen to their world in consequence of the innovations by which they were so vaguely troubled, it seems most likely that every trace of every novelty would have been obliterated, and that Europe would have been sealed off from penetration by such foreign influences as the Arabic numerals and Chinese block printing, just as Islam was actually sealed off from those "graven mages" and China from all the tricks of the "outer barbarians." Indeed, it may be that the wonder is not that Giordano Bruno was burned at the stake but that Copernicus and Galileo were not. The compartmentalization of Western culture may indeed be the price at which alone modern civilization could have been won.

Moreover, the partition, so to speak, by which science and folklore have been divided has been neither fixed nor impenetrable. From Francis Bacon to John Dewey some individuals have always rejected the prevailing dualism. The recently aroused social consciousness of the atomic scientists is a case in point. It is true, too, that throughout modern times the scientific compartment has been constantly enlarged while that of folklore has steadily diminished.

But it is this very fact that gives the tradition of compartmentalization critical importance. During the century which has passed since publication of *The Origin of Species* Western civilization has been moving rapidly toward the realization of a wholly scientific frame of mind. But just as it has begun to seem as though folklore might be dispensed with altogether, a new dogma has arisen: that of the essential irrationality of all judgments of value. The dualistic habit of mind—the compartmentalization of science and folklore—is by no means wholly responsible for the emergence of this dogma. But it does constitute a propitious climate of opinion

—propitious, that is, to the coexistence of scientific knowledge and moral agnosticism.

4

A second contributing factor of great significance is the tradi-tion of economic individualism. It is indeed strange that an economic doctrine should have influenced the world-view of a whole culture. But we must remember that ours is a commercial culture as well as an industrial one. Moreover, though the circum-stances which gave rise to this extraordinary theory were economic, the theory itself has a potency that goes far beyond those circum-stances. More than anything else it is responsible for the willing-ness of the community to believe that clear and certain knowledge of general validity is impossible in the area of value judgments. It is impossible—so we have been taught by the classical econo-mists—because such knowledge would be contrary to the laws of nature.

The situation that brought forth this amazing doctrine was that of the long-continued partnership between the empire-building monarchies and the great trading companies of early modern times, and especially the "mercantilist system" of trading regulations by which these partners maintained their monopoly. As the American colonists had reason to know, and as everyone now realizes, it was a thoroughly bad system—bad for the colonial peoples, and bad for the general run of small businessmen and for the consuming public of the imperial powers themselves. Whatever we may now conclude about the manner of its refutation, all students are now agreed that mercantilism richly deserved to be refuted.

The trouble with the classical doctrine of economic individualism is not that it refuted mercantilism but that in doing so it erected a barrier against all subsequent economic planning and therefore against organized intelligence itself. For mercantilism was a case of economic planning. As we now know, it was bad planning. But classical economic doctrine did not merely expose the errors of the mercantilists. Indeed, after Adam Smith's scathing denunciation of the great trading companies, they were largely forgotten. From then on down to the present time the theory of the "self-regulating market" as the essential mechanism by which all the far-flung and infinitely varied activities of a vast community are automatically guided has been developed for its own sake, so to speak, or rather as a bulwark not against former errors or any particular errors but against the universal error which is thus presumed to be inherent in any and all effort to take thought for the future what we shall eat and what we shall drink.

The ascendancy which this amazing doctrine has achieved and maintained over the minds of the Western peoples is of course due to a variety of circumstances. In particular, it is amazingly plausible, and it is plausible partly because economic individualism has seemed to coincide with religious emphasis on the primacy of individual "conscience" and political emphasis on the individual's "natural rights." Partly, too, the theory of the economy as an automatically self-regulating system has seemed to coincide exactly with the principles in terms of which scientists have been resolving the mysteries of both heavenly and earthly bodies. Meantime, as disenchanted commentators have pointed out all along, the notion that in buying cheap and selling dear everyone is acting for the common good is singularly agreeable to a community all of whose members are engaged in making money, and most agreeable to those who have made the most. To these considerations there must be added another which is perhaps more important than all the rest. The doctrine of economic individualism has prevailed during a period in which the Western world has witnessed a great industrial revolution marked by vastly increased volumes of production and consumption along with a tremendous growth of population, and not unnaturally the prevailing doctrine has received the credit for all this growth—just as Marxist doctrine and the Soviet system now enjoy the credit for the industrial revolution which has been taking place where they prevail.

As everybody knows, the philosophy of economic individualism —the doctrine, as Lewis Carroll phrased it, that what makes the world go round is "everybody minding his own business"—has been the prime determinant of public policy with regard to economic affairs for several generations. What is not so widely appreciated is the moral incidence of economic doctrine. Not only does it subject every proposal for reform to attack on grounds of "creeping socialism"; it also tags every would-be reformer—in effect, everybody who ventures to try to define and formulate the public interest—as a "crackpot" or an "egghead." He is so identified *a priori,* so to speak. For if the only sound definition of the public interest is that which results from the play of market forces, then anyone who ventures to substitute his judgment, however well informed, for the "decisions" of the market is obviously a fool if not a scoundrel. So the saying has evolved: "Scratch a reformer and reveal a would-be dictator."

This is moral agnosticism. In its effect upon the Western mind classical economic doctrine, by far the most formidable body of ideas to be found anywhere in the whole area of the social sciences, is directly in line with the moral irresponsibility which has resulted from the compartmentalization of science. However, great as its influence has been, it would not now be so great were it not for the coincidence of a third contributing factor: the doctrine of cultural relativism.

5

Like scientific separatism and economic individualism, this doctrine also sprang from innocent beginnings. In its age of innocence it represented a sincere and altogether praiseworthy effort to correct what all scholars now consider an egregious and highly regrettable misconception. Time was when Europeans looked down upon all others as at best heathen and at worst beastly savages. The doctrine of cultural relativism had its origin in the correction of this attitude. In a later chapter I shall dwell at some length on the coincidence of the systematic study of "primitive culture" with the Darwinian revolution. But at this point it is relevant only to note that when such study got under way, in the latter part of the nineteenth century, scholars soon began to see that even those beliefs and practices of primitive peoples which contrast most vividly with European culture make sense of a sort to the peoples who hold the beliefs and perform the rites. However nonsensical and even gruesome any particular "culture trait" may seem to us, it can be understood only in terms of the function it performs in the scheme of life of which it is a part, a way of life which may have stood the test of time ten times, or even a hundred times, as long as ours.

From this beginning it was seemingly an obvious and inevitable step to the generalization: there is no general, or transcultural, criterion by which culture patterns can be judged; the meaning, validity, and sanction of all culture patterns derive from the traditions of the community whose traditions they are and from their acceptance by that community. They have no other source or sanction.

The phrase "all culture patterns" would seem to include all the skills and all the accumulated knowledge that go to make up what we now call science and technology. But most exponents of the doctrine of cultural relativism manifest a saving vagueness at this point. Obviously technological designs and skills are culturally accumulated and transmitted patterns, and social scientists sometimes talk about the process of their accumulation and transmission as though it were identical with the process by which tribal legends are transmitted and tribal mores inculcated. As a rule, however, exponents of cultural relativism avoid commitment on this (obviously highly debatable) point by the simple expedient of not raising the issue. But they are in quite general agreement that all moral precepts—all value judgments—derive from the beliefs and attitudes of various particular cultures. Hence such value patterns are functionally significant features of those cultures, but have no general, or transcultural, significance or validity. In short, there is no criterion, and however much our knowledge may increase there never can be one, by which the people of one culture can judge the values of another people. All values are, and of necessity must always be, "subjective," a reflection of the bringing up of those who hold them, and nothing more.

This, I need hardly say, is the quintessence of moral agnosticism. In the doctrine of cultural relativism a tendency that has been implicit in Western thought since the dawn of modern science now finds its consummation. That tendency has many other mainfestations, all to the same effect, for example "the sociology of knowledge" and "logical positivism." Like the doctrine of cultural relativism itself, each of these sets out from a basically sound position. Obviously exponents of the sociology of knowledge are right in arguing that much of what passes for knowledge even today is in fact a codification of tribal tradition, and no less obviously the logical positivists are right in pointing out that the use of words with vague and shifting meanings is still all too common; and since these weaknesses are most prevalent and most conspicuous in the area of those common human interests where values are commonly thought to be defined, both sociologists and logicians have found it an easy step to the conclusion that where such interests and values are concerned human thinking can never be anything else but vague and prejudiced. Thus twentieth-century scholars seem all to be moving toward the same conclusion: the moral impotence of mind and the total dependence of mankind upon prejudice and superstition.

7

These theories form an impressive array, and also a disastrous one; for its effect is to destroy all genuine moral leadership. What hope is there for a community whose intellectual leaders not only cannot demonstrate the superiority of their way of life over that of any other people but have convinced themselves that no such demonstration is intellectually possible?

It is the dissociation of truth and value that defines the moral crisis of the twentieth century. That dissociation itself is the consequence of an error so fundamental that it affects the very meaning of value but so simple that it can be stated in a few words.

Every culture has two aspects, which the terms secular and supernatural identify with sufficient clarity for present purposes. This has always been apparent. Reports of anthropologists make it quite clear that however devoutly and literally even the simplest peoples may believe the figments of their folklore, they are nevertheless well aware of the difference between secular activities, such as preparing the soil and sowing the seed of a new crop, and supernatural activities such as warding off evil spirits and invoking the friendly intercession of the ancestors.

This polarization of all cultures is a basic fact of "human nature," that is to say of the social organization of human behavior. It affects all human activities. Indeed, the error into which the social theorizing of the twentieth century has fallen so disastrously arises from this very fact. Dimly recognizing the polarity of culture, social scientists have been misled by the seeming otherness of science, even in its most primitive and practical manifestations. Thus the dividing line has seemed to fall between technical knowledge and the practical arts on one side, and on the other all the social patterns which comprise the structure of every society—the whole "system of interpersonal relationships" in which human values arise and are defined.

But in fact the organizational patterns of the social structure are neither wholly sacred nor wholly secular. Rather they are oriented in both directions, and so is knowledge. Certainly "knowledge," defined without reference to whether it is true or false as the sum of what people think they know, is neither wholly scientific nor wholly mythological.

The same is true of values and valuing. The significant distinction is not between description and evaluation. It is rather between secular efforts of description and evaluation and those exercises of description and evaluation which employ supernatural premises. Not all that is descriptive is science; mythology is no less descriptive. Nor is science confined to mere description. The essence of scientific inquiry is the effort to determine causal relationships— the processes of mutual affectation which run through all human activities as well as through all the events of nature and so give rise (in the realm of human affairs) to the kind of meaning we identify as value: that is, the bearing of any given human activity or interest upon other human activities and interests. But folklore also is never merely descriptive. It is likewise a fantasy of the interplay of imaginary forces in a system of fictitious causation which gives rise likewise to a system of fictitious values.

In the realm of values as in the realm of knowledge our problem is that of sorting out the secular from the fictitious. This is the problem which has been so vastly complicated by the fundamental error into which modern scholarship has been misled. The basic fact of cultural polarization has been misinterpreted so as to put knowledge (conceived as deriving from descriptive judgments) on one side of the picture, and value (conceived as deriving from normative judgments) on the other side; whereas the real problem is that of distinguishing true knowledge from false knowledge, and true values from false values.

That false values abound, no one can deny—values which are

defined by the sentiments and suppositions of particular cultures and are cherished only by the peoples who have been conditioned by those cultures. We ourselves are by no means free from this affliction. But such values have never had their source in the knowledge and skills of science and the arts and crafts. For it is indeed true that science is not the source of false values. But this does not mean, and cannot mean, that true values are wholly divorced from science. Our cultural enslavement to arbitrary, conventional, and legendary values is less abject than has been true of any other people, and we owe our partial emancipation to the great cultural revolution through which Western civilization has been passing.

What has made that revolution possible is the fact that knowledge is power—power to achieve all that mankind is capable of achieving, not an arbitrary and restrictive power but a capacity for achievement that expands as knowledge and skill increase. The body of knowledge we now call science reflects the uniformities of nature, and so do the values of man's achieving. Such a body of knowledge is possible only because it has been evident from the dawn of human mentality and culture that each new bit of information can be judged true by the same process that has established the truth of previous bits, so that the bits all form a whole and make the process a continuous one. The same is true of values, and for the same reason. Famine and disease are facts, and evils; and the expedients by which mankind has been able, gradually but progressively, to overcome such evils are, by the same token, good. Western science and technology are universally judged to be superior to those of all other peoples and all earlier cultures, and the Western standard of living is universally acclaimed not only as good but as the best to which mankind has ever attained. Quite evidently such judgments are not culture-limited, nor are they confined to man's material existence in any narrowly animalistic sense. Periods of freedom from hunger, plague, and rapine have also and invariably been periods of the flowering of the human spirit. The years that saw the first stirring of modern science and technology have always been known as a golden age of all the arts, and so identified as a rebirth of the glory that was Greece. These judgments are universal precisely because this aspect of culture contains within itself a criterion both of truth and of value that is the same for all ages, all peoples, and all cultures.

If such were not the case, our situation would be desperate indeed, for it would mean that Western civilization, massive as it is, has fetched up in a dead end. But in truth it is not our civilization but only the ideas of a handful of twentieth-century scholars that are at a dead end. To find the way out of our dead end we have only to rediscover that criterion of value which, however hesitantly and stumblingly, human civilization has nevertheless always eventually followed.

CHAPTER IV

WHY FEELINGS ARE ILLUSORY

I

ARE VALUES MADE KNOWN TO US BY OUR FEELINGS? That values do evoke feelings goes without saying. It may even be true that evocation of feelings is a distinguishing characteristic of all values—that what we mean by values is, in significant part at least, the power certain experiences have to move us emotionally. But this is another matter. We are emotional creatures, and as such we have the power to respond emotionally in a wide variety of ways to an infinite variety of situations. Because such emotional responses are indissociable from values of all kinds—even the most intellectual as well as the most explicitly moral or esthetic values— I plan to discuss the significance of these responses in a later chapter. The question I am raising now is not that of the emotionality of values but rather that of the evidentiality of emotions, or (more broadly and vaguely) feelings; and I raise the question at this point because the supposition that in the realm of values feelings constitute evidence is like an axiom by which all subsequent inquiry is conditioned.

This supposition is all the more insidious because it can be made, and usually is made, quite unconsciously. In the preceding chapter I have discussed certain trends in modern thinking which have led the present generation of social scientists into moral agnosticism. The supposition that feelings are self-validating underlies and permeates all these trends. It does not give any of them the particular direction that has led to this agnosticism; but it supplies the motive power, so to speak, without which none could have moved in any direction.

This power derives from what I propose to call the "feedback" principle, on which spontaneity of emotional reactions feeds back impulses which have been amplified by social conditioning. I speak of feelings as well as emotions because distinctions of meaning between these terms are not universally clear or accepted and because all are subject to the operation of this principle. Psychologists are not agreed as to the exact number of "true" or "primary" emotions. But whatever the number, they are agreed that states such as rage or anger, fear, and love or affection all have a physical basis. Each is accompanied by, or is, a certain physical condition which includes the functioning of various glands, vasodilation or contraction, differences of muscular tonus, and the like. The same is true of a number of conditions not ordinarily identified as "primary" emotions but universally classified as feelings, such as grief, disgust, and the like—perhaps even amusement. Grief is accompanied by lacrimation, actual or "subliminal"; disgust, by actual or subliminal regurgitation; amusement, by laughter; and so on. It is in all these conditions that the feedback principle obtains.

For in all these situations something more than a physical stimulus is required to elicit the physical response. This something is social conditioning. As various experimenters have demonstrated, certain conditions, such as those of fear or rage, can be induced in new-born babies as well as in animals. In both, unmistakable physical evidence of fright can be induced by a very sudden and extremely loud noise, and so on. Indeed, this circumstance seems to have been the basis on which such reactions have been identified as "primary." But it has also been demonstrated that even with animals an arbitrarily associated stimulus such as the ringing of a bell simultaneously with the appearance of food can be made to produce the food reaction even when it occurs alone. This is the well-known "conditioned reflex." Human capacity for such association is far greater than that of lower animals. Even in early infancy human babies begin learning to respond to associated stimuli, such as the appearance of a milk bottle. In effect they "know" what the milk bottle "means." These reactions are as immediate and seemingly as spontaneous as any "natural" response. But in fact they are learned responses to social situations.

All social conditioning is of this character. Among all human beings with the exception of new-born babies—that is to say, among all those to whom values have meaning—social conditioning intervenes between physical stimulus and physical response. Animals can be frightened by sudden confrontation with fire, and

54

so can human beings; but in by far the majority of instances human fire fright results from a shout of "Fire!" in a crowded hall, or the sound of a fire siren, or a radio broadcast.

In this respect grief and amusement most closely resemble fear and anger. Notwithstanding the complexity of the social experience through which we learn to respond to various situations with tears or laughter, those responses come to be immediate and virtually instantaneous. Thus we commonly speak of laughter as "spontaneous," as indeed it is in the sense that no appreciable interval of time elapses between stimulus and response during which we might be supposed to decide that the occasion is an appropriate one for a display of sorrow or amusement. The manifest spontaneity of even the organic processes characteristic of such responses is of course what led to the classical formulation of the James-Lange theory, commonly misstated as the theory that we are sorry because we cry and amused because we laugh. Actually, what in one connection we call feelings and what in another connection we call organic states are obverse and reverse of a single phenomenon.

2

The spontaneity of the whole feeling syndrome also gives rise to the "feedback" effect. I call it that on the analogy of the familiar electronic phenomenon. If a public address system is so laid out that sounds emerging from the loudspeaker impinge upon the microphone, these sounds will be amplified along with those currently issuing from the speaker's mouth, thereby causing distortion. This is known as "feedback." The same effect occurs if a record player is so mounted that vibration produced by the loudspeaker is transmitted to the turntable. That vibration, which had its origin in the vibration of the needle, is thus fed back to the needle where it mingles with impulses currently produced by the record's grooves to produce a roar of distortion.

Something of this kind happens in connection with all the feelings to which human flesh is heir. The spontaneity of our reactions prompts us almost irresistibly to feed back to the original stimulus impulses which have been "amplified" by our social conditioning. Obviously the role of the electronic amplifier is not strictly analogous to that of social conditioning, but there is a significant similarity between the two. We do not hear the amplifier, only the magnification it effects. In like manner we do not "hear" the social conditioning. In a sense it "magnifies" the original stimulus by giving it meanings we have been conditioned to associate with such an experience. But since it has done so without our being aware of it, we feed those meanings back into the original experience, much as sound impulses are fed back to the microphone; and the result is that socially acquired meanings now mingle with the original experience and seem to be inherent in it. The more effective and extensive the social conditioning is, the more spontaneous is our response; and the more spontaneous is our response, the more apparent it seems to be that the meanings we give to such experiences are inherent in the raw material of the original experience. Moreover, the stronger the feelings, the clearer the evidence seems to be that such raw material of experience is inherently funny, horrible, or frightful. The greater the gusto with which we laugh, the surer we feel that the incident which has provoked our laughter is inherently funny; and the angrier we are, the more certain we feel that the object of our anger is in fact insulting—and of course the more firmly we are thus convinced of the validity of the insult, the angrier we are.

The error to which emotional feedback gives rise is that of misplaced causality. The spontaneity of our feelings produces a very strong impression that likes and dislikes originate in the feelings themselves. The conditioning through which we have learned what to like is passed over and virtually ignored. This is well illustrated by the widespread belief that great works of art possess the power to move anybody. Thus, for example, an eminent conductor who had recently returned from a tour of the Far East testified that audiences of native Okinawans greeted Beethoven's *Eroica* with much greater enthusiasm than they accorded any lesser piece, thereby "proving" Beethoven's greatness and the "universality" of all great art. This is nonsense, of course. Whatever was the cause of the demonstration in question, we can be reasonably certain that it was not the genius of Beethoven. On the contrary, the evidence is overwhelming that people "like" not what the consensus of informed opinion identifies as best but what they know and recognize and have learned to like—good, bad, or indifferent. The fashionable audiences of Beethoven's Vienna liked Rossini better. This is not to say that the *Eroica* is not a stirring symphony. It is indeed—to those who understand it, even rather superficially. To those whose understanding of it is profound it is one of the greatest pieces of music ever written, and their emotional response to it is correspondingly intense. I assume the conductor in question to be one of these. His error is one of misplaced causality. The intensity of his own feelings leads him to overlook the causal significance of his lifetime of musical experience as a determinant of what he hears and feels, and so to impute to such a work of art a mysterious power to arouse in anybody just such a response as his own.

A wide variety of feelings produce this effect, and the misconceptions to which they give rise are legion; but they all have a common character, that of imputing to the original experience a potency which it does not possess. Indeed, the phenomenon which I am calling "emotional feedback" must have played an important part in the genesis of all supernaturalism. Repeated reference will therefore be made to it in later chapters. It must also be largely responsible for the persistence of supernaturalism even in modern Western civilization. Something more than the authority of received tradition is required to explain the veneration in which the Western peoples have continued to hold their heritage of supernaturalism notwithstanding the continuous attrition to which that heritage has been subjected by the steady advance of scientific knowledge. That "something more" has been the feedback effect. Insofar as supernatural traditions persist at all, they condition the emotional responses of the people among whom they persist; and to those people their own seemingly spontaneous emotional responses to the symbols and rituals of their creed will seem to constitute direct evidence that the power to move men's "hearts" resides in the cultural stimuli themselves. This of course is what is meant by the common saying that one must "open his heart" in order to "know" that power.

3

Among the most significant manifestations of the feedback effect—most significant, that is, in terms of its consequences for

Western civilization—is the feeling of aloneness. This feeling is largely responsible for the persistence of the ancient dualism of "inner" and "outer" worlds: the inner world of "spiritual" or "mental" reality which we know "directly," and the outer world of "appearance" which we apprehend only "indirectly" through the medium of the physical senses. I call it a "feeling" because it is a very familiar experience, and because that is how we ordinarily speak of it, though it may be reducible to a complex of sensations and emotions. By the simple expedient of closing our eyes we seem to have the power to withdraw from present company into an inner aloneness to which no one else can intrude, where we can "commune with ourselves." As a feeling, this experience is genuine enough. Indeed, everyone has the experience. What is illusory is the supposition that it gives rise to special knowledge. It is simply not true at all that any knowing results from any such feeling. That which we suppose ourselves to have learned from such "self-communion" was already "known" to us before we closed our eyes; and it was precisely this "knowledge" that "in reality" each of us is a "spirit," and that we can feel ourselves to be such by the expedient of withdrawal to "within ourselves" which has given us such an eerie feeling when we have closed our eyes.

The classic formulation of the doctrine of self-knowledge is that of Descartes: "I doubt; therefore I am." What makes it a classic is the fact that Descartes reduced a universal experience to a neat formula. The experience was universal because the reality of the inner world of spirit and the unreality and transience of the outer world of appearances had been traditional with the Western peoples since ancient times and because—thanks to the feedback effect—this belief was presumed to be verified in the emotional experience of every man, as all such beliefs are.

The Descartes effect, as it might be called, is largely responsible for the stubborn persistence of a dualism by which throughout modern times all efforts to understand the nature of man have been vitiated, including efforts to understand the meaning of values. It has not been the only factor in the process, of course. In a certain historical sense the burgeoning of science and technology from the dawn of modern times made dualism inevitable. To the extent that the medieval mind was essentially otherworldly, medieval thinking was unitary. It was only as science and crafts-manship built up the importance of the "external" world that the dualism of the "inner" and "outer" worlds, of "reality" and "appearance," "mind" and "body," became increasingly significant. In this historical sense the development of such a dualism was of course a step in the right direction. Better that the "external" world should have been misconceived than that it should not have been recognized at all! But it is nevertheless a fact, deplored by a host of modern investigators, that the price we have paid for the early development of science and technology has been exorbitantly high. For by virtue of the feedback effect the "inner" voice, first of "conscience" and then later of "moral sentiments," became the voice of authority in the modern world.

4

It is this circumstance that gives a sinister significance to the whole philosophy of individualism, that has played so great a part in the development of Western culture throughout modern times. In a very real and significant sense the whole movement of Western civilization has of course been away from authority and toward what Sir Henry Maine called "contract." But that movement has been indirect. Thus it proceeded not by the rejection of authority as such, but rather, as Carl Becker pointed out in his most inspired book, *The Heavenly City of the Eighteenth Century Philosophers*, by the substitution of the authority of Nature for that of an ever-present Creator.

In this process "the individual" played a uniquely significant part. For long before the sentiments of the individual became the voice of Nature, the individual conscience spoke with the voice of God. Rebels against the established order were sustained by the self-validating authenticity of the inner voice.

Modern civilization is to a unique degree the work of individuals: that is, displaced persons, an amorphous assemblage of people, neither nobles nor serfs, who had been, as Pirenne put it, uprooted from their feudal habitat; a sort of intermediate or middle class, who clustered together in extramural settlements. It was as individuals that the participants in this rebellion had been uprooted and displaced. As escapees, they rejected the authority of the institutions, political and ecclesiastical, from which they had made their escape.

But they could not reject the content of the only culture they knew. No people can. As participants in medieval culture, they brought that culture along with them "in their heads." Thus the institutions of bourgeois society which gradually evolved from their activities had an authentic history. But they lacked external authority. It was this lack which was filled by the authority of individual "inner light." More important even than any external circumstances such as historical legitimacy was the conviction of rectitude, the inner conviction of being right, the intensity and effectiveness of which are explicable only in terms of the feedback principle.

In seeking to follow the inner light the pioneers of modern Western individualism were doing two things. They were deliberately rejecting traditional belief and traditional authority, and they were to the best of their ability aligning themselves with the order of nature. Theirs was the spirit of genuine inquiry. As intellectual pioneers they deserve our highest admiration. Beyond question the present level of investigation would have been impossible to attain except as a consequence of such pioneering. Nevertheless we must likewise bear in mind that the conception of individual autonomy, by which Western civilization has been so greatly influenced, was in process of formation between three and four centuries before the time of Darwin. The order of nature to which the pioneer individualists sought to assimilate mankind was a pre-Darwinian order.

That there is some sort of order in nature goes without saying, and it is no less true and obvious that all human arrangements must conform to the uniformities of nature. Men have gone wrong only as their conceptions of the uniformities of nature have been wrong; and those conceptions have been wrong not only from ignorance but even more by virtue of being vitiated by the prejudices and preconceptions of prevailing societies. Our own conception of nature has very largely escaped that curse, and it therefore offers greater hope of an intellectually valid criterion of value than mankind has ever enjoyed before. This is a matter of the greatest importance, to which I shall therefore return again and again. For an understanding of the emergence of the principle of individualism, however, what is most significant is the pre-Darwinian character of the conception of nature, and especially of human nature, that sustained the principle of individual autonomy.

The individual from whom all the institutions of bourgeois society thus derived their authority was not a product of evolution. He was the creation of the Almighty, who had created him in His own image. It was possible for the authority of individual conscience to supplant that of the established Church only because every individual could recognize the voice of God speaking through his own conscience.

Political authority underwent the same transformation. By virtue of the feedback principle it became possible for "individual rights" to assume the same indefeasibility which had appertained to feudal legitimacy. The intellectual apparatus which accompanied the shift was of course complex and varied. But what has lent conviction to the philosophy of individualism in all of its many manifestations has been the common experience of all men: to wit, the feeling expressed late in the nineteenth century by the poet, W. E. Henley, "I am the master of my fate; I am the captain of my soul." In the absence of such a feeling, common to all rebellious spirits, a feeling that is seemingly confirmed by its own vividness, no theory of the autonomy of the individual could have won general assent. Given the feeling, the intellectual details have been, and still are, a relatively minor matter.

5

By far the most important consequence of the feedback effect has been, and still is, the seemingly axiomatic identification of values with feelings. Because individual experience has seemed to provide the ostensible ground for this identification, throughout the ages men who have been seeking to free themselves from common superstition have sought in feelings a genuinely secular criterion of value. They have done so for reasons that are now obvious. As individual experiences all experiences of pleasure and pain, of likes and dislikes, and of good or bad seem remarkably similar; and so they are, if we leave out of account the whole process of social conditioning. Pain is what used to be called a physical sensation, and there is even such a thing as the physical sensation of pleasure. These experiences are common to animals. They involve the functioning of specific bodily mechanisms, and can therefore be designated meaningfully as "natural." Injuries are harmful as well as painful; food is nourishing as well as pleasant; and consequently it seems equally natural to suppose that the injuries are bad because they are painful and the food good because it is pleasant.

Are likes and dislikes similarly natural? That is what hedonists of every stripe have always supposed. They have done so for two reasons: first, because the feedback effect makes all feelings seem as spontaneous and natural as any sensation, and second, because no general theory of moral sentiments is possible unless likes and dislikes are assumed to be as natural as physical sensations. Hedonism has always assumed intelligence. It was just as evident to the ancient philosophers as it is to us that some painful experiences are good and some pleasant ones bad. This offers no difficulty so long as the criterion is still that of physical sensation. The pleasures of eating may be outweighed by the pain of indigestion, and the pain of dentistry may be outweighed by one's escape from more severe and prolonged suffering later on. By this reasoning the good life, both for individuals and for societies, becomes a simple matter of the calculus of pleasures and pains—very complex no doubt in the proliferation of detail, but in principle fundamentally simple. But in order to suppose that such a calculus does constitute the good life, it is necessary also to suppose that what is true of pleasures and pains is likewise true of likes and dislikes—that the agonies of shame and guilt are strictly analogous to those of toothache, and that the pleasures of public approbation are like drink to the thirsty.

This is the assumption which runs through the theory of moral sentiments in all its various manifestations. By the eighteenth century, when the British "empiricists" were laying the intellectual foundations of classical political economy and utilitarian ethics, both of which found consummate expression a century later in the works of John Stuart Mill, modern thought was well settled in the groove of psychophysical dualism. Notwithstanding the organic "basis" of pleasure and pain, the supposition was that even those feelings occur in the "mind." Thus the absence of organic apparatus for the detection of likes and dislikes constituted no barrier to the further supposition that they also occur in the mind. That such is indeed the case every man could easily determine for himself by inwardly contemplating the operation of his own mind. The spontaneity and vigor of his own likes and dislikes seemingly provided the clearest kind of evidence that likes and dislikes are "natural" phenomena—that they are "given" attributes of all mankind, implanted in human nature by the Creator as one of the "pre-established harmonies" of the Order of Nature.

6

Thus the feedback effect provided one of the two foundation ideas upon which the whole theory of the self-regulating market was erected. I have already remarked upon the significance and the amazing plausibility of that theory, which, more than anything else, epitomizes the ideology of modern Western civilization. Its significance could scarcely be greater, for it is nothing less than a theory of man's relation to nature. Moreover, it is in intention a wholly secular theory. As products of the Age of Reason, both of its foundation ideas, man and nature, are seemingly naturalistic. That is why they are so plausible. Nevertheless, both are quite unmistakably pre-Darwinian. Indeed, this whole theory of the interaction of man and nature is a projection of Leibnitzian "pre-established harmony." In effect it assumes that man and nature have been independently created by an omniscient Architect, but so cunningly devised that, guided by the laws of its own being, each will naturally adjust itself to the requirements of the other: man to nature, and nature to man. Needless to say, this conception has completely disappeared from twentieth-century science. It persists only in the classical theory of the economy.

That theory is most commonly epitomized today by its exponents in terms of "The allocation of scarce resources among alternative uses." The supposition is, of course, that the mechanism of allocation is the market, and that what the market does by way of allocating scarce resources among alternative uses cannot be done (or cannot be done as well) by any other instrumentality. Although economists do not ordinarily emphasize the fact, this whole conception of the allocating process necessarily assumes that "scarce resources" and "alternative uses" are independent variables; for if the same circumstances which define resources and determine their relative scarcity or profusion also determine their uses, then it is those circumstances which in actual fact do the allocating, the market being scarcely more than a recording mechanism, like a ticker tape, upon which the decisive circumstances are registered.

We know today that resources and uses are not independent variables. For many years Professor Erich Zimmermann, the leading authority on the subject of resources, developed the thesis that both the identity of resources and their relative scarcity or profusion are determined by the culture of the people in question. For example, even such a common material as aluminum, which exists (as we now know) in all parts of the world, can be identified as a resource only since its identification as a chemical element and, more specifically, since the discovery in 1886 of the electrolytic process for extracting the metal from bauxite.

No student of resources now questions the cultural determination of the identity and availability of resources, and the same is true of "alternative uses." It is the culture of any given people that determines the uses to which all things shall be put—both whether they shall be used at all, in what various ways they shall be used, and in what circumstances and what amount the various members of the community shall use them. Furthermore, culture traits do not vary independently. There is no point on which greater agreement prevails among cultural anthropologists than this. Every culture is an integer of which every part bears a functional relationship to every other part such that no change can occur in any part without all the rest of the culture being affected in some degree. Thus, for example, the invention of the automobile has brought changes in the class structure of American society, by virtually wiping out the distinction between riders and walkers. It has also markedly altered the pattern of urban areas, creating suburbia and making shopping centers grouped around "cash-and-carry" supermarkets the order of the day.

But when Adam Smith wrote his *Theory of Moral Sentiments* and later drafted the first full-scale blue print of the self-regulating market in *The Wealth of Nations*, all this was far in the future. In his day the scarcity of the resources by which man lives seemed to have been decreed by "the niggardliness of Nature," and natural scarcity seemed quite distinct from the sentiments and likes and wants of human nature and the alternative uses which flow from them. Indeed, long before the time of Adam Smith reflective minds had already begun to be fascinated by the subtle adjustments of the market and to seek out the independent variables which might thus be undergoing adjustment to each other. On the supply side, given the face of the earth, labor seemed to be the decisive variable by which "cost" is determined, or even perhaps the "corn" which was thought to be the principal cost of the labor supply. It was Adam Smith's great achievement to systematize this analysis by recognizing land, labor, and capital as "factors of production."

Meantime, on the demand side of the market theory, moral sentiments have continued to reign supreme. Even today economists declare, just as the moral philosophers of the eighteenth century did, that "wants are primary data." That is to say they are what they are because human nature is what it is, quite independently of the geographical circumstances which (presumably) define "natural" scarcity.

7

This dissociation of "resources" and "uses"—and their treatment as independent variables—does more than establish the market as the central guiding mechanism of the economy. It also constitutes the ground for the identification of resources as the "means" to the attainment of uses as an "end," a consummation in which the identification of values with sentiments plays a strategic part.

Obviously the founders of classical political economy were not the originators of the distinction of means from ends. That distinction must surely have its origin in the common day-to-day activities of mankind. Wherever intention exists in human affairs and whatever it may mean, whatever is done with such intention is the means to whatever is intended as the end of that intention; and in the setting of everyday activity means and ends have the meaning, whatever it is, of that intention. By the same token, throughout the ages mankind has in imagination endowed supernatural beings with intentions; and insofar as their powers have been conceived to transcend those of man, the ends which their intentions have been conceived to define have therefore transcended human ends. Hence the conception of "higher" ends of cosmic scope and "ultimate" significance has been a familiar one throughout human history. I shall have more to say about this phenomenon in a later chapter, and only mention the matter at this point by way of noting that conceptions of cosmic ends and of the subordination of human values to such ends have pervaded the Judaeo-Christian tradition of Western civilization. Hence it is not surprising that such a notion should have been prevalent in the eighteenth century. It is prevalent even today.

What is surprising is that it should have persisted in the thinking of the tough-minded "empiricists" who developed the theory of moral sentiments into a theory of the socio-economic organization of modern society. This could scarcely have happened except by virtue of the feedback effect. The "satisfaction" that often accompanies the fulfillment of "wants" is so vivid and immediate that it seems to constitute prima facie evidence of the inherent value of the satisfaction-giving "goods," and the "disutility" of "work" is often no less immediate and convincing. When Adam Smith declared that consumption is the end to which all other economic activity is the means, he felt no need to justify or even to explain such a dictum, nor have later writers done so. Indeed, it would be impossible to do so. Just as everybody (except the very young, the very old, and a very few "social butterflies") is both a consumer and a producer, and just as "consumers' goods" and "producers' goods" can be identified as such only with reference to specific operations, so too every operation involves the consumption of something or other and the production of something else. Even rest and recreation contribute to the productive process if, as advertised, they result in spiritual refreshment, enhanced vitality, and longer life. Economic activity is an aspect of the life process of mankind and as such is continuous. The only ground on which it is possible to maintain the consummatory value of consumption is that of "simple common sense"—the emotional experiences of mankind taken at face value: our grumbling at having to get up in the morning, and our occasional exclamations of "Ah! This is what makes life worth living!"

8

This illusion which has played so large a part in the theory of the self-regulating market—the illusion that built-in sentiments provide natural guidance to mankind—has even survived the Darwinian revolution. No one supposes any longer that likes and dislikes were implanted in mankind by special creation for the guidance of the race. As I have already noted in the preceding chapter, anthropology has supplanted zoology at this point. Only the bodily mechanisms of our feelings are provided by Darwinian creation. Notwithstanding our common experience of the feedback effect, we are now well aware of the role of culture in the conditioning process by which we learn to grumble and exclaim. Moreover, thanks to Freud and his army of successors, we also know how tremendously important are the earliest years of childhood for the development of "Conscience"—the feelings of shame and guilt which later find expression in moral judgments. It is also true, of course, that the heritage of culture includes the vast accumulation of knowledge and skill as well as the material embodiment of past skill and knowledge; and it is true of the earliest years of childhood that they also witness the most important educational experiences of human life, the seeming miracle by which the human infant learns to speak and to manipulate tools—thereby re-enacting the cultural miracle by which man first rose above the animals. But so strong is our feeling of the importance of feeling that we can relegate all such matters to an instrumental role.

In short, the twentieth century has produced a sort of cultural hedonism. Like the hedonistic philosophies of ancient times, and like the eighteenth-century theory of moral sentiments, this doctrine holds that feelings constitute the directives, the rewards and punishments of human life. This twentieth-century hedonism is not a product of modern science, any more than the theory of moral sentiments was a product of economic investigation. In both cases —indeed, in all its manifestations—the doctrine that human life is guided by feelings is an axiom upon which subsequent investigation is based. The only proof of the importance of feeling is feeling itself. Thus modern psychiatry does not undertake to show the primacy of feelings by any sort of medical evidence. Indeed, the medical evidence would seem to show the contrary: that people in whose lives feelings are preponderant become deranged. The more we contemplate our feelings, the more obsessive they become. But the source of the conviction, in all such situations, is an illusion. Anthropological investigation likewise reveals how feelings are conditioned among various peoples. It also exhibits the extent to which the affairs of such peoples are affected by such culturally conditioned feelings. It does not establish that such conditions are the necessary fate of all mankind, nor even that any such people are better off for feeling as they do. On the contrary, just as in the case of psychiatry, the evidence seems to show that they would be better off if they were a little less susceptible to bogus fears and ecstasies. What establishes our belief that all values are made known by feelings is not the anthropological evidence but our own feelings.

9

What the anthropological evidence establishes is the relativity of feeling-values, and therefore—axiomatically—of all values. For if values arise only from feelings, and if feelings give expression only to the beliefs and practices of particular cultures, then there are no values of any general significance. But do values arise only from feelings? After all has been said, we have only the warrant of our feelings for any such "axiom," and we have the best of reasons to distrust our feelings.

That we do in fact make value judgments in quite another way is a matter of common experience—just as common, indeed, as our experience of feelings. Furthermore, such evaluations are judgments in the true sense of the word. What they express is our understanding of the facts of life. If we use the word "subjective" to refer to feelings, as we commonly do, then these are objective judgments, since they are based not on feelings but on facts. Our understanding of facts is never absolute or final, and to the degree that such is the case our factually based value judgments also fall short of absolute finality—but only to that degree; for we judge values by the same criterion in terms of which we establish truth. For example, we judge health to be good and illness bad by the same process of reasoning by which we identify and define health and illness.

That criterion is objective in another sense. Not only does it have to do with facts; what it does is done with tools and instruments. As such, the process of valuation is a cultural process; but it is a different cultural process from that by which our feelings are conditioned. This is the distinction which must be understood if true values are to be understood and distinguished from false values; and since it is the contrasting aspects of **culture** which have to be distinguished, that can be done only through **an** understanding of the nature of culture, to which, therefore, the immediately ensuing chapters will be addressed.

CHAPTER V

HUMANITY'S TWO ASPECTS

I

W ITHIN THE PAST TWO OR THREE GENERATIONS the whole universe of discourse of human affairs has undergone revolutionary change. In making such a sweeping statement I do not
mean to suggest that we have cut ourselves off completely from the
past. That has never happened. Even after the Copernican revolution the stars and planets were the same. Not only are they still in
the same places as before; we still call them by the names they acquired in remote antiquity. Bodies were known to fall even before
the law of falling bodies was established. Fire was known, and
quite a bit was known about it, before it was known to exemplify
the process of combination of chemical elements. The same is true
of the universe of human affairs. The affairs themselves are much
the same as always. Thus, for example, mankind is just as emotional as ever. Furthermore, as I suggested in the preceding chapter,
the assumption that emotions play an essential part in the determination and organization of man's values has persisted into the
twentieth century notwithstanding the cultural revolution. What
has changed is our conception of the whole process of human
activity, the whole setting in which values are conceived to exist.
In a word, culture has replaced human nature as the foundation
idea for an understanding of the actions, thoughts, and feelings
of all human beings.

That the cultural revolution followed immediately on the heels
of the Darwinian revolution is a matter of obvious historical fact;
but why it did so is not so obvious. The central idea of the
zoological revolution that is associated with the name of Darwin
is that of evolutionary change. Indeed, in the generation preceding Darwin's the same idea had already revolutionized the science
of geology. Lyell's "principle of uniformity," which is generally
known to have been a major influence upon the thinking of Charles

Darwin, substituted the idea of gradual, evolutionary change over a prodigious span of time for the then-prevalent notion of earth-wracking cataclysm in the explanation of geological processes; and what Darwin did was to carry over into zoology the same notion of a gradual process extending over the time span of geological epochs. This idea seemed to be directly applicable to the explanation of the development of civilization; and consequently one of the most imrnediate effects of the theory of the evolution of species was the development of similar theories of the evolution of society.

The record of this development is a striking one. When *The Origin of Species* appeared Herbert Spencer was already at the height of his powers. Indeed, under the influence of Lamarck and Von Baer he was already in revolt against the prevailing doctrine of special creation. Hence he welcomed Darwinian evolution most enthusiastically and attached to it the phrase by which it is still popularly identified, "survival of the fittest." This idea—a sort of combination of hedonism with evolutionism—became the central theme of all his major works, the influence of which was of course immense. In the United States it was carried still farther by Lester F. Ward, the founder of American sociology, who coined the term *telesis* to designate the conscious development toward a preconceived end which knowledge of the evolutionary process had now, he thought, made possible. The monumental works of these two writers pretty much span the remainder of the nineteenth century, and were followed, just after the turn of the century, by Benjamin Kidd's *Social Evolution*. By the time that work appeared other ideas were beginning to occupy the minds of scholars, and as a consequence Kidd failed to receive the acclaim of his greater predecessors. Nevertheless *Social Evolution* was very widely read and therefore may be taken as indication of what was generally thought to be the significance of Darwinian evolution for an understanding of social development.

Meantime Tylor was laying the foundations of the new science of social anthropology. His *Primitive Culture: Researches into the Development of Mythology, Philosophy, Religion, Language, Art and Custom*, published in 1871, likewise exemplified what is now regarded as a naive evolutionism, as also did Morgan's *Ancient Society, or Researches in the Lines of Human Progress from Savagery, through Barbarism, to Civilization,* published in 1877. Thus from the very first the attention of students of society was focussed upon the developmental aspect of the Darwinian revolution.

2

In view of the eminence of Darwin's earliest social interpreters, it is not surprising that students of society even at the present day should persist in reading the lesson of evolution as that simply of a process of gradual change. But Darwin did not explain a process by which fixed and immutable species had come into existence through gradual change. His most revolutionary achievement was that of substituting for the classical conception of species a new conception of species itself. It was by conceiving species as tentative, flexible, and continually changing forms that he was able to account for the amazing diversity of organic structures; and it was the application of this conception to man himself that aroused the most violent antagonism. Is man what he is because he was created by the Almighty in His own image, a little lower than the angels? Or is he, as Darwinism held, a sort of super-ape? This was the principal challenge with which Darwinism confronted all students of human affairs, and this was the question to which the concept of culture has at length supplied an effective answer.

For the critics of "Darwin's ape theory" had a point. Nothing is more obvious than the fact that human activities—which is to say the human "mind"—cannot be accounted for in zoological terms, however "evolutionary." The principles of zoological evolution account for the structure of the human body and for the organic functioning of all its various members. But the patterns of human activity and of human thought and feeling are not accounted for by the functioning of any organ nor of all the organs of the body taken together.

It is true of course that the species pattern of the human body sets limits to all human activities. We sometimes say of situations in which we find ourselves that they call for three or four hands. But no machine can be operated by any one man which really does make such a demand. No human being can carry on any activity continuously without interruption for more than a few hours. Our bodies do indeed impose physical limits upon all our undertakings.

It is also true that no two human beings are exactly alike. In recent years researches in such fields as genetics and biochemistry have revealed organic differences between one individual and another of a hitherto unsuspected degree of subtlety. There can be no doubt that such physical differences do affect the performance of various activities by various individuals in many and various ways, and this has led some scientists to make sweeping assertions with regard to the supposed primacy of physical characteristics in the patterning of human activities. But though it may be true that one man's speaking voice has a different pitch and timbre from another's and that one man speaks with greater poise and assurance than another, and though it may be true that such differences derive from physical heredity, surely all those differences taken together are of less significance for the totality of those men's activities than the fact of the existence of the English language, a medium of communication by virtue of which alone they are able to speak at all and so to engage in all the activities to which language communication is a prime necessity.

But a language is not an item of physical heredity. It is a social, or cultural, heritage. This heritage is not a faculty, or function, of the human body, although it exists only by virtue of human existence; nor is it a set of physical objects the existence of which is independent of the existence of mankind, although it does find expression in physical artifacts which do have a physical existence independently of any particular human being or group of human beings. Indeed, it is, as many social theorists have pointed out, *sui generis:* a unique order of entities, neither objects, nor processes, but rather a body of action patterns; one that exists only by virtue of man and is perpetuated only by transmission from one generation of human beings to another; but one that has an objective existence independently of any particular individual, and is assimilated by each individual human being. Every human being becomes human in the behavioral sense only by assimilating such a body of action patterns. At birth he is human only in the zoological sense. His body is that of a member of our species; but he is utterly incapable of behaving as all human beings do (for instance, he is utterly unable to communicate, languagewise) until he has learned a set of action patterns by virtue of which he is able to participate in the activities of a community among whom that set of action patterns already prevails.

3

It is this body of action patterns which has come to be known as "culture." This revolutionary concept has emerged from the study of social anthropology. Whereas all the social sciences, and for that matter all the humanities, are concerned with particular aspects or areas of culture, it is almost altogether through the study of the whole cultures of the many and various primitive peoples by social anthropologists that the significance of culture has come to be understood. Its significance is revolutionary because at long last it resolves the mystery of man's humanness, thus completing the secular revolution that began in early modern times.

For the concept of culture does three things. It squares with Darwinism. The animal species, *Homo sapiens,* carries on the activities characteristic of mankind by virtue of the group elaboration and transmission of culture. It also explains the very great diversity of human societies, a diversity incomparably greater than the individual variations which zoologists have been able to detect. For each society is by cultural definition a law unto itself. Every feature of every culture must be understood not as it appears to representatives of other cultures, but as it actually functions in the culture of which it is a feature. At the same time the theory of culture likewise explains the otherwise amazing stability and persistence of the diverse societies of the world, since each society imposes upon all its members the sanctions by which the continuance of that society is insured.

I have spoken of the elaboration of cultures by the communities among whom they prevail, rather than of the creation of culture, because we have no direct knowledge of any beginning. The most ancient human remains are always accompanied by evidences of culturally organized activity: artifacts, the remains of fires, food refuse, and the like. Social theorists have sometimes pondered the question which came first, culture or society. But as knowledge accumulates this seems more and more clearly to be a hen-and-egg conundrum. Clearly culture, defined as a body of activity patterns, and society, defined as an organized community, are aspects of the same phenomenon. The creation of interpersonal relationships is a function of culture. All cultural action patterns define social relationships. Thus, for example, language communication postulates a speaker and a listener. Otherwise it is inconceivable. Similarly, all social relationships assume the existence of common activity patterns (such as those of speech). Otherwise the relationship would be inconceivable. It was lack of the concept of culture that thwarted the efforts of such intellectual pioneers as Hobbes, Locke, and Rousseau to account for the existence of organized society. We do not know how culturally organized society began; but we do know that from the "beginning," whatever it was, culture and society were aspects of each other.

No important issue turns upon the supposed time sequence of the beginnings of society and culture. But the differentiation of these two aspects of human experience—the supposition that they are two distinct sets of phenomena such that one might conceivably precede the other—has had grave consequences. Like another closely related differentiation, into which also scholars have been led quite innocently, it has resulted in serious misunderstanding.

4

In order to get a clear picture of these misunderstandings we must repeat a little and anticipate a little.

As I have been saying repeatedly, what we sometimes call "human nature," sometimes "society," and sometimes "culture," has two contrasting aspects. This is no new insight. Throughout the ages thoughtful men have pictured the human race as drawn one way by white horses and another way by black horses. The difficulty has always been the clear identification of these two breeds of horses; and what has made the differentiation difficult is the fact which we are only just beginning to see, that it pervades all the activities of life. Thus to think of values as white and knowledge as black is to plunge into utter confusion. Some knowledge is black and some white, and some values are black and some white; and the same is true of human nature, society, culture, or whatever else we may call the totality of human experience. Similarly, any differentiation of human experience into compartments such as "society" and "culture" immediately exposes us to the risk of identifying one as white and the other as black. But if, as now seems clear, white and black run through all human experience, such an identification is bound to be false and so to confuse our whole picture—of values, or knowledge, or society, or culture, as well as of the bi-polarity that runs through all of them.

This is what results from the differentiation of society from culture. An apparently innocent and useful distinction almost inevitably acquires meanings that spell trouble. To see how this comes

What scholars always have in mind in speaking of society is the

What scholars always have in mind in speaking of society is the network of relationships, some immediate and some extremely remote, by which all the individuals of a community are tied to each other. All of these relationships have two aspects or characteristics, to which I have just been referring as black and white. All are in some degree technological, and all are in some degree ceremonial or institutionalized. The degree in each case varies very greatly, of course; and this is of the highest importance. That is, some relationships are predominantly working, operational, tool-skill relationships; whereas some are predominantly status relationships of power and subservience, arbitrarily established by "legitimate" birth, authentically performed ceremonies, and the like.

What most needs to be stressed in this connection is that technology—the tool-using aspect of human behavior—is not something separate and distinct from the societal network of personal relationships. It permeates all such relationships. This is a point of the utmost importance which will be developed further and reiterated frequently in this discussion. The most serious error one can make with regard to human experience, society, culture, and all related matters is that of thinking of technology as "external," outside us, an aspect of the physical environment of individual men and even of societies. In truth it is none of these things. All tool-using is social. What Adam Smith called "the division of labor" is defined and required by tools—required not in the sense of the exercise of arbitrary authority but in the sense that the job in hand can be done only by four or more hands working together, hands which in the

77

Toward a Reasonable Society

nature of the case must belong to two or more persons. One person holds the lump of flint and another taps it with a flaking tool. One pulls the plowing stick and the other guides it.

For "interpersonal relationships" such as these no authority is needed. But every society is permeated with arbitrary distinctions by which authority is defined. Furthermore, such ceremonial considerations are present to some degree in all working situations, so that it is possible to suppose that social rank dictates whatever division of labor may develop. Is pulling the stick menial because women do it? Or do women do it because it is menial? Is housework menial because women do it? Or do women do it because it is menial? All such questions are loaded—loaded, that is, with ceremonialism. Both alternatives assume that the relationships in question are wholly ceremonial, since both ignore the technological necessity that dictates a division of labor.

This is a serious matter. Once the habit of ignoring the technological aspect of all social structures has been well established, the conclusion seems to be forced upon us that all social structure is ceremonial. Thus it appears that social organization as such is wholly dependent upon myths, conventions, and arbitrary traditions. But this is a half truth that is all the more misleading for being one-half true, one into which we have been led (in part) by making the initial assumption that social organization and culture (which includes the heritage of technology) are distinct.

5

This misunderstanding might have been avoided if it had not been accentuated by another seemingly obvious but highly misleading differentiation. The study of primitive cultures, by which all our social thinking has been so profoundly affected, involves two distinct orders of data. One consists of physical objects: the tools, weapons, accouterments, charms, fetishes, ikons, and all the other physical apparatus of life in any given community; and the other consists of all the rest of the culture of that community. The former is called the community's material culture, and the latter its nonmaterial culture.

This differentiation resulted almost inevitably from the circumstances of investigation. The material culture consists of all the

78

objects which investigators can collect and bring away with them and subsequently install in museums. In the case of ancient peoples it is all that remains. Time itself has effected the differentiation for us. But even in the case of living communities there is a sharp contrast between what can be brought away intact and what can be observed only in the actual life of the people themselves.

Now the terms, *material* and *nonmaterial*, by which these two orders of data have come to be known, are innocuous enough. But several sets of circumstances have combined to give them hidden meanings which have seriously aggravated our confusion with regard to the meaning of value.

One of these is the circumstances surrounding the collection of the objects which comprise the material culture of the peoples under investigation. Such a collection will of course include sacred objects, magic charms, and the like, which are thought by the people from whom they came to be endowed with mystic potencies, as well as knives, axes, baskets, pottery, and the like. To the Western mind, however, even to the minds of research scientists, all such objects are alike. The sacred charms are just as inert as the commonest tools. The anthropologist is well aware of the feelings they arouse in the minds of their own people; but the circumstances of collection, transportation, and subsequent scientific study are such as to suggest very strongly that the magic resides not in the objects but in the minds of the primitive people who created them, and that it has remained behind when the objects themselves were removed. Hence even the most careful student tends to disregard such differences of mystic potency, and to put the entire collection in the same cabinet, treating its various items all alike as inert physical objects, and so to lay the foundation for the tacit assumption that the significant distinction is between the material culture, which as such seems to be wholly secular, and the nonmaterial culture, which by inference seems to be suffused with mysticism.

The effect of this sequestration of collectible objects is tremendously heightened by the seeming externality of our own "material culture." As individuals the denizens of modern Western civilization find themselves surrounded by a vast and complex assemblage of artifacts in the creation of which they have had no direct part.

This technological jungle seems to most people virtually continuous with the landscape itself. They think of it habitually as a major constituent of the physical environment in which their lives are lived, and this is no less true of educated people than of anybody else. For example, all those who deplore the proliferation of "gadgets" do so on the assumption that what they stigmatize as gadgets are external to man, that the human spirit is quite distinct from such physical surroundings, and that it is in danger of being suffocated by "things."

Obviously there is a sense in which all artifacts, from the simplest to the most complex, are indeed external to man. Furthermore, this circumstance is highly significant. The externality of all tools, instruments, and apparatus, and all the materials of which all tools, instruments, and apparatus are made, including the apparatus of scholarship and scientific research, is an essential condition of the technological process. It is because tools have a physical existence external to the human body that they accumulate in physical juxtaposition to each other, and so are susceptible to the process of combination and recombination which we call invention and discovery. That all such combining is effected by human intelligence also should go without saying. Though tools are physical objects, what distinguishes them from all the other physical objects in the universe is their character as artifacts—that is, objects upon which human skill has been expended. As artifacts they signalize human skill and human knowledge, and these characteristics are no less essential aspects of the technological process than the externality of all artifacts and of the materials from which they have been shaped. All this is immediately obvious if we focus our attention upon the technological process; and it is so essential to an understanding of that process that I shall necessarily revert to it whenever that process is under discussion.

But notwithstanding the obvious fact that all the works of man bear witness to human genius (or perversity) and condition the human way of life at every point, as individuals we are so conscious of the externality of our own material culture that we habitually think of it as an outer shell within which the "real" life process goes on. Thinking so about our own lives, we inevitably tend to think of the material cultures of other peoples, which we have been able to collect and bring away, as constituting likewise only the outer shell of the "real" life of those peoples.

This disposition is further heightened by another set of circumstances affecting the study of the nonmaterial culture. In the first place, the term *nonmaterial*, though it was adopted only by way of contrast with the collectible objects that comprise the "material" culture, nevertheless carries semantic overtones suggestive of the opposite of "materialism." By verbal implication the nonmaterial is intangible, mysterious, and otherworldly. Doubtless this implication would never have had serious consequences by itself. But it has not been left to itself. Unfortunately, other circumstances have pointed in the same direction.

6

Strictly speaking, the nonmaterial culture includes the entire system of practices, customs, or folkways by which the life of a community seems to be organized. In view of the very great importance which economic organization has assumed in modern Western civilization one might therefore suppose that the chief interest of Western scholars in the social systems of primitive peoples would from the first have been their economic organization: their crafts and skills, their knowledge of materials, their dietary, their division of labor, their system of distribution, and the like. But in actuality just the opposite has been the case. It is only quite recently that such matters have begun to command the attention of the social anthropologists. From the very first the chief object of interest has been the folklore of primitive peoples—their superstitious beliefs and quasi-religious practices, their strange taboos and revolting mores, their animism and their totemism, and generally their obsession with an imaginary world of spirits and mystic potencies.

This interest has of course been no monopoly of social anthropologists. On the contrary, it expresses the "natural" curiosity all men feel in what is strangest and most spine-tingling in the behavior of other people. It is not strange that people living in a forest should hunt and eat wild animals. But it is strange that they should imagine themselves to be related somehow to the beavers, and that they should subject themselves on occasion to gruesome tortures. From time immemorial that is the sort of thing which has been reported by travelers. As Europeans began to travel more widely than any people had ever done before, lore of this kind began to accumulate and to excite the interest of scholars as well as the general public. Thus long before Darwinism had focussed scholarly attention upon the evolution of culture, literary and philological interest had led the Grimm brothers and Hans Christian Andersen to the systematic collection of folk tales and to the recognition of their cultural significance, and this interest carried over into social anthropology itself. Thus, as the title of his chief work indicates, Sir Edward Tylor's interest in primitive culture was focussed on the mythology, philosophy, and religion of primitive peoples, an interest which reached its culmination at the end of the nineteenth century in Sir James Frazer's monumental *Golden Bough.*

No social anthropologist has ever declared explicitly that the nonmaterial culture even of the most primitive peoples consists exclusively of superstitions, taboos, and occult practices. Indeed, as the science has developed, kinship systems and related forms of tribal organization have come in for a great deal of attention. But it is significant that all the interpersonal relationships of all these systems are channeled by taboos of one sort or another, and that it is upon these taboos—incest taboos, endogamy and exogamy, name taboos, mother-in-law taboos, and the like—that anthropological interest has centered; and as a consequence the impression has been created that the nonmaterial culture is synonymous with the occult.

Indeed, this impression came to be so strongly established that the French school of social anthropologists, led in the last generation by Lévy-Bruhl, did explicitly assert that the "mentality" of primitive peoples is essentially "alogical." In recent decades that proposition has been completely abandoned, but not so much in deference to the reasoning power of primitives as in recognition of the very great importance of culturally conditioned "alogical" sentiment in the lives even of the modern Western peoples. Thus the theory that the mentality of primitive peoples is essentially different from that of civilized peoples has been completely supplanted by the doctrine of cultural relativism, the upshot of which is that all peoples are alike in being creatures of sentiment and in having their sentiments conditioned and patterned by their cultures, and that each culture is a law unto itself—in short, that there is no common criterion, let alone any universal law, by which all cultures can be judged.

I do not mean to suggest that modern scholarship reached this impasse merely by reacting against the theories of Lucien Lévy-Bruhl and his disciples. Many influences converged upon this point. Perhaps the most important of these is the doctrine of moral sentiments which, as I tried to show in the preceding chapter, has been endemic in Western thought throughout modern times and is still supported by the feedback effect: that is, by the seeming testimony of our own feelings. Another significant development, to which also reference has already been made, is the line of inquiry of which Sigmund Freud was the great pioneer. This is a field in which wide divergences of opinion, at least in matters of detail, continue to prevail. But certain basic truths have emerged from the study of psychopathology which have come to be accepted not only by all the workers in the field but also by the general public. It is very much more apparent today than it has ever been before that irrational impulses and emotional seizures play a very considerable part in human behavior: that the emotional experiences of early childhood color the whole of subsequent experience; that the process by which animal impulses and emotions are curbed, channeled, and "sublimated" by social conventions is an extremely subtle and pervasive one; and consequently that even our most rational behavior is always subject to the suspicion of being a "rationalization" of hidden, sublimated, and symbolized emotions. The psychopathologists do not assert that man is the helpless victim of his emotions. But their studies do complement those of social anthropology in underscoring the significance of the process by which man's emotional nature undergoes social conditioning.

7

As a net effect of all these circumstances two serious misconceptions have taken deep root in the minds of twentieth-century social scientists. One is the identification of the whole organizational structure of society with the "nonmaterial" culture, and the other is the identification of nonmaterial culture with the cult of ir-rationality. No social scientist asserts either of these identities clearly and unambiguously as a general principle of social organiza-tion. For that matter I do not know of any contemporary scholar who explicitly externalizes the material culture and in so many words denies that tools have any functional relationship to social organization. Obviously it would be impossible to do so. Virtually all the tools mankind has ever made and used involve some meas-ure of organized cooperation. This is true even of the simplest tools and the simplest societies, and the higher the technology the greater is the measure of organized cooperation that is required. But if one begins at the other end of the cultural spectrum, it is quite possible to ignore all this, and that is what twentieth-century scholarship has done.

Thus one may begin with the undeniable proposition that social organization is a necessary condition of human life. Without it life is indeed solitary, nasty, brutish, and short. But in every depart-ment social organization is permeated by arbitrary conventions, irrational beliefs, and the sentiments and attitudes which result from lifelong emotional conditioning, especially that of infancy. This is true of the family organizations and kinship systems which prevail in all societies; it is likewise true of all systems of govern-ment; and it is most emphatically true of all ecclesiastical organiza-tions, all systems of theology, and all sacred rites. Hence it seems to follow that irrational sentiments and arbitrary conventions—all relative to the cultures in which they prevail—constitute a neces-sary condition of human life.

By such reasoning the transcultural significance of all tools and skills and all clear and certain knowledge is simply brushed aside. No one denies that the criterion by which one tool is judged better than another is the same for all peoples—that stone-age savages (a few of whom still existed until quite recently) instantly recog-nize the superiority of a steel knife over a jagged flint. Indeed, archeologists have all along been dating their finds in terms of the levels of technological attainment they reveal (Old Stone Age, New Stone Age, Bronze Age, Iron Age), on the tacit assumption that no people has ever done what Samuel Butler represented his

Erewhonians as having done: deliberately destroyed their machines and voluntarily returned to earlier and simpler—and of course less efficient—tools. These are facts. But facts can be brushed aside if it is assumed that facts are quite distinct from values.

8

This is the consummation to which modern thinking has been led, in significant part by the dissociation of culture from society, and of material from nonmaterial culture. By developing the concept of culture the science of anthropology has taken the lead in a revolutionary advance. No other idea has made a greater contribution to our understanding of human nature. But the circumstances which have affected the further analysis of culture have given currency to distinctions which have become a serious impediment to further understanding. For the distinction of culture from society and of "material" from "nonmaterial" culture coincides with other deep-seated tendencies of modern thought to polarize knowledge and values; and this false polarization has become the chief impediment to our distinguishing clearly between values which are true and rational and those which are irrational and false.

Both are aspects of culture. But the value of a tool is not a function of its materiality. A magic charm is just as material as a digging stick. It is the activity which each signalizes that gives each its significance and its value, in one case genuine and in the other false. The values which the magic charm exemplifies are culture-limited. But the values which the digging stick exemplifies are the same for all peoples and all ages. Even today we use sticks to dig with on occasion, and (if one had survived) we could take a prehistoric digging stick out of its museum cabinet and dig with it just as its prehistoric maker did. By the same token we have better tools today, and by the same criterion human life is better.

The enigma of culture is that of the coexistence of these two contrasting systems of activity, each with its complement of material objects, and both permeating the organization of all societies. Clearly whatever the circumstances are that have made the cultural way of life possible for mankind, those circumstances have made both the aspects of culture possible and perhaps inevitable. It is perhaps inevitable that man the tool user should also be man the mythmaker and the conjurer. If we are to understand what values are and why some values are true and some are false, we shall have to try to understand this anomaly.

CHAPTER VI

HOW REASON AND SUPERSTITION BEGAN

I

THROUGHOUT THE FOREGOING CHAPTERS I have been concerned with the errors of the past. Thus rebuttal seems to have preceded constructive inquiry and exposition. But there is good reason for this. In the first place, the errors under consideration not only continue to prevail at the present time; they dominate the field. Furthermore, they are not vulgar prejudices. On the contrary, they are strictly intellectual errors into which the leading pioneers of earlier generations have been led by the circumstances of resolutely secular inquiry, circumstances by which it would have been virtually impossible for anyone not to have been affected.

The circumstances under which we labor at the present time are different, and consequently it is not too much to hope that we may now avoid the particular blind alleys into which our predecessors have been led. But we shall avoid them only if we know what they are and where they lead. Most particularly, we must discover where the blind alleys branch off from the high road; for if we are to advance at all, we shall be able to do so only by proceeding farther along the way of the genuine advances of the past.

As we look back in this spirit on the achievements and failures of the past we can scarcely fail to be struck by the persistence with which our predecessors have tried to distinguish between what they took to be two contrasting aspects of human experience and activity. We have already noted repeatedly that where they have gone astray is in their identification and differentiation of those two aspects. Working within the limitations of the pre-Darwinian conception of human nature, the greatest thinkers of the seventeenth and eighteenth centuries seized upon the distinction between reason and sentiment, and tried to find in it an understanding of man's system of values. Later, another generation of scholars,

87

working in the universe of discourse of the revolutionary concept of culture, sought guidance in their working distinction between material and nonmaterial culture. It was sheer assumption on the part of earlier scholars that identified value with sentiment, and their error has since been compounded by the further identification of sentiment with the cultural processes through which human sentiments are conditioned by convention, taboo, ritual, and superstition. Nevertheless, both generations of scholars may have been right in thinking that the key to an understanding of man's sys tem of values is to be found in the recognition in human nature and in all cultural activity of two contrasting aspects.

For there is no doubt about it: man is a creature of contrasts. His achievements speak for themselves. But along with triumphs of skill and knowledge which beggar imagination goes a no less appalling degree and amount of self- and mutual obfuscation and mortification. Indeed so general and pervasive are the manifestations of this aspect of human character that it would be impossible to point to any particular exemplification of it without giving mortal offense to large numbers of people.

What is the reason for this? What are these aspects of human character? Why do all men work at such savagely cross purposes, so that their talent for construction is matched only by their genius for destruction?

These contrasting manifestations of human character go as far back as our knowledge goes. It used to be thought that such was not the case. Ardent rebels against the conventions of their own society were so far carried away by revolutionary zeal as to suppose that "natural man" was free of all convention. Hence Rousseau's passionate cry, "Man was born free, but is everywhere in chains!" The once popular theory of "primitive communism" was an expression of that state of mind. The idea was that "originally" man lived in harmony on the bosom of nature, untroubled by supernatural beliefs and "unnatural" conventions. The Garden-of-Eden story serves to indicate the antiquity, and the attractiveness, of such a dream. But modern investigation has established the complete implausibility of that idea, both in theory and in fact. In the whole realm of human affairs nothing is more certainly established than the "artificiality" of all human behavior. Man is born not so much "free" as helpless. His helplessness is alleviated only as he acquires the artifices of organized society, and the evidence shows that even in the most ancient communities these artifices included just such ceremonial practices as Rousseau rebelled against.

Consequently any attempt to understand the differentiation and interplay of the contrasting aspects of man's activities must assume that such a difference has prevailed from the very "beginning." This is a serious difficulty, since we have no record of any "beginning." Indeed, the very notion of a beginning contradicts what we do know of evolutionary process.

However, we do know something of the process. In particular, we have learned a great deal in the last generation or so of what has come to be known as the symbolic process. The indications are clear and strong that this process is the key to an understanding of how an animal species became human. For there is a logic that is inherent in the symbolic process itself. As a process we can see that it works in certain ways, and must do so, just as with the application of heat a mixture of hydrogen and oxygen gases "must" combine to form water. Furthermore, by extrapolating the logic of that process backward in time we can see, at least in a general way, how the activities characteristic of human beings— which is to say, the human "mind"—could have originated; and in doing so we can also see just how "inevitable" it was that, from the very "beginning," those activities should have exhibited the contrasting aspects by which we are still confused.

2

In epitome, the symbolic process is simple enough. It consists in nothing more mysterious or complicated than the response of an organism to a stimulus which is not the "original" or "natural" occasion of that response, nor anything like it, but one which has come to be taken as representative—or symbolic—of it. Clearly the celebrated Pavlov experiment is related to this process. As Pavlov showed, dogs can become so habituated to the ringing of a bell in conjunction with the appearance of food that they can be made to salivate by the ringing of the bell even when no food is present. Probably Pavlov's bell should not be regarded as a true symbol. Probably his dogs would not respond to the ringing of any other bell, or even to the ringing of the familiar one in altogether different circumstances. But there can be no doubt that the susceptibility of the dogs to such conditioning is evidence of the rudiments of the symbolic process.

An associated experience, such as Pavlov's bell, becomes a true symbol only when the association has come to be recognized in a variety of different contexts and by others than the individual who has been conditioned by specifically related experiences. In discussing the origin of language Otto Jespersen suggested that words may have originated in the form of names, and that names may have originated in consequence of the various songlike cries that different individuals may have formed the habit of uttering and by which they may have come to be known. Such utterances would become word-symbols, and so would constitute the germs of language, only by virtue of being reproduced by others to identify the associated individual. Thus true symbols are closely related to associated experiences; but they are different in being independent of specific associated experiences.

Both this relationship and this difference are extremely important for an understanding of the symbolic process. The closeness of the relationship serves to indicate how very slight is the difference between the brain power of man and that of the higher mammals. People who work with dogs and horses (not to mention the great apes) often say that such animals understand English, and lack only the ability to speak it. That is not quite true, of course. Animals do seem to acquire surprisingly large vocabularies. They frequently respond to the familiar words when their trainers use them in conversation, not intending them as cues to the animal concerned. But they do not respond in that fashion to the same words uttered by other people. It is only the word spoken by the trainer in the familiar accent and intonation that prompts the animal. Thus to the animal the word is not quite a true word, through it is very nearly that, but is rather an associated experience. The difference in brain power, represented by this difference between recognition of the spoken word as an associated experience and so as a cue to associated action and recognition of spoken words as symbols (true language), is probably minute. Thomas Huxley once declared that it is so minute that we may never be able to identify the specific brain tissues that make the difference. Nevertheless, that difference, minute as it is, makes all the difference between animal behavior and human activities.

Actually, it is the symbolic process, rather than increased brain power, that makes the difference. To say this is not to deny that increased brain power is prerequisite to carrying on the symbolic process. The point is rather that a very slight difference of brain power makes the difference between almost but not quite being able to symbolize and just being able to do so; but such is the nature of the symbolic process itself that it so greatly magnifies the difference of brain power as to open a vast range of activities to the symbol user from which even the nearest non-symbol user is totally excluded. This explains the contrast between the activities of even the most primitive community and the most intelligent of animals. Archeological evidence reveals that primitive men used to provide themselves with food by driving wild horses over a cliff, where they would fall and be killed or crippled. Even such a rudimentary hunting technique as this involved the cooperative execution of a preconceived plan, and is therefore far beyond the powers of any animal. Some insects carry on activities that seem to resemble those of man, and hence they are called "social" insects. Our knowledge of the mechanisms of such insect behavior is still very slight. But what we do know indicates that the mechanisms of insect behavior are quite different from the symbolic and cultural activities of man.

3

Indissociable from the tremendous magnification of the capabilities of symbol users is the objective existence of the symbol. In discussing the revolutionary concept of culture, in the preceding chapter, I called attention to the insistence of the anthropologists upon the objective existence of culture, and upon its constituting a unique order of phenomena, one that is *sui generis*. This property is inherent in symbols themselves. Once a human throat-sound, gesture, or mark has become associated in the experience of a group of people with some person, object, or operation, its symbolic character is a fact that is independent of any member of the group or even cf the entire living population. A mark may remain after all the human beings in whose experience it became a symbol have disappeared. Thousands of years later its meaning may still be deduced by archeologists. It is, therefore, a symbol still.

A prime characteristic of the symbolic process is its indefinite extensibility. Inasmuch as symbols are physical counterparts of persons, objects, and operations, their numbers increase in direct proportion to the spread of human operations, and by the same process. An inevitable consequence of the use of sharp stones for cutting purposes is the discovery that stones differ—that some are harder than others, and that some fracture in such a way as to facilitate chipping while others do not. Once the naming process has begun, it is likewise inevitable that such differences should be symbolized. Thus the activities of cutting and of selection and the preparation of cutting tools bring about the acquisition of clear and certain knowledge along with technical skills, or as an aspect of such skills.

It is this circumstance that explains the eventual emergence of neolithic from paleolithic culture, and of the science of chemistry from the mumbo-jumbo of alchemy. The uniformities of nature are there, waiting to be discovered; and, given the brain power to identify things by names, man inevitably would begin to discover them. Huxley was right, of course, in declaring that science (and, we may add, industrial technology) began when man first began to pick up sticks and stones and use them as tools. The process of trying stones for weight and shape and durability was just as truly experimental as anything that modern scientists do. The tentative identification of qualities of color and texture with the tool behavior of certain stones was just as truly a scientific hypothesis, and its testing through the use of other stones of like color and texture was just as truly a case of scientific verification, as anything that goes on in modern laboratories.

In a very real and definite sense the whole body of human knowledge and the whole repertory of subsequently acquired skills was rendered possible by the inception of the symbolic process. So far as we know there has been no increase in the brain power of the human species since paleolithic times, and no essential modification of the symbolic process. The vocabulary of symbols has of course increased, and is still doing so (now at a tremendous rate).

But symbol-using—the basic operation of the human mind—is the same now as it was fifty thousand years ago. This is not to gainsay the possibility that the symbolic process was achieved by degrees. Doubtless our species predecessors, such as Neanderthal man, were not as acute as the present species, and carried on symbol-organized activities with somewhat less facility than we do. Their lower "IQ" may be one reason for the prodigious span of time that was occupied by the Old Stone Age (reckoned in hundreds of thousands of years). But the fact remains that since the advent of the present species, something like fifty thousand years ago, there is no evidence of any change in the brain power of the species generally. Our mental operations are the same as those of our remote ancestors. The very great differences in our activities are cultural, and have resulted from the development of knowledge and skills, and of the physical apparatus in which knowledge and skills are embodied.

For it is of the essence of such activities that they are cumulative. This is partly because they consist in the exploration of the uniformities of nature, and partly because the exploring is done with tools and instruments. Since nature is constant, every new increment of knowledge is added to what is already known. Thus what is known serves always as a base for further exploration. The larger the base, the greater is the opportunity for extending it. So likewise tools and instruments and all the physical apparatus of culturally organized existence, being physical, accumulate; and since new and improved tools and apparatus result from the combining and refining of old ones, the more there are the greater is the opportunity for still further development. The next chapter will be largely devoted to this scientific and technological aspect of culture, and so I do no more than mention its cumulative character here in order to distinguish it from another set of consequences of the symbolic process.

4

Whenever reference is made to symbolism, most people—including most scholars—think first of the occult. This does not mean that occultism is the commonest form that symbols take in present-day life. It means just the opposite. I have already noted the fascination which the strange customs, weird ideas, and grue-some rites of "savages" have exercised over the minds of modern scholars. Similarly it is the strange, weird, and gruesome symbols that challenge attention. They alone, seemingly, defy explanation. Once the question is raised, no one denies that tool-using is a symbolic process, or that the commonest symbols are the ones that are employed operationally. Indeed, we pass these over precisely because they seem to raise no problem, thereby compounding the mystery of the mysterious.

For the truth is that the simplest and commonest activities man carries on constitute the supreme mystery of human life. Among all the activities of all living creatures, the deepest cleft is that which divides the activities of man from those of all other animals. Seemingly this cleft is so deep and wide that through all the ages it has prompted the wildest flights of human imagination. Com-pared with the activities of dumb brutes, the operations of even the most primitive community of men are so amazingly efficient as to constitute a distinct order of reality.

At the same time, the symbolic process apparently provides a clue to an understanding of that order. Even today we speak of the magic of words. Such expressions are of course metaphorical. What we have reference to is the remarkable effects which words sometimes achieve. But to the primitive, even the simplest uses of even the commonest words seem—by comparison with what goes on in the surrounding universe—positively magical in their ef-fectiveness. If we suppose, with Jespersen, that names came first, we must then realize with what a sense of supernal power over each other dawn men first began hailing each other by name. There is nothing like it in nature.

In these circumstances it was inevitable that even the commonest operational name-symbols should have seemed to be endowed with supernatural power; and it was likewise inevitable that this im-pression should be confirmed by the feedback effect. For this whole experience must have been highly charged with emotion. With what feelings of anxiety turning to triumph must dawn men have begun calling to each other! The whole procedure of name-calling must have produced in its first practitioners feelings of astonish-ment and even awe, and these feelings must have attached them-

94

selves to the word symbols as their source. Knowing nothing of the symbolic process, or of the nature of tools or of operational logic, primeval man could only suppose that the word-cry itself contained some mysterious potency to seize the attention and command the response of the person called.

It seems highly probable that the symbolic process through which man achieved his intellectual and technological superiority to the whole animal kingdom is also the wellspring of all the phantasmagoria by which all human communities have been haunted since the beginning of time. Through the fallacy of imputation the symbols by virtue of which man has accomplished his wonders have been endowed with a wonder-working magic potency. It is this sense of magic potency which inspires all superstition and all magic. Though we can do no more thàn speculate about man's beginnings, it seems likely that name-signal calls, as Jespersen suggested, came first. But they must have been followed very soon by words of general application. Indeed, given the requisite degree of brain development, language may have developed with a rapidity which, in contrast to developments during the hundreds of thousands of years that followed, would astonish us, if we had a record of the process. It seems virtually certain that manlike creatures could hardly have more than begun to make verbal identification of any stick or stone (such as the most primitive tool must have been) when they began also to see that other sticks and stones possessed the same *mana* (as anthropologists call such a mystic potency, after the Polynesians). Thus the fallacy of imputation, which may well date from the first name-cry, itself leads in the direction of words of general application.

In this regard primeval man may quite possibly have anticipated Plato. We know that primitives impute the efficacy of tools and weapons (Excalibur-like) to their *mana*.* Thus exigencies of designation would lead to the application of the name of one object

*This propensity to mysticize even those activities which we would now identify as most explicitly technological has of course been an impediment to technological development throughout the ages. Even in early modern times various forms of craftsmanship were known as "mysteries," and though the "mystery" may only have been a pretense on the part of the craftsmen concerned, kept secret for the purpose of preventing competition, even so it was an impediment; and the fact that the conspiracy in restraint of trade took such a form is evidence of an earlier and more genuine mystery.

95

or even person to another object or person of similar properties, while the propensity to imputation would give rise to the presumption that generic properties gave evidence of the mystic powers, or *mana*, of the various classes of objects and persons. Thus a stick would be any object that floats on water and a stone any object that sinks, and the power to float would be taken to be mysteriously implicit in the *mana* of the Platonic essence, "stick."

It is not my purpose to offer a theory of the origin of language or of mythology. My point is rather that the apprehension of mystic powers is indissociable from any and all associational, or symbol-organized, activity—activity of which language is representative. It is so because such organized activity *is* so astonishingly effective as to stir the feelings, and because language (and the symbolic process generally) is therefore inherently incantational no less than instrumental. All operational procedures involve recognition and designation of likes and unlikes; and such designation gives expression to the sense of mysterious powers which is evoked by the amazing effectiveness of symbolic operations— operations of which, as even primeval man could plainly see, no animal is capable.

5

If present knowledge of the interrelation of these aspects of the symbolic process gives rise to any theory of origins, it is one of joint origin, or common origin. It seems impossible that creatures capable of uttering name-cries could have failed to use generic terms, since name-cries themselves perform that function. Children say, "Is your Mr. Smith a big man?" meaning "the principal of your school." Similarly, it seems impossible that any creatures capable of symbol-organized, social behavior could have been immune—even for one moment—to the emotional and Platonic suggestion of mysterious powers. The universality of that suggestion is attested by the universality of mythology, incantation, and mystic rites; and its persistence is attested by the practice—still quite general, even in the twentieth century—of solving problems by giving names to them.

It is by this process, surely, that the mysticizing of the symbolic process is consummated. From imputation it is only a step, and seemingly an inevitable step, to reification, or thing-making. By imputation the qualities, or *mana*, of persons and things named become embedded, so to speak, in the names themselves. Names thus assume the personalities of the persons and things named, and seem fresh and lovely, or grotesque, ugly, disgusting. I have emphasized the physical existence of all symbols, in part because of its significance for the delusion of reification. Because the symbol is real, the qualities˙ and even the mystic potencies which have been imputed to it also seem real, a seeming which again is reinforced by the feedback effect. From this sense of imputed reality it seems to follow that whatever is thus named must exist. The personality which has been imputed to the symbol seemingly implies the actual existence of the forces or beings symbolized.

Obviously this propensity to reification of symbols does not stand alone in human experience. We know that all men have experiences which in effect invite that propensity to run riot. The commonest and at the same time the most vivid of these is dreams. Dreams are natural occurrences. Animals appear to dream. Everyone has watched a dog, which is lying fast asleep, suddenly begin to twitch his paws as though in rapid locomotion and to whine as though in eager chase. Is he dreaming of chasing a rabbit? We cannot know, and do not even know whether he knows. But he certainly gives all the outward indications which human beings give when they are dreaming. In human dreams, however, the dreamer seems to have left the scene in which he is lying asleep and to have engaged in all sorts of activities, sometimes pleasant and sometimes unpleasant and even terrifying, in which he seemingly encounters other people, sometimes people who are known to have died, talks to them, hears their replies, and generally has the impression of being very much alive and active, though all the while he is in fact lying asleep—a fact unimpeachably witnessed by others.

Such experiences are disturbing even now. We have every reason to suppose that our earliest ancestors were just as subject to them as we are; and not only had they not read Freud's *Traumdeutung* (published in 1900), they had not read anything. Moreover, the experience of dreams is very similar to that of ordinary reverie (day-dreaming), which is even more common (virtually continuous) though less vivid, and also to that of trance states and pathological hallucination, which are even more vivid though less common. Primeval man must have thought he saw abundant evidence that human personality is not coexistent with the body but leaves the body quite frequently and even persists after the body has died and disintegrated.

In summoning the evidence of dreams (and related states) I do not mean to revive Sir Edward Tylor's theory that all supernaturalism arose from such experiences. On the contrary, recent study of the symbolic process seems to indicate quite clearly that the supernatural interpretation of dreams, and of human experience generally, is contingent upon symbolization and results from the propensity to reify all symbols. According to John Dewey, the most misleading of all symbols is the first person pronoun, the "I," which is seemingly quite distinct from "my" hand and brain and even from "my" body. Doubtless the symbol "I" is especially misleading. But the fallacy of reification is implicit in all symbols.

No fact of primitive life is better known than the disposition of simple peoples to regard names as "standing for" the persons and even the things named not only in what we now consider the symbolic sense but as actual deputies in the sense that what is done to the name is somehow done to the person or thing named. In the course of a discussion of animism R. R. Marrett once questioned whether "a savage who was mentally incapable of regarding anything whatever as unalive" could ever have existed. That is a good question, and one that should be kept in mind in connection with the ability, even of "savages," to distinguish technological and ceremonial activities. The error to which we are prone in our reconstruction of "primitive mentality" is that of supposing that "savages" impute to inanimate objects "souls" exactly like those of persons. Not at all! To simple people the name-simulacra of inanimate objects are just as different from those of persons as the things themselves are different from the persons themselves. What does follow from the process of imaginative reification is the presumption that the names of things serve as deputies of those things precisely as those of persons do.

6

No derogation is implied in attributing such a habit of mind to early man; for after all, the "Platonic idea" is a refinement of the same way of thinking. Moreover, if name symbols partake of the reality of the subjects and objects named, it follows that even now whenever any name comes into common usage it carries the presumption of existence. Lewis Carroll's snark is a case in point. The author of "The Hunting of the Snark" was a mathematical logician, and as such was well aware of the effect of repetition upon men's minds. ("What I tell you three times is true!") Once a group of people get to discussing a snark (or a "flying saucer"), the presumption that such a thing exists is extremely strong. In one of his most charming stories Anatole France told of a family who invented an imaginary person to whose thievery and other depredations all the misadventures of the household were attributed, with the result that this poor fellow took on a reality quite as vivid as that of any citizen. So also I believe it was Edith Wharton who had one of her characters drop a book into the Xingu River. Subsequently, in commenting on the book he stated that it was "saturated with Xingu," a remark which gave rise to general discussion of this peculiar literary quality.

I take these instances of reification from our own culture by way of indicating that our own thinking is still saturated with Xingu. We share the symbolic process with primeval man, and are therefore likewise subject to the propensity to reification. But the imaginings of simple peoples are magnified by their experience of dreams (and related phenomena) and by their total ignorance of any rational explanation of those experiences. It is this interaction that gives special significance to such experiences, and to many others of which the same is true.

Two types of experience in particular have long been noted in this connection. One is that of the mysterious crises through which all mankind must pass: birth and death, loss of vital fluid, the mysteries of respiration, ingestion, and elimination. To the present-day scientist none of these processes is any more mysterious than the enervation of the voluntary muscles by virtue of which the commonest motions of hand and foot are organized. But, as the word "voluntary" itself suggests, we seem to have such actions under control in a sense that is not true of "involuntary" processes. At the same time, those processes are accompanied by emotional states which further accentuate their strangeness. They are at the same time vital, mysterious, and moving. Small wonder that they should seem to give clear evidence to simple people of the action of more-than-natural forces!

The more horrendous manifestations of nature, also, work to much the same effect. Thunder and lightning, forest and prairie fires, earthquakes, volcanic eruptions, typhoons, and tidal waves all seem to transcend the operation of the ordinary forces of nature. Such events are upsetting even to animals, and all the more to man, the most temperamental of all species. Furthermore, even more than the succession of the seasons and the phases of the moon, they seem to be aimed directly at man. Why is one man struck by lightning, while his companion is unscathed? Why do hurricanes strike directly at human settlements? People still ask such questions, and to primitive man, saturated as he is with Xingu, the answer seems all too obvious.

Such are the promptings which impelled primeval man to surround himself in imagination with supernatural forces, and to devise mystic rites and ceremonies and incantational procedures for dealing with such forces. Symbols themselves are the vehicles of flights of fancy, and flights of fancy—perhaps inevitably—are intensified by man's emotional sensitivity, and by those natural events to which emotions inevitably respond.

7.

The persistence through the ages of supernatural beliefs and occult practices is another story. One part of that story is well known. Throughout the ages such beliefs and practices have been embedded in the cultures by which the activities of all communities are patterned. Thus they are objectified in the very structure of society itself, which purportedly derives its sanction from the "higher powers." Hence the perpetuation of any social system involves the perpetuation of the beliefs and ceremonies of which that system purports to be the literal embodiment. It is not only their antiquity that gives force to the supernatural traditions of any society; it is primarily the fact that to doubt the validity of any such belief or the efficacy of any such practice is in effect to challenge the authority of the social order itself.

But no less important is the veridical quality of all supernatural beliefs and occult practices. All strong emotions are inherently self-validating, and all supernatural beliefs and occult practices are inherently hair-raising. Indeed, if our reconstruction is correct, emotional excitation played a significant part in their inception. The feelings of awe which are induced by participation in the performance of "mysteries" seem to give evidence of the authenticity of the whole affair. That such evidence is logically worthless is now obvious, and through the ages skeptics have had their doubts. To the mass of mankind, however, feeling is believing.

It is also of great importance that in the case of supernatural beliefs and practices this propensity to credit the promptings of emotion is not immediately checked and corrected by the facts, as is the case with tool-using. All supernatural forces are presumed to constitute a causal nexus and to interact causally with natural forces. Their whole significance derives from the fact that they are presumed to do so. The gods can strike a man dead. The spirits of the ancestors can stimulate the growth of the crops or ruin them. But at the same time the supernatural causal system is sufficiently remote from matters of fact to escape the immediate and constant check of inescapable fact. If an arrow is warped, that fact is noted in advance of its being shot, so that when it fails to hit the mark the causal relation between those two circumstances is definitely established. But what is established by the success or failure of the crops? Does success prove the efficacy of the invocation of the spirits of the ancestors? Can anyone prove that failure is not due to the anger of the gods?

This causal isolation of the "higher powers" has a great deal in common with the causal isolation of "higher values," and I shall therefore return to it in a later chapter. For the present all that I have tried to do is to point out that in the bifurcation of culture the dividing line is the line between fact and fiction, and that we owe both our knowledge of facts and our talent for fiction to the symbolic process by which all human behavior is organized. That circumstance does not establish the validity of facts, nor does it establish the value of fictions. The significance of each aspect of culture still remains to be explored.

CHAPTER VII

THE KNOWING-AND-DOING PROCESS

I

A S I TRIED TO POINT OUT in the preceding chapter, the symbolic process endows mankind with two sets of powers: the power of organizing facts and the power of creating fictions. These two sets of powers condition each other. It would be impossible for man to imagine fictions if he did not possess mastery over facts— the facts of which the fictions are imaginary projections. It would likewise be impossible for man to organize the facts of his experience except by use of symbols, which are themselves fictional, symbols the fictional character of which is the root-source of all fictions.

Both of these processes—that of organizing facts and that of creating fictions—give rise to systems of value, and the values of each system have the character of the process in which they occur. As I shall try to show in the next chapter, one set of values and one conception of the meaning of value, which constitute an important part of every culture and play a significant role in the lives of all communities, are essentially fictional. They do not exist except in the imaginations of the people who imagine them. Moreover, as I shall try to show also, such meaning as they have necessarily derives from the matter-of-fact world and from the matter-of-fact values which pervade that world. Whatever meaning angels have is an imaginary combination of the facts of man and bird; and whatever meaning ceremonial cleanliness may have is a similar projection of the fact of physical cleanliness. In order to understand the fictional and derivative character of ceremonial values, it is therefore necessary first to understand the meaning and significance of the genuine values of the matter-of-fact world. Consequently it is to these that the present chapter will be addressed.

2

In all the contexts in which it is ever used "value" is a relational word. The relationships differ widely. In various special situations this word is employed to refer to relationships that are understood to be limited to those particular contexts. Thus mathematicians speak of "values" when they mean numerical relationships; painters and photographers speak of "values" when they mean relationships of light and shade; and economists and businessmen speak of "values" when they mean the relationships of various prices to each other.

In each of these instances it is also true that the relationships to which reference is made constitute a system. In one instance it is the number system; in another, the system of gradations from pure light to total darkness; in another, the price system, to use a phrase which is universal among economists. Moreover, all these systems are related. At first thought numerical values and the values of which artists speak may seem to have nothing in common. But on further reflection we are bound to notice that all the situations in which we commonly employ the term *value* do have something in common. Not only do the values in question constitute a system; all such systems are causal systems. The price system is so called because prices are subject to change in consequence of changing conditions, and because such changes interact upon each other. The values of which painters speak are all causally related to the lighting of the subject and to the mixing of pigments on the palette. Even the values of the mathematician are operational. All have to do with consequences of performing various operations—of counting, adding, multiplying, integrating, and the like.

Thus we no sooner begin thinking about the meaning of the concept "value" than we are brought almost immediately to realize that all the experiences of human life are causally related to each other, and to see that this is what we are talking about when we talk about value. Everything we do affects everything else we do, in greater or less degree; and everything any one of us does affects what other people do, and is affected by what they do. In short, human experience itself is a causal system, one that includes an indefinitely large number of subsystems, all of which are parts of the whole system in the sense that each affects, modifies, and conditions the others.

It is the realization of this basic fact—the realization that every human act affects all other human activities—that is the foundation stone of all morality, the fruit of the tree of knowledge.

3

What is this causal system? Why are all human experiences causally related, or why should we suppose that they are? What necessity, intellectual or metaphysical, ties our activities to each other in such a causal network, or requires us to imagine such a thing? Throughout the ages philosophers have puzzled over the mysterious compulsion that seems to be implicit in the very idea of causation, and it is for this reason that discussion of value commonly begins with a theory of knowledge. This in turn assumes a theory of reality. Judgments of value constitute a form of knowing and can be understood only through an understanding of the whole process of knowing; and since knowing is a relation between a knower and the known, it can be understood only insofar as we can understand both the human mind and the universe in which it operates.

As the monumental works of the philosophers attest, this is a formidable task. But it has been so in large part, if not altogether, because both the human mind and the natural universe have been taken as given. So taken, both are indeed mysterious. It is only within the past century that we have been able to view both man and the universe in the perspective of the evolutionary process and to simplify the problem still further by interpreting the human mind in terms of the symbolic process and the patterns of culture. So interpreted, both reality and knowing lose their traditional mystery; or rather, the traditional mysteries are products of man's imagination.

Culturally considered, knowing is a function of doing. As we have already noted, the symbolic process enables mankind to shape and use tools, a process which imposes the necessity for knowing something of materials and their properties and something of the processes of pounding, cutting, abrading, and the like. That necessity can be simply and completely rendered by the expression, "That is the way things are." In short, in searching out stones for use as tools, primeval man first becomes aware of the uniformities of nature. Those uniformities are "real" in the sense that every feature of the situation is just as real as every other. The stones are as real as the sticks. The fact that the sticks float in water and the stones do not is just as real as the fact that the sticks burn and the stones do not. No one of them is any more or any less real than any other; and in dealing with them man "must" take account of all such properties because they exist—because sticks do uniformly float and stones do uniformly sink.

Nothing that has happened since the day of primeval man has altered such reality or such necessity. Modern science is the elaboration of just such knowledge, and by just such means; and the phenomena it has revealed are just as real as the sticks and stones of primitive man, and no "realer." The moons of Jupiter are as real as the wooden tube and globules of glass through which men first peered at them. But no realer! It may be, for all we know, that some aspects of the universe are beyond our reach, and always will be. But it is quite literally true that "What we don't know won't hurt us."

Why then has mankind worried about the unknowable? Quite unmistakably, the answer to such questions is to be found in the other aspects of our culture. What has worried mankind throughout the ages is not the unknowable but the imagined: the "realms of being" which the use of symbols has enabled the human imagination to conjure up. These range all the way from the supernatural forces of primitive mythology to the abstractions of the philosophers, and at both ends of the scale they are mental aberrations—the consequence of the reification of symbols.

Because symbols (like culture) exist and have a being of their own, it is almost inevitable that we should think of them as existing in the same fashion as sticks and stones; and since the existence of the symbol "stone" is independent of any particular stone and contains within itself all the qualities of all possible stones, there is a sense in which the idea, "stone," is more real than any particular stone. Moreover, since the supernatural forces of primitive mythology consist (in a sense) of ideas, as do the dreams which throughout the ages have seemed more real than the commonplace experiences of waking life, philosophers have been tempted to treat these two senses as one, and to declare without qualification that ideas are more real than the things of which they are ideas and that the starry heavens above are such stuff as dreams are made of. In this fashion the philosophers have raised themselves above the vulgar superstitions of the ancients and at the same time above the "naive empiricism" of their scientific colleagues: a very satisfactory position!

But in fact we have no warrant for supposing that ideas are more real than things. If we approach the problem of reality in the full light of our knowledge of the symbolic process, it becomes quite clear that the reality of idea-symbols, though genuine, is in no sense superior to that of things. Symbols are a different order of reality from things, but not a "higher" order. If percepts without concepts are meaningless, it is likewise true that concepts without percepts are blind—which was only Kant's way of saying that symbols could not exist without things any more than man could make use of things without symbols. In short, there is only one form of knowledge, the knowledge man has acquired in the course of his technological activities, activities in which things and symbols are fruitfully combined. Apart from those activities, symbols lead only to illusion.

4

Having made this brief excursion into metaphysics, we can now return to value theory with some hope of being able to find our way. For what is true of reality is also true of causation. The causal system in which all human activities are related is nothing more, nor less, than the manifestation of the uniformities of nature in the experience of mankind. One human act causally affects other acts of the same person and of other persons in the same fashion and for the same reason that the motions of the planets affect human acts, and human acts affect the motion of the planets, in however slight degree. It is the rotation of the earth on its axis that produces the alternation of day and night and so maintains a relatively even temperature all over the earth within the limits of which human life is possible, and it is the progress of the earth around its orbit that produces the succession of the seasons, to which virtually all life, vegetable and animal, responds, and by which all mankind is therefore continuously affected. So also, when a man drops an apple it falls toward the earth, and the earth, in however infinitesimal degree, rises to meet it.

This does not mean that values exist in nature, any more than it means that the planets have kindly intentions toward mankind. Such confusions have persisted through the ages for two reasons: historically, as an accompaniment of superstition; and logically, as a consequence of the failure to distinguish between things and symbols. In this regard, causation is one of three closely related foci of confusion, the other two being "purpose" (or intention) and "freedom." It is true of all three, just as it is of reality, that the confusion is easily resolvable through an understanding of the symbolic process.

Purpose is a characteristic of human activity—in a sense a manifestation of the (symbolic) knowing process by which human beings organize their activities. Not only do human actions have causal effects; human beings know they do, and consequently they act with foreknowledge of the probable effects of their acts. To some slight extent this is true of certain animals. Dogs can be trained to attack intruders; and we often say in such an instance, "He bit me on purpose!" In contrast, when a man is struck by lightning, educated people do not say the lightning struck him on purpose. But simple people, both ancient and modern, do; and this is not such an egregious error as it appears to be, for it does register an awareness of man's continuity with nature and participation in the uniformities of nature. One need only disregard the uniqueness of the symbolic (cultural) organization of human behavior to arrive at the conclusion: since human acts have causal effects just as the motions of the planets do, and since human beings intend such effects, therefore the planets likewise intend their effects. However, this is so obviously an error that long ago resolutely secular philosophers recognized as spurious the purposiveness which immemorial tradition imputed to the natural universe and therefore insisted that the meaning "purposiveness" is quite distinct from the meaning "uniformities of nature" and is wholly absent from the natural universe.

Some philosophers, such as Hume, and some scientists, such as Helmholtz and Mach, have even gone a step further and suggested that the term *cause* be abandoned altogether in all its forms. But fundamental confusions are not likely to be eased by verbal tricks. The important thing is to distinguish between things and symbols while recognizing that both exist—in this instance to distinguish between the uniformities of nature, a nature that includes man, and knowledge of those uniformities, which is limited to man and is a function of human culture. Thus the sentence, "What is the purpose of the planets?" though it is interrogative in form, is actually meaningless, since only human beings have purposes. One might as well ask what is the sex of the seasons!

5

Mankind, no less than the planets, is subject at every moment and in every particular to the uniformities of nature. Does this mean that there is no such thing as "freedom of the will"? This question has plagued secular inquiry throughout the ages; and since it is fundamental to the whole theory of value, it must be faced. For it seems that values imply choices, and choices imply freedom to choose; so that if there is no freedom, there can be no value. Thus it seems to many people that if man is subject to the uniformities of nature, then he is not free; and if he is not free, then value as well as choice is meaningless. But what we have here is a confusion of the order of nature and the universe of discourse of human culture.

In all its forms the apparent enigma of free will results from the confusion of two different contexts, or universes of discourse, each of which is meaningful only when carefully distinguished from the other, like the familiar case of a supposed collision of an irresistible force with an immovable obstacle. No such collision is conceivable, since each party to it by definition excludes the possibility of the other. The enigma of free will first arose in the lucubrations of medieval theologians who were puzzled by the apparent conflict between the concept of divine omnipotence and that of human responsibility. How can man be held responsible for his sins if everything that happens in the universe happens in consequence of divine omnipotence? Like the irresistible force and the immovable obstacle, these two concepts seem to exclude each other, and the enigma is soluble only on the presumption that divine omnipotence is beyond the puny powers of the human intellect to understand.

In the case of the secular problem of free will and determinism both concepts, like those of the irresistible force and the immovable wall, are well within the competence of the human mind to understand; but each has its meaning in a universe of discourse quite distinct from that of the other, and in each case a universe to which the other is irrelevant. The concept of determinism has to do with the uniformities of nature as revealed by science. What it asserts is the unbroken continuity of cause and effect in the natural universe, of which man is a part. Its opposite is not freedom but indeterminacy.

The concept of freedom, on the other hand, is meaningful only in the universe of discourse of human affairs. Its opposite is not determinism but slavery. There is a sense in which no one is absolutely free, just as there is a sense in which slavery cannot be absolute. The Greek philosopher, Epictetus, himself a Roman slave, declared that his mind was free though his body was enslaved, pointing out that his master might break his arm but he could not break his will. It is likewise true of everyone that the assumption of responsibilities of any kind constitutes a limitation of freedom. Anyone who becomes a citizen of Canada loses his freedom to vote in the United States. But all these degrees of freedom and obligation are irrelevant to the issues raised by the scientific account of the unbroken continuity of cause and effect. In asserting that his mind was free Epictetus was not asserting that it acted causelessly, nor do scientists assert that man is a slave to gravitation. The two meanings, determinism and freedom of the will, do not contradict each other. Each is meaningful in quite a different context from that which gives meaning to the other.

Freedom of the will has a clear and definite meaning; but it is a social meaning—one that makes sense only in the universe of discourse of socially organized human activity. Socially organized human beings must treat each other as responsible, and in that sense "free," since doing so is a basic "rule of the game" of all social organization. The division of labor necessitates allocation of responsibility, and so does the maintenance of order and the observance of any sort of routine in public and private life; and these necessities require us to treat other persons as responsible individuals. No social organization is possible otherwise.

As these necessities indicate, these two contexts—that of the uniformities of nature and that of effective human action—are closely related. Indeed, that relationship is the key to an understanding of the nature of real values. Like intentions and purposes, values have meaning only in the context of human activities. But all human activities occur in the natural universe of which man is a part. The causal interrelatedness of all human activities is a fact of nature, and the life process of mankind is a natural process.

6

The life process of mankind, in which values have meaning, is a process of doing and knowing. I have called it a technological process because human doing involves the exercise of skills in the use of tools, and because all tools likewise serve as instruments of human knowing. By dint of his power of association and the symbolic process to which it gives rise, man is able to organize his activities on a scale that distinguishes him from all the rest of creation; but all those activities are still subject, as we often say to the rule of trial and error. The object of such a trial is to determine whether any given expedient of doing and knowing is in accordance with the "laws" of nature. If it is not, it is an error.

This process is a continuous and cumulative one. It is continuous by virtue of the human power of retention, or memory, which is a function of the symbolic process and is manifest through the use of language. It is cumulative by virtue of the objective existence of all tools and instruments.

That the technological process is continuously and progressively developmental is fully attested by the evidence of archeology and the facts of history. In every archeological excavation the lowest deposits—those left by the earliest peoples—contain the simplest, roughest, and most primitive tools, implements, and other artifacts, whereas those found in higher strata invariably give evidence of development and improvement; and the evidence of history is even clearer. In every field of creative endeavor history records a process of continuous, progressive development—continuous in the sense that in the creative activities of man as in zoological evolution retrograde development never occurs, and progressive in the sense that every development is a refinement and amplification of earlier patterns by the same process which led to the creation of those patterns from still earlier ones. This does not mean that every achievement of every human being is better than any that has preceded. At any given level of any art there will of course be some performances that will be better than others, some that are commonplace and even shoddy, and some that are supreme examples of that art and style. Moreover, any given style is liable to deterioration in the course of mass production. But, contrary to popular belief, no knowledge and no art has ever been lost, though any one may have disappeared from some particular locality. The creation of new patterns does not mean that old ones have been lost, but rather that a new dimension, which extends the possibilities of the old ones, has been added. As the Cathedral of Saint John the Divine attests, twentieth-century masons can still build pointed arches in the medieval manner, though structural steel, glass, and sheet aluminum now make possible buildings such as medieval masons never dreamed of.

Moreover, the process of technological development also is now well understood. Although every development of knowledge and skill is of course the work of human genius, it is not to individual genius alone that we owe such development. Men's minds are no brighter now than they were fifty thousand years ago. But knowledge and skills accumulate. They do so for the reason that has already been indicated: because knowledge and skills are objectified in tools and symbols. This was true even before the development, comparatively recently, of written language. Having found a primitive artifact, archeologists can infer what it was used for, and so, to some extent, how the people who made and used it lived. But since the development of written language, and especially since the development of alphabetical printing (both revolutionary achievements, precisely because of the new dimensions of activity they opened up), everything men do and think has become objectified.

The importance of such objectification of this whole aspect of culture is not merely that of accumulation. Rather accumulation is only the minor premise to innovation. The major premise is the combining of previously existing "culture traits" to form new ones. This process is basically the same at all levels. An Einstein who brings the tensor analysis of Riemann and Christoffel to bear upon the discoveries of Michelson and Morley with regard to the velocity of light is proceeding basically as did the dawn man who combined a stick and a stone to produce the primeval ax. In both instances the combination was possible by virtue of the fact that a hand-held striking stone *(coup de poing)* and the Riemannian four-dimensional manifold not only existed in somebody's "mind," but also took their places in culture. Thus, instead of perishing with their creators they were available to all for further combination.

The range of possible combination is of course that of the natural universe. Granted that it takes a genius to see the possibilities that are implicit in applying Riemannian analysis to the space-time continuum, or in attaching a stone to the end of a stick; still it is undeniable that neither would have been possible save for the uniformities of nature, which in both cases define the compatibility of the materials in question. Sticks and stones are in fact compatible, and so are the space-time manifold and the Riemannian analysis. Throughout the whole development of the technological process man is exploring and exploiting the uniformities of nature.

7

It is in this, the life process of mankind, that values arise. To recognize this fact is not to say that nature "intends" the development of human culture. Nature does not intend anything. Intention is an aspect of human behavior. But it does mean that the value judgments which emerge from this process have a basis in fact. When we judge a thing to be good or bad, or an action to be right or wrong, what we mean is that, in our opinion, the thing or act in question will, or will not, serve to advance the life process insofar as we can envision it. All such judgments are of course more or less limited. Just as what seems to be a fact in a limited context may prove not to be one in the light of further knowledge, so what is judged to be good (or bad) in a limited context may prove to be the opposite in the light of further experience. But in all cases value judgments are judgments with regard to the causal relations between present choices and the future activities of the chooser and of other people.

Causal relationships—the uniformities of nature—do not of themselves constitute values. Only human judgments, more or less well informed, more or less intelligent, translate the uniformities of nature into values. Hence even the most judicious judgments are "subjective." This circumstance has contributed mightily to prevailing misconceptions. For the very fact that all value judgments are by definition thus "subjective" has a tendency to turn attention in the direction of those social influences by which judgment is distorted. I repeat, and keep repeating, such influences do indeed exist. Value judgments are by no means exclusively dictated by facts. Quite apart from errors arising from misinformation, incomplete information, and "honest" mistakes of reasoning, human judgments and choices do frequently and extensively express beliefs and attitudes that originate not in attempted observation and understanding of the facts but in the folklore and mores of tribal tradition.

It is very important that we should understand how this comes about and what it means, and I shall therefore devote the next chapter wholly to this problem. But it is even more important that we should not allow the "subjectivity" of all value judgments to conceal the fact that all human activities are causally related, that mankind has always been aware that such is the case, and that—notwithstanding all the delusions and distortions which have flowed from the propensity to reification and from the exigencies of tribal life—men have always tried to understand the facts of life and to make their choices and decisions in accordance with them.

8

Values are "ends," the ends for the attainment of which antecedent activities are undertaken, activities which are therefore identified as the "means" to those "ends." They arise in human experience in consequence of man's ability to understand the uniformities of nature sufficiently to foresee some of the immediate consequences of his actions, and so to act with the intention that certain consequences shall come to pass.

These words, *means* and *ends*, are extraordinarily misleading. Since in human experience calculation of this kind goes on continuously, it is inevitable that some such terms should be used. Everything we do is a means to something else and an end relatively to what has gone before. I hurry in order to catch a bus; but I hurry also to keep up with a companion and to keep later an important engagement. But the propensity to reification impels us almost irresistibly to imagine that both means and ends exist independently of their place in the continuum of experience and have unique qualities by which each could be independently recognized.

That such is not the case is easily demonstrable for any particular segment of experience. Do we work in order to eat, or eat in order to work? Or do we do both in order to listen to great symphonies? Obviously each of these alternatives is just as absurd as either of the others. The greatest symphony ever written is just noise (defined as "any unwanted sound") from the point of view of those who have discovered that the hall is on fire. Only the satirical genius of a Max Beerbohm could imagine a group of players and an audience so consecrated to the "spiritual value" of great music as to allow themselves to be barbecued rather than interrupt their symphony. The whole value of music, and for that matter of work and food, derives from the presumption that people have other experiences to which these are causally related.

The interconnectedness of all human interests and activities has led some writers to emphasize the continuity of the process of valuation, and the "continuum" (as John Dewey called it) of means and ends. The flow of values in human experience—of ends-in-view which in turn become means to other ends-in-view—is of course an uninterrupted process. No less important is the harmony that prevails in varying degree among the multifarious activities of mankind. Work makes play possible, and play makes work possible.

Neither the continuum of means and ends nor the harmony of values is a fact of nature antecedent to man, yet both have the uniformities of nature as their basis. Both signalize man's discoveries of the uniformities of nature, such as the discovery that some things are foods and others are poisons. Knowledge is always incomplete and judgment always liable to error. Harmony of course implies dissonance. Human experience is full of discordant notes. But in life as in music they are so only in relation to other notes and other experiences, and most particularly to the whole experience of the community, time-bound as it is in the common medium of culture.

9

To restate the theme with which this chapter opened, values form a system. What we refer to when we speak of values is the systematic organization of all the activities of mankind; and since this is the case, there is a sense in which man himself may be regarded as the focal point of the system of values. Whatever men through the ages have learned to value is as valuable as it is because of the contribution it makes to human life, and for no other reason. This is conspicuously true of what we still call the basic necessities of life. Even today in the most highly industrialized countries of the world the basic articles of diet—wheat, corn, rice; beef, pork, mutton, fish—are still those which have been man's food for many thousands of years. Not only has their value been established by prodigiously long experience; it was recognized long before written language had been developed.

This is not to say that food is more valuable than anything else. For the organized activities of large communities of men written language is no less important, and therefore no less valuable, than food. Many specific activities of such communities would be impossible otherwise than by use of written language, so many as to raise a doubt whether such communities could exist at all without that expedient.

The key word here is "system," for it is in the *system* of human activities that values have their meaning. Some writers, noting that all values are man-centered, have therefore been led to make candid avowal of what they have called a biological criterion of value. Even John Dewey sometimes seemed to derive all human values from the biological struggle for existence. An important element of truth inheres in the biological conception. It is no less true of man than of any other animal that all his interests and activities are contingent upon physical survival. Can anything be truly valuable that does not contribute to survival, directly or indirectly? But such a question can also be misleading, since it seems to suggest that survival is the supreme value from which all lesser values derive. But this is nonsense. As Thomas Huxley pointed out many years ago, the evolutionary struggle for existence, with the survival or extinction of any and all species, including man, has no moral significance whatever. Moral significance arises only *within* the *system* of human activities. Given our existence as a species, and given the system of activities by which we live and to which we are irrevocably committed, the problem of values is that of the relation of any given activity or interest to that system. The system may be conceived as a biological expedient, but the things we value are not valued for the sake of biological survival. They are valued as figments of a system: the life system of mankind.

Recognition of the fact that all values come to focus upon man does not mean that the animal necessities of the human body outrank the values of the mind. But it does mean that values of the mind, no less than those of the body, are valuable by virtue of their participation in and contribution to the system. Throughout the ages wise men have insisted that no values rank higher than knowledge, understanding, wisdom; and this has been generally interpreted by lesser men as meaning that such attainments of the human mind, or "spirit," are of supreme value "in themselves." But nothing is valuable "in itself"; for the literal meaning of such a phrase is a flat contradiction of the interrelatedness of all human activities, and so of the very meaning of value. That knowledge is fundamental to all human activities is more apparent today than ever before. Only a little while ago it was still possible for the community at large to misconceive knowledge as a badge of distinction by which "learned" men were set off from their less gifted, or favored, fellows. But today not only does everybody realize how directly the lives of all are affected, for example, by understanding of the causes of epidemics, knowledge of means of checking them, and the wisdom to apply those measures; every schoolchild knows that it was knowledge of the properties of fire and flint that set mankind on the road to civilization.

Furthermore, what is true of knowledge is no less true of all the "higher" achievements of "the human spirit," such as poetry, music, and the graphic arts. We are still prone to think of art as something that is to be enjoyed, and of enjoyment as an "end" that is not a "means" to anything else. At the moment of enjoyment this is a natural and wholesome attitude. Who would want to read a poem or listen to a symphony, all the while thinking to himself, "I am doing this only to sharpen my faculties so that I shall be able to do better work tomorrow"? Nevertheless, our feelings at the moment of enjoyment do not constitute a full assessment of the significance of the experience. If anyone doubts this, let him try to justify opium-smoking on the ground of enjoyment. That also is said to be very enjoyable while it is going on. The trouble with it is that it results in general deterioration. Cultivation of the arts has the opposite effect, and therein lies the key to the value of the arts. It is no more true of music than it is of food that its value derives from our liking of it. In both cases it is much closer to the truth that we like it because we have ourselves experienced its enhancement of all our faculties.

10

This enhancement has led another group of writers to seize upon the development of human personality as the criterion of value. There is much to be said for such "humanism." It recognizes the causal interrelatedness of all values, and does not set up any particular values as metaphysical absolutes, but assesses all values by their functional—systemic—significance. Moreover, it is no less resolutely secular than the so-called biological standard of value, recognizing that value is an aspect of human experience and has no meaning outside the universe of discourse of human activity; while at the same time it avoids the narrow "scientism" of the biological standard by its realization that it is not merely the organism but the activities and experiences of mankind that constitute the system that gives meaning to value.

But human activities and experiences are always social and cultural, whereas "personality" is individual. In focussing their attention upon the development and enrichment of personality, the humanists run two serious risks, each of which accentuates the other. On one hand is the "divine spark" by virtue of which man is traditionally supposed to be set off from all the rest of creation, and human life is therefore supposed to be sacred. This, too, is individual. Inevitably, therefore, emphasis upon the preciousness of human individuality is liable to confusion with just that supernaturalism from which, to do them credit, the humanists seek to free themselves. On the other hand is the socio-cultural aspect of the activity system in which all human values arise. To the extent that they glorify individual personality, the humanists are liable to disregard and overlook what is perhaps the most important aspect of the human value system, namely its social character; this is true increasingly as their conception of human individuality becomes tinged with mysticism.

This is a most serious shortcoming. For what we have to understand is not only the existence but the creation of values, which is an unmistakably social process. Not only is the social value system the medium in which individual personalities are nurtured and enabled to grow from infancy to full maturity, and in some cases enabled to reach extraordinary heights of individual development; the system itself grows by a process that can be understood only as a cultural phenomenon.

II

What is at issue here is the criterion of value. This issue has been traditionally couched in terms of authority. So stated the question is this: By what authority do we hold some things good and others bad, some actions right and others wrong? I call this statement of the issue "traditional" because it derives from tribal traditions which impute such authority to tribal priests and the Higher Powers of which they are believed to be the spokesmen; and in this connection we should recall the supposition of many modern social scientists that value judgments can be made only by the authority of the societies which make them. This supposition in effect perpetuates the tradition of authority.

Why should it be supposed that value judgments involve authority? The only basis there has ever been for such a supposition is that of tribal belief. Seemingly, modern social scientists do not subscribe to the tribal beliefs they discuss. They do not cite Mammon or Belial, but do cite instead the authority of the tribes that believe in such authorities, apparently under the impression that value judgments can be maintained only on some authority. But the only authority for this impression is the tribal belief which the social scientists themselves purportedly reject.

Unfortunately the same supposition is also perpetuated by many humanists, and even by those who hold a biological theory of value. In effect the biological criterion substitutes the authority of Nature (which should therefore be spelled with a capital letter) for that of Higher Powers. But without the capital letter nature does not exercise authority. The "laws" of nature do not compel obedience. They state facts, which is a very different matter indeed. By the same token the citation of Human Personality, or Individuality, as the criterion of value is a mistaken attempt to find adequate authority for the value judgments of mankind, in this case the supposed authority of Human Nature, which also should therefore be spelled with capital letters.

But values do not require capitalized authority, any more than facts do. There are indeed many beliefs which various communities hold solely on the authority of their traditions. But no one supposes that a substitute authority must therefore be found for every fact. To be sure, people sometimes speak of the authority of Science. But actually no such authority exists, and spelling *science* with a capital letter is therefore false and misleading. The actual criterion of scientific truth is a process, the process of inquiry in which mankind has been continuously and cumulatively engaged throughout the ages. The substantial truth or falsity of every scientific fact is determined by its apparent consistency with the whole vast continuum of scientific investigation. None is absolutely true, since the investigative process is by definition incomplete. Further investigation may require the modification of any and every scientific truth.

In a sense, therefore, all scientific truths must be held tentatively. Hence the question is sometimes raised (chiefly by theologians and metaphysicians) whether the whole vast structure of human knowledge does not rest on a foundation of belief—belief in the evidence of the senses, or even belief in the construction which the human mind places on the supposed evidence of the senses— and whether such belief is not on a par with any other belief. But the answer to this question also is obviously No. However incomplete and tentative the results of scientific investigation may be, the investigative process which is the criterion of scientific truth is utterly different from such other beliefs. For in contrast to "other beliefs," the investigative process is one in which all mankind has been continuously engaged. Even the questioner himself, in raising the question with regard to the criterion of scientific truth, is engaged in the process of inquiry, and by asking his question he has invoked that process as the criterion of the meaningfulness of his question and therefore of the validity of the answer.

The same is true of value judgments. Genuine value judgments (as distinguished from tribal fancies) invoke the criterion of the same investigative process, which itself is inseparable from the technological process generally. That process defines the human way of life. Knowledge of good and evil is in the first instance knowledge: knowledge that every human act affects the continuance and furtherance of the system of activities by virtue of which such an act itself is performed. That act itself commits the actor to that system, just as any utterance commits the speaker to the system of articulate speech. To say "I hereby refuse to abide by the rules of the English language" is to utter nonsense. Such a statement itself has meaning only by virtue of being a manifestation of the cultural system known as the English language. But to "abide by the rules" of a language such as English is not to "bow to authority." There is no question of authority. The question is one of making sense. All human utterances constitute an effort to make sense, and so do all human acts. As I shall try to show in the next chapter, this is true even of acts which are guided by tribal fancies. The tribal fancies themselves, however misguided, represent an effort to make technological sense.

Whether any particular human act does make sense is always open to debate, just as the truth of any particular statement is always open to discussion. That discussion itself invokes the life process as its criterion, just as the statement or act under discussion has already done. By discussing the problem of values we are seeking to enlarge our knowledge of good and evil, just as men have always done. When we seek to determine whether anything is good or bad, or whether any act is right or wrong, we are seeking clear and certain knowledge of its causal bearing on the life process of mankind. The criterion of value, like the meaning of causality and the criterion of clarity and certainty, derives from the process itself.

CHAPTER VIII

MYTHS, MORES, MAGIC, AND STATUS

I

THROUGHOUT THE AGES WISE MEN HAVE PUZZLED over man's moral nature. How does man know right from wrong? And why does he feel so strongly about it? The tribal legends of every people provide answers to these questions, answers that are entirely satisfactory to those who believe the legends. But wise men have always entertained misgivings with regard to the literal verity of tribal legends, and their doubts left these questions up in the air. It was of course possible to suppose that man had somehow been endowed with moral sensibilities which other creatures lack; and despite its obvious shortcomings that supposition has therefore been the foundation of all the efforts of the philosophers to give rational (nonsupernatural, or secular) answers to these vital questions. As I have indicated in an earlier chapter, such were the efforts of the most powerful minds of the seventeenth and eighteenth centuries.

Darwinism gave the *coup de grâce* to all such efforts. But, as I have also indicated, it gave rise to quite another type of explanation of the age-old mystery, one that is wholly in keeping with twentieth-century scientific knowledge, as the special-creation theory was not, and one that is still entirely adequate to account for the extraordinary intensity of man's moral convictions.

This modern scientific explanation of man's moral nature combines our present knowledge of the phenomenon of culture with all that we have learned from physiology, psychology, and psychiatry about emotional processes. All known cultures contain prohibitions and compulsions to which all the members of each cultural community are conditioned. Some of these negative and positive commandments are held with very great intensity, and that intensity of feeling is likewise transmitted by cultural conditioning to all the members of each given community. Thus in every cultural community all individuals are conditioned from earliest childhood not only to regard certain acts as right and certain others as wrong but also in certain instances to feel and manifest violent indignation, or equally ecstatic approval, at the wrong-doing or right-doing of others, and correspondingly strong guilt or pride with regard to their own behavior.

All this does indeed occur. The common use of the word *taboo* signalizes the general recognition of these cultural facts at the present time. That word has been derived from the Polynesian language. Its acceptance into English and into common use gives clear indication of general realization that taboos prevail not only throughout Oceania but throughout the Western world as well. To be sure, the word *taboo* refers only to the negative aspect of cultural compulsion. This is, perhaps, a very significant fact. As I shall try to develop later, all cultural compulsions of this sort are singularly restrictive, a circumstance which is of very great importance for an understanding of their bearing upon the whole life process of man; and it is therefore significant that so restrictive a meaning as "taboo" should have won such general acceptance as the generic designation of cultural compulsions. It suggests that the community has all along dimly sensed the restrictive character of all ceremonial compulsion. But for the present, in order to avoid prejudicing the issue, we would do well to use another word which is equally applicable to positive and prohibitive compulsions. There is another word, also borrowed from another tongue, which has this broader significance. William Graham Sumner took the word *mores* from the Latin to designate those customs which have the force of moral law; and his use of it in *Folkways,* a book which because of the introduction of this term has become a sociological classic, made it a part of the vocabulary of social science.

People who have given no special thought to the matter are likely to think of taboos, or mores, as mere conventions—"mere" in the sense of being arbitrary, that is, of having no connection with anything else. But nothing could be farther from the truth. Sumner was fascinated by the wide variation between the mores of different peoples, and he devoted the greater part of his energies to accumulatng instances culled from reports of a great many different cultures and calculated to exhibit the extraordinary contrasts among their mores. Thus he showed that what one people regard as shameful another make obligatory. One people condemn as shameful the exposure of the female face; another not only see nothing shameful in the face but even condemn its concealment. One people condemn exposure of the female breasts; another regard such concealment as the height of salacity. One people enjoin tender care of the aged; another require that they be put out of their misery. The parade of such bits and snippets of cultural practices does inevitably give the impression of arbitrariness. But Sumner nevertheless insisted that mores differ generically from "ordinary" folkways precisely in being integral parts of a system of beliefs, and of occult practices sanctified by those beliefs.

2

All present-day social scientists agree that mores invariably constitute a system, and are themselves part of a larger system which includes a system of beliefs. Virtually all social scientists are now functionalists, in the broad sense of that term. All recognize that any given practice, or value, of any given people can be understood only in terms of its interconnectedness with all the other values, beliefs, and practices of that people. Indeed, it would scarcely be going too far to say that the establishment of this principle—of the integral character of every culture—has been the chief concern of social inquiry during the half century just past. So single-minded has been the focus of social inquiry upon this point that very little thought has been given to the evaluation of the mores and of the beliefs to which they give effect. So fully convinced have social scientists become that all moral values have their origin in, and derive their sanction from, the beliefs and practices of their communities that they have not yet got around to inquiring what this means.

And that is very unfortunate. For, as we cannot fail to see when we push our inquiry in that direction, it means first, that insofar as a people's values derive from mores they are founded upon falsehood. There is no escaping this. The tribal beliefs to which all mores are functionally related are, all of them, beliefs in mystic forces and supernatural powers, and are directly contrary to what we now know to be the truth. Furthermore, as systematic analysis is also bound to reveal, the whole mores system is self-contradictory, since it constitutes an unwitting affirmation, even by primitive peoples, of its direct opposite—namely, of the truth of science and the validity of technological values. This is because the "ceremonial adequacy" of mores and mystic rites is always thought to be attested by actual physical consequences, just as acts of skill are known to be. Thirdly, the adequacy of mystic rites is always contingent upon scrupulous observance of the hierarchical status of the several ministrants. All mores define what is right and proper for persons of designated status. This is the point at which their restrictive character is most significant. As an organization its principal function is not that of getting things done, but rather that of preventing change.

In short, this aspect of human behavior does manifest a system. But it is a system that rests on a foundation of falsehood. Since its ceremonial procedures simulate tool operations, it is inherently self-contradictory. And as an organization its actual effect is the preservation of the social and cultural *status quo.*

Let us, then, consider these aspects of the mores-determined value system.

3

It is certainly true that mores always have an ideological penumbra. Indeed, Sumner's classic definition of the mores made this their distinguishing characteristic. Whereas, according to Sumner, folkways are the habits communities have fallen into without much thought or serious concern—merely, perhaps, as matters of convenience—the mores are those habitual practices with regard to which people do feel great concern for reasons that can be cited at some length. In speaking of these "reasons" that various peoples give in justification of their mores Sumner used the word *philosophy,* and seemed to be under the impression that such philosophies developed gradually around social practices, originally mere folkways, with regard to which various peoples gradually came to feel more and more concern. Although he was never quite explicit on the point, he left the impression with his readers that all folkways may be incipient mores—that the only difference between folk-ways which have become mores and those which have not yet done so is one of degree of development, perhaps even one of age.

But is this the case? What Sumner called "philosophy" must not be confused with the highly abstract disquisitions of the great philosophers. Neither primitive folk nor the folk of our own time indulge in metaphysical speculation. Sumner's mores-philosophy consists of tribal legends: folk tales about gods and demons and tribal ancestors; stories of the creation of the world and of the human race—stories in which the progenitors of the tribe in question play the leading roles.

I do not mean to question Sumner's conviction that all such stories are pregnant with meaning. They are, of course. In imput-ing philosophical significance to tribal legends (and folklore generally) Sumner was building on one of the major discoveries of modern anthropology: the discovery that the folklore of every culture does have a quasi-philosophical significance and in particular that it does constitute for each people a sort of "explanation" and justification of that people's being the sort of people it is and behaving as it does. An integral relationship does indeed exist be-tween a people's folklore and its mores. What is nevertheless high-ly questionable is Sumner's implied timetable and most particularly the implication that "mere" folkways have no special character of their own by which they are clearly and permanently distinguished from mores.

Doubtless it is true that simple people do not feel called upon to explain why a stone cracks when it is struck, or why sticks float but stones do not. Malinowski once remarked that if one were to ask a primitive why his people performed a fertility rite, he would explain at length; whereas if one were to inquire why the soil is loosened and seeds planted in the loosened earth, the primitive would only laugh. As Malinowski went on to say, that laughter does not mean that primitive peoples are totally lacking in what we would call scientific knowledge. Rather it means that they take such knowledge as they have so much for granted, as being so well known and so definitely established, that any question with regard to it strikes them as laughable ignorance.

As a matter of fact, anthropological investigators do know quite well why Trobriand Islanders cultivate the soil, and therefore for the most part do not ask any questions about such matters. But if they return from their investigations with their notebooks full of tribal legends and nothing else, we are not justified in drawing the inference that the Islanders know nothing of agronomy. On the contrary, what they know in this regard is clearly indicated by what they do, just as present-day scientific knowledge of nuclear physics is clearly indicated by the detonation of the bombs. Conceivably the inhabitants of another planet may be able to detect the detonations, and so may infer the present state of our knowledge of physics even though they cannot read our scientific journals. So also the fact that primitive peoples do not publish scientific journals must not be taken as indicative of total ignorance. On the contrary, the scientists (like Huxley, for example) who declare that primitive man laid the foundations of modern science are of course right.

The significant difference between the mores and "mere" folkways is not that mores are explainable while folkways are not. It is rather a difference in the character of the activities and likewise in the character of the explanations which they elicit. But even this is not a total difference. Both "philosophies"—the seeds of scientific knowledge that are implicit in the skills of even the simplest peoples, and the explicit legends that accompany the mores—are in effect causal systems. The gods and demons and the spirits of the ancestors all do things, and their doings have cause-and-effect consequences. There is an unmistakable similarity between the sequence, man throws stone, and the sequence, Thor hurls thunderbolt.

In discussing this analogy scholars have usually emphasized the imputation of human characteristics to natural forces. This is what is called "animism." But all superstition likewise posits a sort of reverse animism. Even supernatural beings are subject to the laws of cause and effect. The acts of the gods have consequences which even they are powerless to prevent. Moreover, the gods themselves, as well as the demons and the spirits of the ancestors, can be acted upon in ways that virtually compel their compliance. This causal principle is the basis of all magic, all mystic rites, and all devout observances.

Anthropologists distinguish between what they call "magic" and what they call "religion," defining the former as a set of procedures by which (presumably) a specific result is achieved (for example, the restoration of a sick person to health by casting out a devil), and defining the latter as a set of procedures by which only very general results are sought (namely, the well-being of the tribe, or even of the whole human race). But it is important to note that the presumption of causal efficacy is present in both cases, and also that in both cases the causality is fictitious.

Human thought, like human activity, presents two aspects. In one of these man reasons toolwise from cause to effect, and the product of his reasoning is knowledge, however limited, of the uniformities of nature. Thus the rubbing of a bronze lamp invariably removes the tarnish and produces a high polish, no matter who does it, and no matter what the concomitant circumstances may be. In the other aspect of his thought man fictionalizes the causal relationship, reasoning from pseudo cause to pseudo effect, with results very much more dramatic and startling and therefore presumably more significant than those of any ordinary act of skill. Thus the rubbing of a lamp conjures up a jinnee, who then proceeds to work wonders—always by a process of cause and effect, but one in which ordinary acts of skill and familiar uniformities of nature are in imagination wildly exaggerated.

The "philosophy" with which mores are identified is unmistakably of the latter variety. That of course is why the mores have such a powerful grip on the emotions. The mores define acts in which Higher Powers take an interest, and that interest is (causally) manifest in ways that are indeed inherently moving. Nature is singularly given to extremes. As the saying goes, it never rains but it pours; and this is true of blessings as well as curses. Crops sometimes multiply far beyond reasonable expectation. Great herds of game appear, apparently out of nowhere. At other times mankind is overwhelmed by unimaginable disaster: floods, tempests, vast clouds of insects, frightful epidemics; and if we assume, as all simple people do, that nothing ever happens by accident, then the emotional grip of the mores becomes entirely understandable. In short, we have a case of the feedback effect. The delight and dismay which the excesses of nature inevitably arouse are read

129

back into the acts of piety and blasphemy to which extremes of good and bad fortune are believed to be causally related. Not only is association between the emotionally moving event and its sup- posed cause fixed in tribal memory by legend and proverb; by the familiar process of symbolic transference the causative act itself comes to be suffused with emotion, so that the contemplation, even in imagination, of acts of piety, nobility, and heroism, brings a foretaste of the approval of the gods, while merely to think of violations of the mores arouses fear, horror, and revulsion.

That cultural communities which have experienced this process, as all communities have to some extent, should therefore judge the values so defined to be not only the supreme values of human life but the only real values is not surprising. What is surprising is the readiness of twentieth-century scholars to echo this opinion. For such values are not only community determined; they are derived from a world view that is essentially false. In declaring that values have the sanction of the communities which hold them modern scholars are not telling the whole story. It is much closer to the truth to say that values have the validity and meaning of the value system from which they derive. The people who hold them dear do so by virtue of holding the entire system—of beliefs as well as mores—by which those values are defined; and if those beliefs are false, the values likewise partake of that imperfection. To say that values can arise only through the development of mores is as much as to say that values are inherently false.

Indeed, the proposition that values derive only from the mores is self-contradictory; for the mores themselves assume the existence of the technological process and the existence of technological criteria of value. As we have already noted, the beliefs upon which mores are postulated themselves constitute a fictitious system of cause and effect. This fiction assumes the existence of a system of genuine cause and effect. The presumption that nothing ever hap- pens by accident is a misconception and falsification of the basic scientific principle, *Natura non saltum facit.* So also the notion of ceremonial adequacy is a distortion of the principle of technological efficiency.

I do not mean to suggest that man was a matter-of-fact practi- tioner of technical skills *before* he became superstitious and ritualistic. As I have already noted, we have no knowledge of the time-table by which our species and its immediate predecessors became human. But we do know something of the processes which comprise characteristically human and cultural activities and we can draw significant inferences from our knowledge of the interrelations of those processes. Thus we know that the symbolic process underlies both acts of skill and acts of ritual, and that in all probability neither could have developed otherwise than in the presence of the other. The use of symbols and the misuse of symbols (by reification) are obverse and reverse of each other. It is inconceivable that man could have learned to use fire without using words, such as *fire, burn,* and *stick*; and it is likewise inconceivable that man could have used words—those magic talismans!—without declaiming, "Fire, fire, burn stick!"

4

The same sort of mutuality prevails between rites and mores as between mores and the tribal legends which justify them. Sumner's notion that mores begin as casual habits and only gradually become mores as a "philosophy" accumulates around them is almost certainly in error. The same symbol-sustained mentality that makes it possible for man to understand the causal relationship between sticks and fire also makes it possible for man to imagine lightning as a vast firebrand hurled across the sky; and the same mentality that makes it possible for man to recognize friendly overtures and to distinguish them from hostile gestures, also makes it possible for man to make friendly overtures toward the Higher Powers he imagines as the hurlers of thunderbolts, and to take defensive measures against hostile cosmic forces.

Such measures would of course be conceived in terms of the chain of supposed causes and effects, and the same is true of mores. Mores define human acts which are conceived to be pleasing in the sight of Higher Powers, or offensive to them. Thus mores are a product of the same mentality that thinks in terms of Higher Powers. The supposition that beavers are taboo and the supposition that they are the progenitors of the human race necessarily arise together in the human mind (and culture) and are inconceivable otherwise; and so does the supposition that the Almighty

Beaver will be placated by the ritual cleansing of the tribe through ceremonies conceived in the spirit of the causality of taboo violation.

Such being the case, none of the terms we use to designate the various aspects of this complex is an adequate designation of the whole. This is just as true of the term *ceremonialism* as it is of *mores* or of *myth* or *legend*. Ceremonial observances assume the existence of the value system of the mores; and they likewise assume the "world-view" that is postulated by mythology, and are otherwise inconceivable. But the term *ceremonialism* has certain advantages nevertheless. For one thing, by shifting emphasis from the mores to another aspect of the complex this term serves to bring the entire complex into clearer view. But more important than that, by focussing attention upon ceremonial adequacy as the objective of the whole complex activity—of belief, compliance, and propitiation—this designation points up the quasi-technological significance of the whole complex.

In every cultural community ceremonialism is a way of getting along, a means of survival, and ideally of achieving a heaven on earth. It is certainly true, and has been noted repeatedly by students of culture, that the strategic objective of the mores value system, and of the system of beliefs and ceremonial observances of every people, is the survival and progressive well-being of that people and through them of mankind generally. This is the keynote of the doctrine of functionalism. In the apprehension of every people bountiful crops, a plentiful supply of fish and game, human fecundity, immunity from catastrophe and from marauding enemies, all depend upon scrupulous observance of taboos and equally scrupulous performance of the prescribed ceremonies.

Indeed, so clear and definite is this objective in the minds of all peoples that many scholars have been led to conclude that ceremonial systems do actually produce the desired results. Otherwise, they ask, how could these various communities have survived as they have? Sumner even went so far as to suggest that all cultures are subject to the evolutionary process, and that their survival is evidence of fitness.

In a sense, of course, all cultures are subject to the test of survival. But this is not true in any teleological sense. That is, it can-

132

not be assumed of cultures any more than of zoological species that survival means progressive betterment. Survival means only survival. In the case of a culture it may mean only that the practices of that people are not quite disastrous enough to have resulted in their extermination—as is evidenced by the fact that they are still alive. What more can it mean?

In discussing the functional significance of ceremonial practices some anthropologists (Malinowski, for example) have insisted that it is not fair to primitive peoples to dissociate ceremonial from technological activities. Since those peoples (Trobriand Islanders, for example) regard their sacred rites as being essential to the growth of their crops, we are not justified in attributing that growth solely to their agronomy; for if they were to desist from the rites, they might quite possibly desist from cultivation too. In short, the rites are justified by the crops. This amounts to outright acceptance of the technological criterion of value, as becomes evident if we compare such a judgment with that of an orthodox adherent to the tribal mores.

Such a defender of the faith would certainly insist that it would be better that the tribe should pass away than that it should abandon the way of righteousness. That is the position taken at this very moment by the elders of various American Indian tribes. But in arguing not only that primitive cultures must be taken as wholes and that the cultural totality must be judged by the physical well-being it assures (in the form of crops), anthropologists are in effect inviting comparison between the total product of such a culture and that of others—for example, that of industrial society. We, too, are entitled to be judged by the crops we raise; and the fact is that crops which are raised without benefit of mystic rites but in the full light of modern science are incomparably superior to those of the Trobriand Islanders by the very criterion according to which it has just been insisted that we must judge those primitives.

The point is that ceremonial values do not exist in isolation. Always they constitute a system. That system is a quasi-causal system. In origin it is an extrapolation of tool causality and hence of the uniformities of nature, of which it is a simulacrum. Hence the validity of the ceremonial system cannot be asserted without indirect assertion of the reality of the technological process and the validity of technological values. When social scientists assert that values derive solely from the convictions of the peoples who adhere to them, they are necessarily and inevitably asserting the contrary.

5

They are also, however contradictorily, endorsing status as the bedrock foundation of all social organization.

It used to be supposed that the social structure of human society had its origin in physical dominance, the dominance of some powerful, crafty, and irascible old male who was able (for a time) to subdue all other males and to lord it over all females and their children. The source of this notion is obvious. It is a picture of an animal herd, but of animals who walk on their hind legs; and no less obviously it exemplifies the effort to think of man in Darwinian terms before the meaning and significance of culture was fully understood. For in all human societies dominance is cultural. The authority of a chief, a shaman, the head of a family, derives not from physical strength but from mana.

Although the word *mana,* like *taboo,* has been taken over from the languages of Oceania, unlike *taboo* it has not found its way into common use, even by social scientists. And that is unfortunate, since it designates the positive of which *taboo* is the negative: the mystic potency with which persons of superior status are endowed and for lack of which those of inferior status are inferior. Thus, as various anthropologists have pointed out, most especially R. R. Marett, mana is a cultural constant, a force to be reckoned with in all societies. It may accrue to different persons in different ways: by inheritance, like the divinity of kings; by ordeal, like university degrees; or by unique personal experience, like military decorations. Similarly, loss of mana may result from violation of taboo, and may be confirmed by ceremonial degradation.

Thus the concept of status is implicit both in the mores and in all ceremonial observances. Indeed, it is impossible, as we have already seen, to define mores without taking note of the fact that they are schematized in terms of status. That is, they determine what is right, and what is wrong, for persons of stipulated rank to do. What is right for children (playing with dolls) is wrong for adults; and what is right for adults (playing with fire) is wrong for children. In like fashion ceremonial observances can and must be performed only by persons of designated status; otherwise they are wholly ineffective.

Indeed, this constitutes a key difference between ceremonial and technological activities in general. Because ceremonial activities commonly employ artifacts—charms, fetishes, ikons, vestments, and consecrated edifices of all kinds—and because these are included in the roster of collectible objects which anthropologists identify as "material culture," the question has sometimes been raised whether there is any essential difference between a tool and a fetish, such for example as a throwing stick for killing game and a whirling stick for making noises (that is, a bullroarer). Not only is there a clear difference between the causative forces (supposedly) employed, natural in one case and mystic in the other—a difference which might be said to be imputed in terms only of modern Western culture—there is also a difference of status involvement which would be even clearer to the primitive mind than to our own. A tool is an artifact which will perform to much the same effect whoever wields it, one that anybody can employ. A fetish, on the other hand, is wholly ineffective in any but consecrated hands. Profane hands may whirl the bullroarer in defiance of taboo and may produce a noise; but that noise will not summon any spirits. Only when the bullroarer is whirled by persons of designated status will mystic forces respond to its supplication.

That the concept of status likewise permeates the "philosophies" which are indissociable from all mores and all ceremonialism, goes without saying. As we have already noted, all supernaturalism implies not only the imputation of human characteristics to natural forces but also a sort of reverse animism according to which supernatural forces intrude upon human affairs. In like fashion the supernaturalism which results inevitably from symbol reification has the logically inevitable effect of imposing supernatural distinctions upon the human community. It was not the physical prowess of the herd bull that gave human society its characteristic structure but the mystic power of the "anointed keeper of the code."

Is all social organization necessarily of this character? In recent years a great many social scientists have been so far under the influence of the mores concept as to hold not only that values derive solely from mores but also that social structure as such derives solely from status. This misconception arises from failure to understand technology and consequent failure to distinguish technological from ceremonial organization. As I have indicated in an earlier chapter, tool activities set up organizational patterns quite as definitely as ceremonial activities do; but they are different patterns. Indeed, the two types of organizational patterns exhibit the same contrast that distinguishes tool skills from mystic rites. Tool activities postulate a division of labor the sole criterion of which is efficiency, whereas the sole criterion of status is ceremonial adequacy.

It is true that efficient teamwork necessitates a clear "chain of command," and that any smoothly operating team—athletic or industrial—bears a superficial resemblance to a ceremonial hierarchy. On a well-organized assembly line every man must know his place and must perform all the functions, and only those, that are appropriate to the place to which he has been assigned. It is also true that organizations which began as efficient teams sometimes degenerate into ceremonial hierarchies. Successful generals sometimes become dictators. I call this "degeneration" from the technological point of view because such a development never occurs in response to any requirement of efficiency but always through the contamination of teamwork by pre-existing traditions of status. It was of course the tradition of Bourbonism that made Napoleon's imperial pretensions possible. Hence it is not surprising that even the most careful scholars should have been misled into supposing that all social organization is hierarchical.

But in actuality the requirements and criteria of these two types of social organization are directly contrary to each other. Technological teamwork is efficient only to the extent that all considerations of status are ignored in single-minded commitment to getting the job done. The performance of the Brooklyn Dodgers and the New York Giants would not have been improved if Jackie Robinson and Willie Mays had been required to step aside and doff their caps when encountering a White Man while running bases; nor would it have been improved by once more limiting team membership to White Men. (I use capitals as standard practice requires, to show that the distinction is ceremonial rather than physical.)

Moreover—and this is the most important consideration of all—ceremonial organization is necessarily static. This means that it stands in inevitable opposition to the dynamism of the technological process. Technological activity continually gives rise to innovations resulting from the putting together of things in new ways by people who have no business doing so. Not only do such things happen in defiance of the established ways of doing things; quite commonly they force the devising of new organizational patterns. New positions must be filled for which there are no traditional, authentic, hereditary occupants. In short, organizational fluidity is a *sine qua non* of technological progress.

Status is the direct opposite of all this. Its keynote is not efficiency but ceremonial adequacy, and ceremonial adequacy requires that tradition shall always be honored regardless of consequences —that is, of mere technological consequences. The rule of seniority must be maintained regardless of the technical efficiency of the persons concerned, and no woman must ever be permitted to do "man's work" regardless of her apparent qualifications. In each case, however, all "right-minded" people would "know" that the apparent advantages of following another course are illusory, and that in the end only the righteous prevail. They know this because the prophets of old have proclaimed it so. Every system of status is static precisely because it is oriented toward the past. Its keynote is authenticity, and authenticity derives only from the past, in which nothing can be changed. "As it was in the beginning, is now, and ever shall be, world without end. Amen."

6

Such is the ceremonial system of values. That such values do exist and play an important part in the life of all communities, no one doubts. No individual can afford to disregard the ceremonial system of his community, even for a few minutes. To do so would be to give intolerable affront to the sensibilities of the entire community. In noting this fact I do not mean to be cynical. It is a fact that every individual spends a considerable part of his life—especially of his early life—in learning what sort of behavior the community expects of a person in that station in life in which circumstances largely beyond his control have somehow conspired to place him. It is also true that the sudden nullification of the ceremonial system of any community would produce a grievous state of disorganization. Many instances of this sort are on record. Conquest of primitive peoples by Europeans and subsequent prohibition of head-hunting and similar manifestations of "savagery" has often had this effect, and so has migration of peasants to industrial centers to which peasant mores were entirely inappropriate. I therefore repeat: recognition of the nature of mores and of the functional significance of the entire ceremonial system has been one of the great achievements of modern social inquiry.

But it is not the last word. Because tradition and tradition-grounded values play a large part in the lives of all individuals and of all communities, it does not follow that all values are tradition-grounded or that all communities and all human beings are equally tradition-bound. On the contrary, rigorous analysis of ceremonial values themselves reveals the coexistence at all times of another and different system of technologically determined values; and the experience of the Western peoples during the past few centuries (as well as that of other peoples in other times) reveals quite unmistakably the progressive displacement of superstition by knowledge and of prejudice by reason. This trend is the hope of all mankind.

CHAPTER IX

REASON AND ECSTASY

I

DURING THE PAST FIVE CENTURIES the secular trend of Western civilization has become increasingly pronounced and therefore increasingly evident. This is true of the process in both meanings of the word *secular*. The trend is one of extremely long range, and it is also one of steadily decreasing otherworldliness, or supernaturalism, and steadily increasing naturalism, or matter-of-factness. Notwithstanding the persistence of ancient traditions and long-established institutions—a heritage of which, at least as scholars, we are more fully cognizant than any earlier community has been—Western civilization is now secular to a degree that would never before have been thought possible; and it gives every sign of becoming progressively more so, while at the same time its influence is spreading with unprecedented rapidity to all parts of the world.

Many sincere, informed, and thoughtful people find certain aspects of this trend extremely disturbing, all the more so because they recognize the truth of science and the value of modern technology. They would not deny the major thesis of this book, that all human activities and interests are causally interrelated and that knowledge of the causal consequences of our acts gives rise to value judgments. But they would insist that values are never merely known, they are also felt; and that merely intellectual apprehension of various chains of cause and effect is not enough to account either for the moments of ecstasy which make life worth living or for the sense of dedication which sometimes impels men to lay down their lives for some higher cause.

This rejection of what might be called, after Santayana, "the life of reason" arises from a misconception of the role of emotions in both aspects of human behavior: the supposition, in one case, that the spontaneity and intensity of our emotions lends significance and even validity to esthetic and moral judgments, and in the other the supposition that intellectual judgments are entirely devoid of such feelings. It is perfectly true, of course, that likes and dislikes, approval and disapproval, do not establish the truth of any scientific proposition or the efficiency of any technical device; but it does not follow at all that scientists and craftsmen are therefore coldly unemotional creatures, or that mankind views the products of hand and brain wholly without feeling. The feelings which unquestionably do accompany such activities are, in a quite definite sense, secondary and derivative. But so are the feelings which accompany observance or infraction of the mores, common supposition to the contrary notwithstanding.

Man is a highly emotional creature. Present knowledge of emotion leaves much to be desired. But certain things we do know. One is that all emotion has an organic, or physiological, basis. We love, fear, hate, delight, and abhor with our bodies. Another thing we know is that all such feelings are subject to conditioning by experience. Whom we love and what we abhor are culturally determined. This does not mean that all the members of any cultural community love and fear exactly the same people and things—that all are as exactly alike as a boxful of tin soldiers. On the contrary, no two members of any community ever have exactly the same experiences or cultural exposures. But all are in infinitely various ways conditioned by their equally varied experiences.

As I have tried to indicate in earlier chapters, nobody knows this better than the social scientists, and especially the anthropologists, from whom we have all learned the significances of culture. Furthermore, nobody knows better than they how false are the fictions of tribal legend and how restrictive are the mores and the caste systems of ceremonial tradition. Consequently it seems to me astonishing that social scientists should now appear as advocates of continued acceptance and practice of such traditions. What is most astonishing is the catholicity of these advocates of primitivism. They seem to argue that it makes little difference what people believe, what ceremonies they enact, or what mores they impose on their communities, so long as they believe something or other of a supernatural character and observe some regulations or other which are sufficiently arbitrary and discriminatory to be susceptible of no reasonable justification.

Their argument seems to run like this. Emotion is one of the inevitable and necessary components of human life. Mores (and ceremonialism generally) arouse emotions. Therefore ceremonialism is a necessary component of human life. Nothing else can take its place. Without it mankind would be lost in an intellectual waste land.

The same argument has a popular variant which has received even wider circulation. The impartiality with which scientific knowledge has called in question the inherited beliefs of all communities and sects has given rise to a similarly general and impartial condemnation of unbelief. Many leading adherents of all sects now agree that nothing is worse than unbelief. Purportedly believers can get on very well together, however contrary their several dogmas. It is only heretics who are beyond the pale.

2

But is it true that only "believers" are capable of dedication? A leading and otherwise highly respected American philosopher has recently invoked the case of the four chaplains to illustrate this principle. During World War II a troop ship was torpedoed and was sinking rapidly. Many soldiers were without life preservers. The four chaplains who were on board—a Roman Catholic, two Protestants, and a Jew—took off their life preservers and gave them to four soldiers, and then stood at the rail with their arms linked as the ship went down. All four were drowned.

Beyond question this was an act of sublime heroism. The question is: Were these four men inspired to this act of heroism by their various sectarian beliefs? The fact that all four were chaplains suggests that conclusion. But is no other conclusion tenable? Do these four stand alone in the annals of disaster? I cite this case because it seems to me to suggest a conclusion directly opposite to that for which my colleague has invoked it. The truth is that the annals of maritime disaster are full of instances in which captains have gone down with their ships after rendering every possible assistance to others. They have done so for what I would call reasons of logic, and entirely without any sort of ceremonial inspiration.

The captain is responsible for the ship and for the lives of all on board. It is not necessary that he should die; but it is a logical necessity that he shall not fail to do everything within his power to save every other person on board; and if the discharge of this responsibility means that his death is inevitable, then he must be prepared to die. Joseph Conrad's *Lord Jim* is a celebrated study of the fate of a ship's officer who dodged this responsibility. The four chaplains were not deck officers. But they were officers whose peculiar responsibility it was to set a personal example of courage and steadfastness. It was their supreme triumph that they did so, at the cost of their lives, and knowing that such would probably be the case. Certainly they gave a magnificent example of the force of conviction. But the source of their conviction—what they were convinced of—was the responsibility of officers for the lives of others in their charge.

I cite this case because it seems to me to give clear evidence that the emotional fervor which makes it possible for men to rise to acts of heroism does in actual fact derive from understanding of what I would call technological necessity. No one doubts that the emotional dynamism which, in widely varying degree, suffuses all values is therefore an essential component of human life. No one doubts that tribal beliefs, loyalties, and mores are a source of emotional galvanism. This is amply attested by the case of Shadrak, Meshak, and Abednego, and the myriad instances of their fellow martyrs, as well as by that of the Baal worshipers who threw them in the fiery furnace—for we must not suppose that people burn each other up for fun. But to recognize one source of emotional inspiration is not to prove there is no other. The whole argument I have been examining rests on an assumption: the assumption that emotional exaltation (which we all agree is an essential component of all value) can spring only from mysterious sources. It is that assumption which is contradicted by the case of the four chaplains.

As a matter of fact, it is continually contradicted. Another celebrated case of disaster at sea, the sinking of the *Titanic,* which so magnificently exemplified the principle of "Women and children first," is a reflection of a simple matter of fact. Generally speaking (and in moments of disaster there is no time for anything but generalities) men are larger and stronger than women and children. Any man who in such circumstances saved himself by thrusting aside some small child would therefore be the object of universal obloquy, like Conrad's Jim, who saved himself at the expense of his passengers. In *A Pail of Oysters* Vern Sneider vividly portrays the feelings of a family of Taiwanese coolies, all of whom are suffering semistarvation, but who nevertheless still farther reduce their portions of rice so that a young wife who is pregnant may have more. Modern medical science could do no better.

All these are extreme instances. But they differ only in degree from all experience of values, experiences that are so common in the lives of all of us as to seem quite commonplace. That is one reason why they have been ignored. But the principal reason is the ascendancy which throughout the ages tribal beliefs and ceremonial traditions have exercised over the human mind. Because ceremonial traditions have purported to define the supreme values, and because all lesser values have therefore purported to derive their value from their hierarchical relation to the "supreme values," and also because conspicuous emotional crises in the lives both of individuals and of communities are commonly ceremonial in origin, the achievement of knowledge and skill has seemed to be emotion-free.

But such is certainly not the case. Present knowledge of emotion alone would justify us in making this assertion without any further inquiry into the particular emotional states which accompany technological behavior. As we now know, our emotional apparatus functions continuously through life. Absence of what the French call "crises of nerves" most certainly does not connote absence of nerves. The condition of emotional tranquility is just as much an emotional condition as any other. Even if this were the emotional state in which all intellectual inquiry and all exercise of skill took place, we would still have to recognize this state as an emotional one. Indeed, we would then be justified in placing a high value on tranquility. We might well argue that it would be better for disasters not to occur than for them to occur even though accompanied by acts of heroism.

3

However, as everyone who will take the trouble to examine his own day-to-day experience must realize, neither the intellectual life nor technological activity is characterized by uninterrupted tranquility. On the contrary, the technological process is accompanied by a wide range of emotions, and the value judgments which emerge from that process are in fact held with quite as great a force of conviction as any of which mankind is capable. So wide is the range of emotional experience, and so limited is our present knowledge of this function, that it would be impossible for anybody to give a definitive account of the emotional reactions which occur in conjunction with technological activity. But anybody who cares to try can easily identify at least three main types of emotional experience which owe nothing whatever to mystical beliefs or ceremonial conditioning.

The commonest and most extensive, and therefore perhaps the most significant, of these is the anxiety and exasperation which accompany the uncertainty of result, or failure, in all technological effort, and the feeling of triumph which accompanies success. I use the singular number because all these feelings seem quite definitely to be closely related. That is, the sense of triumph which accompanies success is directly proportional to the degree of anxiety, annoyance, and exasperation which has accompanied the previous effort.

By way of clear identification of this set of feelings let me call attention to a very common experience: that of the stubborn recalcitrancy of inanimate objects. No one who has ever used a tool—and every human being has done so virtually throughout life—has failed to have the feeling on countless occasions that the materials he is dealing with are deliberately eluding him. This is not a holdover from primitive animism. We are not annoyed with our automobiles and our television sets because we learned about gremlins at our mothers' knees. The real source of our annoyance, as we all know quite well, is the difficulty of the prob-

perience some faint echo of the excitement of the original discoverer. The suggestion has sometimes been made, even in recent years, that the phenomenon of appreciation is explicable only on the supposition of a special faculty. But this is true only on the further supposition that there is nothing to appreciate—that the object of appreciation is so mysterious as to be accessible only to an equally mysterious "intuition." In simple truth, appreciation, conceived as an emotional response to whatever is being appreciated, is indissociable from understanding. It is impossible to understand Archimedes' discovery of the phenomenon of specific gravity —to put oneself back some twenty-two centuries, wiping one's mind clear of all present knowledge of all the apparatus of a modern laboratory, and so to imagine the discovery of a way of determining what the insides of a solid object are made of without cutting it open or even so much as scratching it, and to do so simply, neatly, but with irrefutable certainty with ordinary materials that are universally available—without experiencing excitement, wonder, and delight. It was in fact a wonderful discovery.

The indissociability of thinking and feeling, or of understanding and appreciation, extends throughout all experience, and characterizes all human values. It is the common element that links truth, beauty, and goodness. That pure intellectual appreciation closely resembles esthetic experience is a commonplace. At the same time, no one argues that truth and beauty are identical. As I shall try to show in the pages that follow, this is because esthetic values contain an element that is absent' from pure intellectual values. But they also contain a common element that is a *sine qua non* of both—indeed, of goodness too. The emotional exaltation which sustained the four chaplains would have been impossible if they had not known with a certainty approaching mathematical demonstration that they were doing the right thing; and our appreciation of their heroism would likewise be impossible if we also did not understand something of the responsibility of officers. The exaltation which is indissociable from the quintuple counterpoint of the finale to Mozart's *Jupiter Symphony* is generically the same as that which is likewise indissociable from Napier's "analogies." To those who understand music, as to those who understand trigonometry, each is an amazing *tour de force*, a consummate achievement of unity in diversity—neat, compact, definitive; completely and profoundly right.

The meaning of rightness in music is somewhat different from its meaning in mathematics. But there is also a meaning that is common to both, and also to goodness. In all three sets of values the criterion of rightness is technological, or intellectual; and in all three situations emotional excitement is the invariable concomitant of technological achievement (as depression is likewise the concomitant of failure). It may well be that Mozart conceived his finale first, employing his themes in the opening passages of the movement only after he had worked out their contrapunted possibilities. We do know, because he said so, that he possessed the power of what might be called synoptic imagination, by which he was able to conceive an entire composition as a whole. Does this mean that in developing his themes one after the other and then assembling them in simultaneous array he was merely playing a trick? By no means! It was a trick, certainly; but what a magnificent trick! According to legend, Archimedes filled his bathtub too full, so that when he got into it, the water slopped over. What a squalid performance! Nevertheless, Archimedes' sudden realization that the water he was slopping on the floor was a function both of the volume of his body and of its buoyancy made this (if the legend is true) one of the golden moments in the whole history of civilization. His excitement was the inevitable concomitant of his correct apprehension of this fact.

5

No values, not even the most abstrusely intellectual, are emotion-free. That is why scientists speak of a "beautiful" experiment and chess players refer to a "beautiful" series of moves leading to a checkmate. But when we speak of beauty as it is revealed by the fine arts we have in mind something more than problem-solving. The problems artists seek to solve are clearly different from those of scientists. Both groups deal extensively with symbols, but the two sets of symbols are quite different in character and function. Whereas those of the scientist stand for substances and operations each of which taken by itself has no emotional significance, those of the artist are explicitly and intentionally emotional in character, since they stand for emotional experiences.

One is tempted to say that the symbols of the arts stand for emotions and nothing else. This is most evident, perhaps, in the case of music. The sound patterns which musicians weave are calculated (more or less successfully, as the case may be) to evoke various feelings. Such feelings are suspended, so to speak, in an experiential vacuum. The music may be mournful or joyous, but it can never give us anything to mourn or any cause for rejoicing. The sound patterns by which moods are induced are of course conventionalized versions of the sounds people do actually make in various emotional situations. Some of these have an organic basis, and some are cultural. Thus march time reproduces the sound of marching feet, which is the same for all members of this bipedal species. By its tempo, the timbre of the instruments employed, and even by the character of the thematic material, march music may further suggest a military band or a funeral march; but it can do so only to the ears of people who are culturally familiar with brass bands and funerals. Only within the narrowest limits can music "tell a story." The familiar strains of Chopin's "funeral march" do suggest an interment, but they do not inform us who has passed away.

Even in the case of the graphic arts, and still more that of literature, it is not so much what is represented, or narrated, that is esthetically significant as how it is represented. A color photograph of the scene immediately following a serious traffic accident might be shocking, but would it be art? With virtual unanimity artists say no. Art consists in the evocation of emotions by symbols —in the case of the graphic arts, graphic symbols—not by streaming blood and spilling entrails.

The contemporary revolt of painters and sculptors against "representation," though it has been carried through exaggeration into preciosity and even faddism, has its origin in a valid distinction. The art (or technique) of using symbols to evoke emotion, like all other forms of technology, is in a continuous process of development. Hence the most important contributions to any art are those which enlarge our vocabulary of symbols. Actual traffic accidents, and actual love affairs, do not do so—only the poems, the paintings, the music which open our eyes and ears to the emotional significance of new ranges of color, form and mass, of sound patterns, and of the magic of words.

Artists and art lovers object to crude representation (such as that of the lingering death of Little Nell) not merely because the perpetrator is violating their union rules, and not merely because he is loafing on the job, but most especially because he is perpetrating a fraud. The people who buy pictures because they portray Texas bluebonnets, and because as Texans they love bluebonnets, but still under the impression that such portrayal is art, thereby receive, on what they suppose to be good authority, a false impression of art—one that will close their eyes rather than open them. It is this hoax which nonrepresentational art foreswears.

6

The art of evoking emotions by the play of symbols is both ancient and mysterious. It is an amazing thing that one creature should be able to direct the attention of another creature to a specific object by making a particular kind of noise with his throat; but it is still more amazing that one such creature should be able to bring tears to another's eyes, or "cause his blood to boil," by tapping a hollow object in an appropriate manner. In an earlier chapter I have tried to show how the mystery that is implicit in the symbolic process itself may have given rise to all the lore of mystic forces. It seems clear that the central mystery of all art likewise must have stemmed from the central mystery of the symbolic process. No doubt that is why all the arts had their origin in ritual and fetishism.

This association has persisted through the ages. Notwithstanding the secularization of the arts, it still persists. We can never be quite sure to what extent the feelings with which we respond to a portrayal of the Madonna or a rendition of our national anthem signalize the hold of ceremonial tradition and to what extent they are a measure of the skill of painter, sculptor, or composer. Nevertheless, many circumstances combine to establish the validity of the distinction. The world is full of sacred objects which are almost totally devoid of artistic significance; and we are likewise surrounded by more or less distinguished works of art—some sublime, some extremely humble—the ceremonial significance of which is so slight as to leave no question but that their artistic merit is quite distinct from their sacred character, if any. But more conclusive than any of these end products are the facts of artistic development.

The progressive development of all the arts, though it is not as conspicuous, perhaps, as that of science, is no less a fact. I shall not argue with those who maintain that modern artists cannot equal, let alone surpass, those of some "golden age" of long ago except to remark that it is quite obviously a form of ancestor worship. As such it persists in all walks of life and is an incubus wherever it persists. Architects are in perennial rebellion against Parthenon worship, sculptors against Phidias worship, painters against Raphael worship, and musicians against Beethoven worship.

In all the arts imitators have demonstrated times without number that any fairly skillful practitioner can reproduce the achievements of earlier artists so perfectly that it requires spectroscopic analysis to detect the hoax, just as any school child can now prove that the sum of the squares of the legs of a right triangle are equal to the square of the hypotenuse just as conclusively as Pythagoras could do. In all the arts, likewise, quite ordinary practitioners are now employing symbolic techniques which are far beyond the cultural horizons of the Elizabethan age, or the Renaissance, or the glory that was Greece. Whether any individual "great" was, or was not, greater than any particular "great" of another age is a question no one can answer with assurance. But it is most certainly a fact that Beethoven could no more have written Bartók's quartets, or Raphael have painted Cézanne's portraits, than that Leonardo could have flown.

The advantage which Bartók enjoyed over Beethoven was exactly the same as that which the Wright brothers enjoyed over Leonardo: each came later in a developmental process. Like scientists and artisans, all artists learn from their predecessors. Their discoveries and inventions, like those of science and the mechanical arts, result from the combination and recombination of previously contrived instruments and processes; and this must always have been the case.

The secularization of the arts is a consequence of the inherently technological character of the artist's job. The fact that the arts of symbolic evocation of emotion were from the first associated with ceremonial mystery-making does not testify against their technological character, just as the fact that simple peoples have from time immemorial eaten poisonous berries to induce hallucinations to which they have attributed supernatural significance does not testify against the biochemistry of poisoning. Obviously there have been embryonic biochemists and embryonic artists among even the most primeval savages, practitioners who have dimly recognized such tricks for what they are. Otherwise how could they have been able to improve upon them, as subsequent history proves they must have done?

7

This does not mean that the artists of any age are coldly calculating technicians. Rather, it means, as I have only just now tried to show, that no person is devoid of feeling in his work, and that technicians are never as frigid as is commonly supposed. Indeed, they are so excitable that they run naked through the streets shouting "Eureka!" I have dwelt at some length on the case of esthetic values because it is the exact converse of the values of science and the "useful" arts. Everyone agrees that the value of an idea or an instrument is not established by our feelings, and consequently we are tempted to ignore the fact that pure intellectual achievements (and failures) do excite strong feelings nevertheless. Conversely, everyone agrees that esthetic values do excite feelings, and consequently we are tempted to ignore the obvious fact that our feelings do not establish the validity of esthetic values either.

As everybody knows, feelings are extremely unreliable witnesses. They are so even in the realm of the fine arts. Years ago Carl Van Vechten had his Peter Whiffle declare repeatedly and oracularly, "Tingling is the test." Nothing could be farther from the truth. It was not because the youthful Brahms made him tingle that Robert Schumann wrote, "Hats off, gentlemen! A genius!" How could he have dared risk such a pronouncement if he had no notion of what Brahms was doing, or how he was doing it?

It is true, of course, that in the case of esthetic values feelings are strongly indicative. This is true because what we call art is the art of evoking feelings by the manipulation of visual and auditory symbols. But how indicative the feelings are depends on whose feelings they are. When a man like Bernard Berenson declares that he has spent his life seeking thrills, we must not make the mistake of confusing him with a motorcycle racer, or with the people who say "I don't know about art, but I know what I like." The point is precisely that Mr. Berenson did know quite a bit about art, and consequently he was not likely to be taken in by the meretricious or the derivative.

Furthermore, contrary to a widespread impression, there is a surprising degree of agreement between Mr. Berenson and other knowledgeable people. A number of circumstances combine to support the notion that esthetic values are matters of taste about which people are bound to disagree. One is the fact of feeling-involvement. Another is the fact that knowledge of the arts is not as widespread as many other forms of knowledge. Still another, and one of paramount importance, is the persistent association of the arts with tribal traditions, loyalties, and rituals. But these difficulties only serve to underscore the very considerable measure of agreement which nevertheless prevails. Nobody supposes that Sargent was a greater painter than Cézanne, or that Chaminade was a greater composer than Chopin, or that Edgar Guest was a greater poet than T. S. Eliot.

Like the fact of artistic development, such agreement is explicable only on the assumption of a common technological criterion of artistic excellence. Moreover, there is still another respect in which esthetic values join hands with those of truth and righteousness. The symbolic evocation of emotion is universally judged to be a good thing—good, that is, in the broadest sense of conducive to the good life, and so good for all mankind. In this respect modern psychiatry sustains the Aristotelian theory of catharsis. Man is an emotional species. Furthermore, man's cultural way of life is highly complicated. Inevitably it produces emotional strains. But at the same time it frequently dictates the suppression of the emotions it arouses. As Aristotle realized, and modern psychiatry confirms, this is an unwholesome situation. It is well for all of us—"well" in the hygienic sense—to laugh and cry occasionally, if we are not to go crazy. Throughout the ages all the arts have helped to keep us sane. Not only that. By relieving our tensions and sharpening our perceptions they have contributed to the zest and skill with which we have addressed ourselves to all our other activities.

Here, too, emotion plays its part. We enjoy good health, as the saying goes. But we do not value it because we enjoy it. In a very real sense we enjoy it because we value it. What is most enjoyable is the certainty that our sense of well-being is not an illusion. Euphoria can be produced by drugs; but such drugs are known to have harmful aftereffects. We set a low value on the enjoyment of opium and a high value on enjoyment of the arts because we know that one is harmful and the other beneficial—harmful and beneficial for all our other activities. This does not mean that what we "appreciate" in a great painting is our own heightened sensibilities—that anybody listens to a symphony thinking to himself, "Isn't this fine! I'll surprise the boss tomorrow!" What is at issue here is not any particular esthetic experience but rather the ground on which as a community we have placed a high valuation on esthetic experience generally, and my point is that we have done so not because particular esthetic experiences are enjoyable, but because we know it to be fact—attested by all and denied by none —that all experience of this kind is beneficial.

Such a judgment of fact does not supplant emotional experience or deny its genuineness. Obviously there can be no appreciation of beauty without emotion. But it is no less true that (leaving aside ceremonially conditioned emotion) there can be no emotional response except as an accompaniment of a technological judgment. In part, the exclamation "What a beautiful picture!" gives expression to the same meaning as "What a beautiful experiment!" or "What a beautiful pipe wrench!" In each case what is expressed is the excitement—the thrill—we all feel in the presence of what we recognize and know to be a strikingly successful achievement. But in addition to this feeling which accompanies all values, whether intellectual, esthetic, or moral, the picture excites those particular emotions which the artist's skill has enabled him to symbolize. Thus, if it is a somber picture, we feel both elation and depression. But the depression is no less inseparable from, and contingent upon, our recognition and understanding of the artist's symbolism than our appreciation of a beautiful pipe wrench is contingent upon our knowing what a pipe wrench is used for and wherein this wrench is superior to others we have known.

8

The same is true of moral values. It is with regard to these, of course, that technological judgment is likely to seem least adequate; and it is toward this point that the whole of the present discussion has been directed. However, with the predicate that has now been laid, the conclusion should already be in sight.

Moral values are of course suffused with emotion. But, as I have been trying to point out all along, they are not in this respect utterly different from considerations of "mere" mechanical skill. When we say to somebody who is beating a child, presumably for disciplinary reasons, "That is the wrong way to go about it," our meaning is substantially the same as regards both fact and feelings as it is when we use the same words to reproach someone who is trying to loosen a bolt by turning it clockwise. True, our feelings are not quite the same in these two cases. Just as esthetic symbolism brings feelings into play in a manner that is foreign to intellectual experience, so also issues of moral right and wrong bring into play feelings of affection and compassion, indignation and revulsion. These feelings are somewhat different from those of esthetic experience, and they are invoked in a somewhat different fashion. But it is just as true of moral as of esthetic experience that feelings do not serve as the criterion of right and wrong. They do not supplant judgment but are contingent upon it. In the realm of right and wrong, as in that of true and false and that of beautiful and ugly, the criterion in terms of which we judge is a projection of the continuum of causal interrelatedness that runs through all human activities. Beating a child is bad for the beater and bad for the beaten.

In one sense what we mean by moral value is the larger significance of any value—its relation to the continuum of value. In this sense, the loosening of a bolt may have moral significance, like that of the nail for want of which a kingdom was lost. But there is another sense in which moral has the meaning "personal" and "intimate." These two meanings are not mutually contradictory. The continuum of value necessarily includes all the most personal and intimate concerns of all members of the community, and in doing so it takes on the emotional significance that inevitably distinguishes all intimate personal relationships.

I say inevitably meaning organically. We are so made that all intimate personal relationships are fraught with emotion. Even animals form personal attachments and likewise "rub each other the wrong way." We know comparatively little about the physiological and biochemical mechanisms which intimate personal contacts set in motion; but we do know that they are pervasive and insistent. These two circumstances—animal attraction and repulsion, and pervasive mystery—unquestionably play a large part in the development of mores, and so of ceremonialism generally. We "like" the smell of the people of our own village, and abominate the smell of the people to the south of us—garlic-eaters and opium-smokers! (Our favorite poison is alcohol.) And being articulate (symbol-users), we rationalize these affinities and aversions. Thus it seems that the outlanders are filthy savages, since instead of speaking a proper language they communicate with each other by means of a jumble of nonsense syllables, and they do not isolate their women during menstruation.

This is not to suggest that ceremonialized conventions are a biological necessity. (In the process of development of culture they may have been an inevitable concomitant of symbol-using, as I have already tried to indicate; but that is quite a different matter.) But it is true that intimate personal relationships are biologically suffused with emotion, and that this circumstance accounts for the peculiarly emotional flavor which inevitably suffuses what —on that account—we identify as "moral" values. Thus it is no accident that the word *immorality,* unless otherwise qualified, has the connotation of sex. We know—thanks to modern psychiatry, better than ever before—that in one way or another sex colors virtually all personal relationships; and we know—thanks to modern anthropology, better than ever before—that sexual taboos (for example, incest taboos) play a large part in all systems of mores and are enforced with savage ferocity. But this does not mean that moral values are universally and exclusively irrational, and of necessity must be.

On the contrary, it is not true of the distinctively moral values any more than of any others that feelings dictate judgments. That feelings are present, and that they are important, goes without saying. It is our emotions that lend the force of conviction to our judgments, and not only in the area of intimate personal relationships. But even in that area the causal interrelatedness of all human activities constitutes a criterion in terms of which technologically objective judgments can be made—can be, and always have been—upon which feelings of approval and disapproval are contingent.

9

Let us take an example. Because of its seeming irrationality, and because of the intensity of feeling it arouses and the corresponding savagery with which it is enforced (as attested, for example, by Sophocles), the incest taboo has been the subject of general investigation and discussion among anthropologists; and it may therefore serve a useful purpose here. The "philosophies" with which various peoples have rationalized their incest taboos have indeed been quite irrational, and they remain so even at the present time. Thus it is quite untrue that unions between close relatives are bound to be genetically harmful. Animal breeders get some of their best results from "line breeding." Nevertheless, a good case for the prohibition of sexual relations among members of the same household (other than husband and wife) can be made on quite different grounds.

As everybody knows, sexual interests are obsessive to a degree. It would be true of any social structure—any system of family organization—that the spontaneous occurrence of random sexual relationships would be destructive of the existing order, since it would establish loyalties tangential to those defined by the existing system. That, I think, is the reason for the universality of the incest taboo, and also for the wide variation of the definition of degrees of kinship which are subject to the rule. The latter of course vary with the structure of the family—that is, of the group who live together—and of the social order of which it is a part.

Whatever that structure may be, incestuous relationships would be, virtually by definition, a nullification of it.

This is not to say that all the peoples who have prohibited incest have done so as a matter of cold-blooded reasoning from sociological principles. Whatever the mystic forces may be which are conceived by any people to preside over their social order, the nullification of that order will of course be seen as an offense against those forces. Nevertheless, the fact remains that it is an offense. However wrong any people may be in their notions of what it is an offense against, they are right in judging it to be offensive.

Furthermore, this is true of a wider range of moral offenses than is generally realized. Many moral offenses are so regarded by all peoples. Taking the life of another person is such an offense. Notwithstanding the paradox that what one people regards as murder another considers justifiable homicide, no culture regards with complete indifference in all cases the taking of human life; and the same reasoning is applicable to taking life that is applicable to incest. As I remarked several chapters earlier in a similar connection, death is in fact irreversible and disruptive of human activities generally. This was just as true of simple peoples among whom matters of life and death were enshrouded with superstition as it is now of advanced secular societies. We may discard the superstitions of those simple peoples; we may deplore their methods of crime detection, by sorcery and the like; we may repudiate their ways of meting our justice, by blood feuds and the like; but we must admit that the fact of death is the same for all peoples, ourselves included.

But if the factual basis of moral judgment is the same for all peoples, it is no less true that vigor of emotional response is likewise the same. The progress of knowledge, in particular of knowledge of the cultural organization of human behavior, and the concomitant eradication of ancient superstitions do not mean that people are any more indifferent to each other than formerly. To suppose that such must be the case is to assume not only that emotions are subject to conditioning by tribal mores and their associated beliefs but even that they have no other source; and such an assumption is contrary to the most obvious facts.

We know as well as we know anything that human emotionality

is antecedent to all ceremonialism. It originates in the organism. The system of culture patterns only gives form and direction to our vital forces. To be sure, such shaping of emotional fixation and expression is tremendously important; but it is never final. Because one society directs the affections and repugnances of its members in certain directions, it does not follow that another society may not direct the same feelings with equal intensity in other directions. In one society the affections of the children may be directed toward their physical father, in another toward their mother's elder brother. But in both, affection is the fruit of intimate association. In each case what the patterns of culture do (among other things) is to determine who shall live together in intimate association, and (purportedly) why.

The substitution of knowledge of the basic facts of life for folklore does not alter those basic facts. Parents do not love their children less for knowing that the children's responses to their endearments are the fruit of propinquity and not a manifestation of any mystic force. People do not abhor murder any the less because they regard it as an irremediable disaster and not the work of evil spirits; nor is the urgency of their demand for the execution of justice any the less because they regard a murderer at large as a public menace and not as the corporeal agent of an evil spirit.

10

These are concrete values, highly individual in character. But industrial society is becoming constantly more impersonal as the scale of social organization constantly increases. Does this process involve a loss of the feeling of immediacy, a weakening of the emotional force of conviction, by which moral values are defined? Many people think it does. Indeed, their arguments are all too familiar. They point to such widely varying manifestations as the indifference to the common good exhibited by the horde of "litter-bugs" who infest our public parks, both local and national, and the appalling inhumanity of the atom-bombing of Hiroshima and Nagasaki. But is such evidence conclusive? Does it represent a genuine effort to understand the moral character of industrial society, or have ancient prejudices been allowed to stack the cards? Which is more significant: the bombings, or the moral uproar they set off? If the bombings had occurred without expression of concern, a moral observer might justifiably conclude that they betoken a loss of moral sensibility such as might well be attributed to the "impersonality" of modern life. But they did not so occur. On the contrary, never have so many of the earth's inhabitants been so deeply stirred by so few incidents—so few and so remote from the centers of Western civilization.

Trivial as it is in comparison, the case of the defacement of public parks and highways raises the same questions. Which is more significant: the defacement, or the vast and growing public outcry against it? In trying to answer such a question we must remember that the people who throw beer cans out of automobiles have not had either the cans or the automobiles very long. With regard to such things we are all like infants with new toys. We have barely begun to learn the possibilities of these toys for good and evil. Nevertheless, it is already beginning to be clear that the freedom of movement which the automobile confers also imposes responsibilities. Already many people feel such responsibilities very strongly, and we have good ground for supposing that the time may soon come when littering a park or highway will be universally regarded with the same disgust that would be felt toward an adult who threw food leavings on the floor—as ladies and gentlemen did only a few centuries ago—and will be just as rare.

Unbiased observation should be sufficient to convince anyone that the force of moral conviction is just as strong today as it has ever been, notwithstanding the increasing secularism of Western civilization. But logic also points to the same conclusion. Owing to the scale of modern organization, the objects of significant emotional attachment are increasingly broad abstractions: the public welfare, the United States of America, Western civilization. Is it possible for mankind to entertain towards entities as vast and indefinite as these such an intensity of loyalty and dedication as has served in the past to sustain tribal cultures? The answer to this question must be Yes, and first of all, as I have just said, on grounds of common observation. The annals of war bear witness that the dedication of modern Americans to their country's cause is just as strong as that of primitive tribesmen. But more significant is the increasing power of intellectual abstraction and its accompanying force of emotional conviction.

Abstraction as such is no new thing. In considering the immediacy of the primitive tribesman's personal loyalty to his chief we must not forget that the strongest feelings of even the most primitive peoples are focussed upon mystic forces. Even the chief commands the loyalty of his people not merely because they know him personally but much more because of his mana: because his people know him to be the embodiment of a mystic force. Such forces are abstractions, however imaginary they may be—ceremonial abstractions, to be sure, but abstractions none the less. But the power of the human mind to create abstractions is not limited to the mythopeic imagination. There are also the intellectual abstractions of creative intelligence; and if anybody supposes that intellectual values are devoid of feeling and so have no power to command the loyalties of men, let him try a simple experiment on a ten-year-old child. Let him deny that the sum of two and two is four. I say a child because an adult would dismiss him with a smile of contempt, but a child would be so baffled by the conflict between the ceremonial respect owing an adult and his intellectual conviction that the sum is four that he would manifest acute emotional irritation culminating, quite likely, in a paroxysm of rage.

The fury of the child who faces contradiction of what he knows to be true is significant because it is a true expression of the ethos of industrial society. No people have ever adhered to their tribal superstitions with a stronger force of conviction than the Western peoples now feel for science and technology. All values—all human activities—are suffused with emotion because they are the values of an emotional species. It is our emotional nature that infuses into our value judgments the emotional force of conviction and even the sense of dedication. But it is not the intensity of our feelings that determines what is valuable. For all peoples the basis of judgment is the causal interrelatedness of all human activities, which is to say the uniformities of nature as they affect mankind. People do not adhere to their superstitions out of mere habit of conformity. They adhere with passionate intensity to what they suppose to be true. Such being the case, it would be ridiculous

—it would be contrary to everything we know—to suppose that the intensity of our conviction must fade to the extent that our knowledge is warranted by fact and to the extent that our judgments of value are correct.

Knowledge is always incomplete, and all judgments of value are subject to correction. But this does not mean that all knowledge is equally incomplete, nor does it mean that all value judgments are equally fallible. We do quite incontestably know more today about the uniformities of nature and the interdependence of all human activities than men have ever known before, and we are therefore no less incontestably in a better position to make sound judgments of value than men have ever been before. This does not make sound judgments automatic. The menace of illusions of pride and grandeur is no less for us than it has been for any of our forebears. In human life, as in that epitome of human life which we call science, every answer raises an indefinite series of further questions. The more we understand the significance for all mankind of such universal values as those of freedom and abundance, the more difficult their realization appears.

But this is no reason for despair. In spite of the growing complexity of all human affairs, the task is now what it has always been throughout the ages: that of pressing on. There is only one way to resolve confusion, and that is by moving steadily forward. Our knowledge is incomplete and our skill inadequate, and this condition can be relieved only in one way: by the acquisition of more knowledge and greater skill. The present book is intended as a contribution to this effort.

PART FOUR

CHAPTER X

THE UNITY OF VALUE

O NE OF THE MOST UNFORTUNATE CONSEQUENCES of twentieth-
century sophistry is the habit of thinking of value always in
the plural. I call it a "habit" because that is all it is. No one has
ever established, either by logical analysis of the nature of value
or by the natural history of the origin of value in human experience,
that particular values come into existence independently of each
other and lead separate existences either in society or in the lives
of individuals.

Bad though the habit is, there is a reason for it. Those in whom
the habit of pluralizing value is most firmly established are themselves chiefly concerned about the clash of conflicting values and
the process of adjustment which modern life entails. They have
good reason to be so concerned. Values are cultural phenomena,
and under the conditions of modern life contacts between different cultures—in some cases very widely different cultures—
are the order of the day. Moreover, even within the confines of
Western culture, changes of unprecedented magnitude are occurring with unprecedented rapidity. A process of intercontinental
admixture is going on. Scraps of value torn from their original
setting are finding their way into the lives of peoples whose value
systems are quite different from those in which the migrant values
originated; while at the same time medieval values persist in even
the most advanced industrial culture. It is these circumstances, of
course, and all the strains and stresses they entail, that have given
rise to the habit of thinking of values in the plural, as though they
were distinct and separate doses of cultural medicine, or infections
by cultural viruses.

But in spite of all the confusions of acculturation, the unity of
value is inherent in the meaning of all values. As I have tried to
show, this is true even of ceremonial values. Tribal mores and the

tribal superstitions which sustain them are of course culture-limited; and to those who recognize no other source of value this circumstance provides a powerful impetus to thinking of values always in the plural. But to the people of each culture even their most arbitrary conventions form a system, a hierarchy even, ostensibly headed by some "ultimate" value or *Summum Bonum*—salvation or nirvana. In the apprehension of the community all things good and evil are so by virtue of contributing to, or impeding, the attainment of the supreme good.

In short, values are never a random assortment. Even on the supposition that all values are culture-limited, the alternative is between one value *system* and another. To the extent to which values become detached from the systems which gave them meaning, they cease to be values, and the resulting situation is a confusion—the *anomie* of sociological theory: an absence of pattern in which choices and decisions become meaningless. However distinct such value systems may be conceived to be, and however arbitrary their cultural imposition, value is always unitary.

Moreover, there is a larger sense in which all value systems are related. All are causal systems, either in fact or in supposition. The beliefs of which a value system is the embodiment are beliefs with regard to causal efficacy: that all good things work together for the supreme good, which is the Final Cause. This means that underlying all ceremonial values are the actualities of cause and effect. It is the actual blighting of a crop that signalizes the enormity of the taboo, infraction of which is supposed to have caused the crop to wither, an actual illness that gives evidence of witchcraft. Underlying all the false values of all systems of superstition and convention are the true values of science and technology.

These are the same for everybody. The meaning of a "good" crop is the same in all cultures. Good health is so regarded by all peoples. Food is universally accounted good, and notwithstanding all the vagaries of dietary taboo all the peoples of the world eat virtually the same things. It is this basic fact that has made the taboos of alien peoples seem outlandish and so has fastened the attention of scholars upon differences, to the neglect of obvious and universal values.

Such values are by no means limited to animal existence. All peoples prize knowledge and skill. Falsehoods flourish and are infinitely varied; but all peoples mean the same thing by "true" and "false," and all attach the same values to both. Among some peoples (ourselves included) the art of deception is widely practised, and the skilled deceiver is greatly admired. But the very meaning of deception implies that the truth is known at least to the deceiver, and that the victim of the deception is victimized precisely because truth is great and will prevail. It prevails because, like the uniformities of nature of which it is a projection in human experience, it is the same for all men.

All peoples prize tools, and value skill. Cultural barriers sometimes prevail against the adoption of the strange tools of alien peoples, and strange skills are sometimes abhorred as witchcraft. But no people has ever abandoned the use of tools, just as no people admires clumsiness or honors ineptitude. These meanings are the same for all. The artistry we admire in the work of primitive craftsmen—those, for example, who painted the bison on the walls of the cave at Altamira—must certainly have been admired by their contemporaries, and in part for the same reasons. Granted that the paintings were ceremonial, and that the craftsmen were almost certainly credited with occult powers (as many people still credit contemporary "genius"); the fact remains that they must have known what they were trying to do with line and mass and color, and that their genius too could only have resulted from an infinite capacity for taking pains.

True values are trans-cultural—they are the same for all men—because they are all interrelated. All are manifestations of the same process, the life process of mankind. All knowledge is related to and conditioned by all other knowledge, and all skills are mutually contributory. Good health, freedom from disease and famine, is contributory to the acquisition of skill and knowledge; and the growth of knowledge and development of skill are contributory to good health.

All true values define and fortify each other. It is this circumstance that has made civilization possible. If such were not the case, mankind would be a species of animal, long since extinct. Man does not live by bread alone, for the good and sufficient reason that bread never comes alone. Bread is a highly sophisticated nutrient which man achieved only after several hundred thousand years of accumulation of knowledge, skills, equipment, and organization.

What an irony it is that in the twentieth century our chief ground of self-reproach should be that our lives lack any common purpose, any clear sense of general direction! Certainly, if this were true, it were a grievous fault. But if it were true, how could we have reached the present level of civilization? Only a few hundred generations divide us from the men who first made bread. Could we have amassed the vast store of knowledge that we now possess if knowledge had been of dubious value? Could we have achieved our present degree of mastery over the elements and processes of nature, or brought into existence all the formidable apparatus of twentieth-century technology, if the value of these activities, the worthiness of these "gadgets," were truly subject to doubt?

Obviously our doubts arise not from the secular achievements of industrial society but from the shadow those achievements cast across the idols of the tribe. Throughout the ages men have pursued common purposes that were inherent in the logic of their secular activities. But they have imputed their common purposes to their tribal fetishes and have attributed all their successes to tribal piety. They have done so for reasons which are only now beginning to be understood; but they have done so for so long a time and with such assiduity that the eclipse of tribal piety and superstition has produced a general sense of moral vacuum.

In fact, no such vacuum exists. Industrial society is not morally bankrupt. The comfort and security of modern life, the amazing decline of the death rate, especially of infants, and the prodigious increase of life expectancy, have not been achieved at the expense of higher values, nor have they led to the neglect of higher values, except insofar as "higher values" may be dogmatically defined in terms of some particular tribal piety.

It is generally recognized that certain values have been idealized by all the "great" religions of history. Those values are universally recognized as the highest of which mankind is capable: loving kindness, gentleness, nonviolence, brotherly helpfulness to all others irrespective of race or creed or physical condition. The universality of such values is more than a coincidence. The human way of life is essentially cooperative. Mutual aid is a basic condition of the technological process. In spite of all the confusions and divisions of tribal superstition and taboo, this has always been realized, more or less dimly to be sure, but nevertheless more or less persistently and even continuously. Just as the fantasies of tribal beliefs and mores, being themselves quasi-causal, invariably appeal for their final authentication to the actualities of cause and effect, so the ideals of mutual aid and common brotherhood have persisted through the ages notwithstanding all the barbarities of tribal separatism.

It may be that the hazard of mutual destruction is greater at the present time than ever before in the history of mankind; but it is also true that awareness of this danger is more intense and widespread than ever before, and for the same reason. What has arrayed mankind in hostile camps is not the atom bomb. Hostile camps are always a manifestation of tribal parochialism, today no less than in the Old Stone Age. It is of course the immensity of the forces which modern knowledge and technological cunning have placed at the disposition of mankind that makes the parochialism of the twentieth century so much more hazardous than that of the Philistines and the Ishmaelites. But the knowledge that has made those forces available has also made known to people throughout the world the appalling dangers that reside in them.

Moreover, this knowledge is an inseparable part of knowledge in general. The passion for freedom that has been spreading throughout the world in recent years is a manifestation of a sort of intellectual epidemic. Even in remotest Asia and Oceania, even in darkest Africa, people are becoming aware of a way of life that is far superior, in certain obvious respects, to their own. However dimly, they realize that the freedom the Western peoples have achieved is a function of the abundance they enjoy—and vice versa. Just how these values are related is by no means clear to them. Indeed, it is still far from clear to us. But it is increasingly clear to all of us that the fruits of skill and knowledge are good, notwithstanding the dangers they entail, and that the values they signalize and foster are all interrelated, since they are all functions of scientific knowledge and technological competency.

That the values of industrial society are real is attested by the eagerness of other peoples to share them, and also by our own common determination, notwithstanding various ideological misgivings, to press on to their fuller attainment.

What are these values? Since this question encompasses the whole of human life, no answer to it can hope to be complete. I am confident that the values I have chosen for discussion in the chapters that follow are representative. Certainly they are mutually complementary, and in this sense I think it is reasonable to suppose that what is true of them is true of value in general. By the same token, their meaning is the same for all. These are values all mankind has sought. Their validity for all is attested by the life process of which they are a manifestation.

CHAPTER XI

FREEDOM

I

NO VALUE IS CLOSER to the heart of Western civilization than freedom. None is held more dear, and none is more truly characteristic of our way of life. It is therefore significant that no other value reflects the moral confusion of the twentieth century more fully or more vividly.

The causes of this confusion lie deep in the roots of Western culture, as the preceding chapters have indicated. But they are manifest in the contrast between the simple, obvious, and primitive conception of freedom and the much more difficult, complex, and subtle conception which has been emerging gradually in the course of the development of the secular society of the Western world. Most simply stated, it is the contrast between the conception of freedom as a "condition," and its conception as a "process."

In the primitive sense, freedom is the absence of coercion. To anyone who is aware and resentful of being coerced, such a definition when first encountered is likely to seem wholly adequate. But deeper consideration indicates its apparent inadequacies. Not only is such a conception of freedom wholly negative, it is therefore wholly noncommittal. Denunciation of coercion is a pleasant enough exercise, since most of us are aware and resentful of being coerced in one way or another. But it sidesteps the question whether in any larger sense the individuals or groups in question deserve to be free—whether the world would be better off for the termination of the coercion in question.

All men are egotists, and all societies are by their very nature self-assertive. It seems almost as though self-admiration were the curse mankind has had to bear in compensation for the blessing of social organization. All communities believe themselves to be the chosen people of some Higher Power, and seek to preserve their ancient traditions, which prove, to their own satisfaction, that such is the case; and all peoples therefore resist domination by other peoples and absorption into their cultures. This is the fact which throughout the ages has sustained and informed the primitive conception of freedom—the principle cited in Woodrow Wilson's classic phrase, "self-determination of peoples."

The appeal of that resounding phrase is very great, since it elicits a sympathetic response from our own cultural egotism. We too have sought, and perhaps achieved, self-determination. But in effect such a principle implies the cultural fragmentation of mankind, and therefore it stands in opposition to all those historical forces which have brought about the consolidation of the nations and given rise to the ideal—cherished by Woodrow Wilson himself—of the unification of all peoples. If self-determination is the highest good, what about the Confederacy? What about the League of Nations? Clearly the fragmentation to which the doctrine of self-determination leads has no stopping place short of the individual, and stops there only because the individual is by definition indivisible.

2

"The individual" was freedom's standard-bearer. It is for this reason that the metaphysics of individualism has obsessed the Western mind throughout modern times. Modern Western society had its origin not in the feudal system but in the medieval towns. These were communities of "freedmen" which grew up outside the walls, so to speak, of medieval society. These freedmen were quite literally runaway serfs. Each and severally, their first interest was the highly practical one of making good their getaway. But as the towns grew and began to constitute a challenge to the feudal lords, lay and ecclesiastical, their need for a convincing justification of their situation grew.

This need is itself clear evidence of the inadequacy of the primitive conception of freedom. It is not enough to escape coercion. To be secure in his freedom the free man must show cause why he should not, or cannot, be coerced; and since no man can resign from the human race or detach himself altogether from his ancestral culture, this can be done only by representing the values of that culture as having their origin and sanction in his individual-

172

ity. Precisely that has been the purport of the Western philosophy of individualism. Those who made good their escape from feudalism had no wish to abrogate medieval culture *in toto*. After all, it was the only culture they knew, and its values and beliefs were those of the families they left behind and of the ancestors they still revered. What they required was rather some reorientation of the prevailing culture by which their freedom would be assured. In an age of theology, any convincing justification must be theological; and since it was a community of detached individuals who required metaphysical relocation—detached not only from their families and forebears, their former occupations, the political authorities, and their spiritual advisers—this situation inevitably led to the apotheosis of the human individual. Just as the claims of individual conscience were opposed to those of the Church, so the claims of human individuality, flowing directly from the fatherhood of God and implicit in the doctrine of freedom of the will, were opposed to the claims of feudal tradition.

As Western society continued to develop, the theology of individualism burgeoned into the philosophy of natural rights. This doctrine, too, had theological origins. Indeed, it is the logical corollary of the metaphysics of individualism. All social structures include status systems which are graded systems of rights and obligations, and in all social traditions these are held to be of supernatural origin. According to medieval theology the whole system of feudal rights and dues was divinely sanctioned. With the rise of national states both political authority and divine sanction came to be concentrated in the person of the sovereign. To modern minds the doctrine of the divine right of kings is so patently absurd that people are liable to forget that it was the embodiment of an ancient tradition which Western society gave up with extreme reluctance, and only by substituting the counterdoctrine of natural rights.

The essence of this doctrine is that all rights derive from human individuality. They are inalienable in the same sense that individual identity is inalienable. Most especially are individuals endowed by nature with the right of owning property. One of the most amazing, and at the same time most highly characteristic, features of both of these ideas—of the nature of human individu-

ality and of the nature of rights—is their amenability to secularization. By the seventeenth century, when (in England at least)
the final confrontation of the old order by the new occurred,
science was coming of age. The same generation that witnessed
the "bloodless revolution" also witnessed the founding of the
Royal Society. The human individual could now be regarded not
so much as the son of God as a fact of nature, and the same was
true of his inalienable rights. As Locke declared in his classic
defense of the Whig revolution, man establishes his right to
property by mixing his labor with the soil. His freedom to do so
derives from his very nature—from the faculties with which he
has been endowed since the Creation. Man's freedom, signalized
by the right to own property, is by this time held to be as much a
fact of nature as the law of gravitation. Thus the whole weight of
the new science was brought to bear on the side of freedom.

3

For property meant freedom. It did so for a very definite reason,
though one which later generations have been prone to forget. The
absolute power of kings by divine right includes power over both
the persons and the possessions of all subjects. The freedom of
the individual from arbitrary arrest and confinement is a circum-
scription of that power, and so is the guarantee of the individual's
right to security in the possession of property. Thus the assurance
to all citizens of "life, liberty, and property" constitutes the virtual nullification of the absolute power of the sovereign. That,
of course, is why the right to own property received so much emphasis in the seventeenth and eighteenth centuries—an emphasis
which has survived even into the twentieth century.

I do not mean to suggest that class interest played no part in
such emphasis. Obviously it played a very considerable part. It
was the property-owning class, rather than the "proletariat," who
took the lead in the long-drawn-out battle against the feudal order; and since this was the struggle in which the modern conception of freedom was shaped and tempered, it is not surprising
that the interests of that class should have been identified with
that conception of freedom.

But the traditional emphasis upon property rights does reveal the inadequacy of the classical (Lockeian) conception of freedom to meet the contingencies and requirements of an expanding industrial society. Intellectually, at least, the struggle against feudalism is over. Not that Western society is no longer in danger of a relapse into tyranny! As recent events have demonstrated, that danger never ceases. No doubt eternal vigilance is the price mankind will always have to pay for every kind of progress. But however important it may be to exercise vigilance against slipping backward, as a guide to the future vigilance is inadequate. Like the primitive conception of freedom, it is essentially negative: the preservation of the *status quo*.

Thus the fatal weakness of the classical conception of freedom lies in its premises. Immensely effective as they were against medieval dogma, metaphysical individualism and the doctrine of natural rights throw no light whatever on the confusions of the twentieth century. In a very real sense—as we should all understand by now—there is no such thing as an individual. That is, human individuality does not antedate social experience, and therefore social principles such as freedom cannot be derived from the supposedly prior existence of the individual. Epictetus declared that his master might beat him; he might even break his arm or leg; but he could not change his mind. But was he then free from coercion by the "law" of gravitation? Could his mind operate independently of the multiplication table? Would a mind that was innocent of arithmetic be freer than one for whom two plus two must always be four? Rousseau's passionate assertion, "Men are born free . . ." is quite untrue. Men are born wild, and become human only by a process of domestication which begins virtually at birth and continues throughout life. No man is "free" from this process. Whatever freedom means, it cannot mean that.

So it is also with rights. The notion of rights, and the recognition of particular systems of rights, are of course features of the various social systems into which human infants are all inducted. Rights are established by law and by tradition, and they undergo alteration as traditions change and laws are modified. The history of the Western peoples in recent centuries is a record of such a process of change. But this process, far from establishing the inalienability of any rights, is rather clear evidence of the mutability of all human institutions. No informed and thoughtful person can possibly assert today that men are free because nature intends it so, or that any particular freedom—from arbitrary molestation or confiscation—can be said to derive from the nature of man or of the universe. All freedoms, like all coercions, are social.

4

By itself, alas, this proposition too is wholly negative. As we have already noted at length, it is their recognition of the social matrix of all values that has prompted many leading thinkers of our time to abandon the effort to find any general conception in terms of which such a value as freedom might be understood. Accepting as final the relativity of all values to the traditions of the peoples who hold them, and failing to distinguish between cere monial and technological traditions, they declare simply that freedom is a basic value of Western society, one to which (for various historical reasons) the Western peoples have dedicated themselves, and that is all there is to it.

But this is not enough. It is not enough to enable us to define specific freedoms, and it is not enough to sustain any effective commitment to defend them. Granted that the right of any citizen to be secure in the ownership of property—implicit in the saying that a man's house is his castle—is one of the building blocks of freedom. That saying conjures up a picture of a yeoman staunchly defying a bailiff. But however much we cherish such a memory, how are yeomen and bailiffs going to help us to determine whether the Tennessee Valley Authority is another building block of freedom or whether it is "creeping socialism" and therefore an erosion of our ancient freedom? An eminent exponent of the yeoman theory declares that ". . . the most formidable enemy of civil liberty is modern democracy," and that ". . . when it succeeds in destroying the old traditions for any long period of time the resurrection of such a sentiment as that of civil liberty becomes fairly hopeless." If freedom has nothing to support it but sentiments evoked by old traditions, its case is indeed hopeless.

5

The truth is that freedom is not so much a condition as a process. It is not merely a denial of coercion, by alien peoples or by tyrannical sovereigns. As it has been achieved by the Western peoples in recent centuries, the concept of freedom is bursting with positive content; and that content has been poured into it, generation after generation, by the scientific-industrial revolution.

Our freedom is virtually synonymous with the fullness of life as it has been realized by industrial society. For example, discussion of the free enterprise system has always emphasized the individual's freedom to choose his employment or the line of business in which he wishes to engage, and likewise his freedom as a consumer to buy whatever he pleases. But any such choice is only as wide as the number of industries and occupations that exist, actually or potentially, at any given time and place, and by the relative profusion or paucity of consumer goods. Considered in these terms freedom of choice has been increased prodigiously in recent generations in direct consequence of industrial growth and diversification. The same is true of limitations of time and space. Mobility, upon which also economists have laid great stress, is largely conditioned by existing means of communication and transportation. The freedom of movement which denizens of industrial society now enjoy is incalculably greater than that which conditions made possible only half a century ago—and many more times greater than that of five centuries ago.

Such freedoms can of course be regarded as corollaries of the integrity of the free individual, as in fact they were. The question is one of causal sequence. Did the doctrine of individual integrity come first? Did the founders of classical liberalism first create the conception of the free individual and then derive the corollary freedoms of economic choice and mobility; or did people first begin to move around, to change their occupations and their consumption patterns as changing circumstances permitted, and did they then defend the new freedom, opposing force to force and ideas to ideas?

One of the corollaries of the supposedly "fundamental" freedom of the individual is freedom of communication, and especially freedom of the press. Throughout modern times a free press has been the hallmark of a free people. But very little was heard about this before the time of Gutenberg. Did the ideal of free communication inspire the invention of printing by movable types, or vice versa? For many years freedom to print the Bible, and especially to print translations of the Latin text into the common speech of the various Western peoples, was a fighting issue. Was it the ideal of religious freedom that prompted such publication, or was it the technical possibility of publication that raised the issue of religious freedom?

I submit that in every case it was the progress of science and industry (as we now call them) that defined and inspired the freedoms which Western society wears so proudly, and that the perpetuation and extension of those freedoms is a *sine qua non* of the further development of science and technology and so of all the values that flow from them. Freedom is not an ultimate, or a primary assumption. It is an aspect and a condition of technological process.

6

In a very real sense Western society owes its technological advancement, and so its freedoms, to an accident of history. This is not the place for a recapitulation of the history of the Western world. But it is impossible to understand the meaning of freedom as a feature and an ideal of Western civilization without taking cognizance of the nature of the process by which it came to be so.

During Roman times the Western peoples received from their conquerors the whole of the vast accumulation of knowledge and skills which the Romans had inherited from the ancient civilization of the Mediterranean world. This the "barbarians" fully assimilated. They also received the institutional patterns and ceremonial traditions of the Romans. But these were alien institutions and traditions which therefore rested far more lightly on the Western tribes than they did, for example, upon the Greek-speaking people of the Byzantine Empire, who regarded Homer and Plato as their own folk heroes and at the same time identified themselves as Romans and their empire as the Roman Empire, as indeed it was.

After a relatively brief period of Roman tenancy (about one-fourth as long as the period that has since elapsed), during which the Western province was swept by repeated waves of "barbarians," the Western peoples cast off the authority of "Rome" (actually, now, Constantinople-Byzantium); and thereafter the authority of the Empire was never again successfully asserted over the Western peoples. Thus was created a unique situation: that of a large and for those days relatively populous area in which the technological heritage of thousands of years of continuous development had been thoroughly established but in which also prevailed a unique degree of institutional fluidity.

I realize that such a characterization is in complete contrast to the conception of the Middle Ages on which most of us grew up. Until quite recently medieval society was quite generally supposed to have been an extreme manifestation of institutional rigidity. There are two reasons for the prevalence of this notion. One is the fact that at its apogee, in the thirteenth century, feudalism—in theory, at least—was authoritarian. Later generations have therefore tended to take feudal society at its own valuation, forgetting not only the contrast between medieval ideals and the spotted actuality but also the long period—seven centuries or so—in which the feudal "system" (and contemporary authorities now agree that it was anything but that) was in process of formation. The other reason for the subsequent prevalence of misconception derives from the efforts of later generations, beginning with the Renaissance and the Humanist revival, to break away from medieval authoritarianism. Such efforts always exaggerate the evils they deplore. Thus it is only within the last generation or two that historians have begun to realize how different the experience of the Western peoples has been from that of the peoples of India or China during the same centuries, or even that of the Byzantine Empire.

Furthermore, the centuries of turmoil and institutional improvisation that followed severance from "Rome" coincided with a series of culture contacts through the agency of which a process of acculturation was set going that was of unique significance to the Western peoples. Two or three examples of this process will be sufficient to indicate the character and the importance of this process. One is the introduction of the Hindu-Arabic numerals into Western Europe. Another is the introduction of the Chinese art of printing. Still another is the blending of the arts of ship-building and rigging developed by the ancient Mediterranean peoples, the Arabs, and the Vikings. In all such instances the culture contacts in question made little difference to the other participants. This was due in part to technological circumstances. In the case of printing, for example, the fact that the Western peoples had inherited a phonetic alphabet from their Mediterranean forebears made possible first, printing from movable types, and then the uniquely rapid spread of literacy. But in all cases the fluidity of Western culture meant that the Western peoples were uniquely receptive to new things. Even in the case of printing it was by no means technologically impossible that some Chinese genius should have done for his people what the Cherokee Sequoyah did for his. But the passionate adherence of the Chinese to their ancient ways and their corresponding contempt for the crude devices of the "outer barbarians" would almost certainly have proved insurmountable obstacles to the adoption of a phonetic alphabet—as in fact they did to similar developments.

Thus the ingredients of the cultural explosion of the fifteenth century were accumulating throughout the Middle Ages. It was a cumulative process. The development of each new device called for the use of tools and materials which were by no means universally accessible but were to be found in the medieval towns, thanks to other aspects of the general process. For example, the printed word could not possibly have spread with such astounding rapidity (something like twenty million books of varying sizes printed in the half-century following the Gutenberg invention) had not the manufacture of paper already become general; and the inking of metal type faces would not have been possible had not the Renaissance painters already developed linseed oil as a medium for paints. Thus each art reinforces others.

7

In describing the inception of the industrial revolution as a cultural process I do not mean to belittle the individuals who played leading parts in it. Obviously, everything mankind does is done by culturally oriented individuals. But for an understanding of the process, as distinct from the award of honor, the cultural orientation is all-important. This is especially significant for an understanding of the growth of freedom as a concomitant of industrial revolution.

For one thing, industrial development is the locus of power, and not only in the age of atomic fission. In its earliest stages the industrial revolution affected weapons no less than plowshares. The medieval towns not only afforded an immediate haven to freedmen; as the spawning ground of industry the towns were able to generate the power that enabled their citizens to stay free and eventually to dominate their countries. The forging of swords is a handicraft, but the casting of cannon is an industry.

But another aspect of the process is even more important, since it is qualitative. Freedom, it has been said, begins in the hearts of men—more truly, perhaps, in their minds. Certainly the most important freedom is freedom of the mind; and freedom of mind is both a prior condition to invention and discovery and a further consequence of all technological development. Throughout the foregoing discussion I have emphasized the unique combination of circumstances by virtue of which it became possible early in the life of the Western peoples for technological novelty to prevail against institutional inhibition. This process, too, was cumulative. The first use to which the Hindu-Arabic numerals were put was in the reckoning of merchants, and the first use to which the art of printing was put was in the publication of the Latin Bible. In each case the new art had direct effects upon its users. As we have already noted, the printing of the Bible was a step in the direction of religious freedom. The simplification of arithmetic by use of the Hindu-Arabic decimal system likewise led directly to the invention of double-entry bookkeeping, and so was a step in the direction of free enterprise.

But even more significant was the stimulus which all such innovations gave to the development of scientific inquiry. As every schoolchild knows, simple arithmetic is the foundation of the natural sciences; and it is no less true that publication is the lifeblood of all scientific inquiry. The dawn of the age of science coincided with the dawn of the industrial age. The same process that endowed the free cities with industrial power also brought enlightenment. Throughout modern times political freedom and freedom of the mind have gone hand in hand.

The process of industrial revolution has another aspect that is equally important for understanding and attaining freedom. Starving men are not free, nor are starving communities. If the universe were so constructed that enlightenment could be won only at the permanent sacrifice of the comforts and necessities of life, mankind would have remained unenlightened. It is only because knowledge gives immediate, automatic, and cumulative access to man's necessities and comforts that any degree of intellectual advancement has been possible. The enlightenment to which Western society has progressively attained from the dawn of modern times is a direct function of the increasing opulence of industrial society. In a very real sense the freedom we have achieved is in direct proportion to our wealth. This is what the Marxists have in mind when they speak of freedom as a "bourgeois" perquisite; but in doing so they miss the central truth of the relationship of freedom and enlightenment to wealth. It is not only men of wealth who are free, but communities of wealth. Freedom is a function of the technological process, and as such it is a community function in a far more significant sense than Communism dreams of. The machine can tolerate neither ignorance nor poverty.

Such a statement is symbolic, of course. Freedom is not in any literal sense machine-made. It is rather a function of a process that runs through all the fabricating activities of all mankind in greater or less degree. I have called this the technological process; but such a phrase also must be taken in the broadest sense as including all the tool-using efforts of the race. It must also be clearly understood that among the most important tools are the tools of inquiry. But they are so because as instruments of inquiry they are still tools—because all inquiry extends the boundaries of man's command of tools. What the machine symbolizes, therefore, is the vast area that is now included within the boundaries of the possible. The extent of this vast area is significant because it represents the extent of human freedom; and the positive significance of freedom is defined by the scope of human activities. Freedom does not stand outside the life process of mankind as a sort of message from another world. It is significant and precious

182

because it is an essential part of the meaning of that process. That is what the commitment of Western civilization to industrial revolution really means. In seeking to extend the limits of the possible, we have sought freedom; and in seeking freedom we have committed ourselves to industrial revolution.

8

We may well say that the most important freedom for every individual and for any society is freedom from ignorance. But it is so, for the individual as for society, because knowledge—warranted and demonstrable knowledge—means freedom from prejudice and dogma, from superstitious fears and from enslavement to the past. Such freedom is good for the individual and for society because it means a release of energies and an enlargement of the area of the possible. Knowledge, as the saying goes, is power— not merely power over other people but power to do things. For the individual, as for society, freedom from ignorance means freedom from want; while at the same time freedom from want means, both for the individual and for society, greater access to knowledge.

This is the reason for the extraordinary emphasis that has been put throughout modern times on freedom of inquiry and freedom of communication. Such freedoms have usually been stated, especially in earlier centuries, in terms of the inviolable rights of the individual mind, or conscience; and those concepts have figured so largely in our literature that they have become a part of language and hence persist as the idiom of freedom, even after the concepts themselves have been largely discarded. But all the while it has also been evident to thoughtful men that freedom of thought and expression is a condition *sine qua non* to the continuance and continued development of a way of life.

Thus John Stuart Mill pointed out that society can never safely suppress dissident opinion, however small a minority it represents —even a minority of one—since we can never be sure that the dissident may not be right. This is soundly functional reasoning. In effect he has said that any infringement of freedom of inquiry is bad because it puts the whole process of inquiry, and with it the technological process as a whole, in jeopardy. But then he went on to declare that even if we could know that the dissident opinion is mistaken, its suppression "would still be evil." This is resounding rhetoric, but intellectual nonsense—resounding, because an echo of a grand tradition; nonsense, because a contradiction of all that has gone before. It is enough that freedom is the condition *sine qua non* of all intellectual, scientific, and technological development.

The converse is true of tyranny. Neither individuals nor societies achieve genuine and lasting freedom merely by throwing off constraint. The individual who seeks freedom from domination by withdrawing from all social relationships finds not freedom but emptiness, and the society that seeks freedom merely by throwing off the yoke of authority creates not freedom but a power vacuum into which some other authority is bound to flow. As I remarked at the outset, such freedom is negative. The great achievement of the Western peoples has been the progressive filling of the power vacuum that follows the removal of the tyrant not with another tyranny but with another way of life.

9

That way of life is technological. Beginning in early modern times, coincidentally with the first stirrings of industrial revolution, the Western peoples have been replacing authority with automation. That is the significance of government by laws rather than by men. From generation to generation some have always opposed democracy as being nothing more than the substitution of the authority of the many for the authority of the few, or even one. But that is an egregious misconception. The sovereignty of the people is a totally different kind of sovereignty from that of any king or ruling class by divine right. The sovereignty of the people is the sovereignty of the facts. It is true that no representative body is a perfect instrument for ascertaining the whole truth. But however imperfect, it is a more effective instrument than any other.

As one generation has succeeded another the democratic government of the Western world has become more and more sensitive to facts and more and more responsive to them, less and less an exercise of authority. With the increasing complexity of modern industrial society the business of ascertaining facts becomes more and more complex and extensive, and governmental organization becomes correspondingly complex and extensive. To some people such a development seems fraught with menace. But this also betokens a misconception of the meaning of democracy and the meaning of freedom. Freedom is not absence of organization. For individuals as well as for societies it is a function of organization—of the relations of husbands and wives, parents and children, employers and employees, and of all citizens with each other —in terms of sound working arrangements based upon true assessments of the abilities and proclivities of all rather than upon the authority of some and the subservience of others.

Is the Census Bureau an instrument of oppression? A recent writer has pointed out that for a century and a half humble clerks in the Bureau of the Census have effected a revolution every ten years, moving the focus of power steadily westward as the American people have grown and spread. But, as Don K. Price points out in *Science and Government,* what this means is that we have been governed by the truth. We see progressively more of the police, even in America, than former generations did. Indeed, there is a policeman on every busy corner, ordering citizens about and issuing *lettres de cachet* to those who get out of line. But in fact these officers are there to keep careful count of the flow of traffic and to direct it with maximum expeditiousness. They are in effect machines, adjuncts of a system of electric lights.

We expostulate over the imposition of having to make out income-tax returns. But this too is a device—more or less successful but of quite unmistakable intent—to organize the assessment of taxes on the basis of the facts. Through the evolution of democratic institutions the once tyrannical authority of the tax collector has long since been tempered by standardized techniques of assessment which in turn are subject to appeal to "equalization" boards. But by making each individual responsible for reporting his own income, the new system in effect replaces authority with automation. It is thus one of the many milestones in the achievement of free government.

Freedom does not mean absence of government. To conceive it so is to lapse into primitive negativism. Organization we must have; and the more complex our activities become, the more complex and extensive the instrumentalities of organization are bound to be. It is only through that process that true freedom can be achieved: the freedom of government, and indeed of all the instrumentalities of organization, from the tyranny of status; operational freedom; constructive freedom; the freedom to inquire; and the freedom to create.

CHAPTER XII

EQUALITY

I

LIKE FREEDOM, EQUALITY STANDS HIGH among the values that are most prized by the Western peoples; and like freedom, however incomplete its realization, it is one of the distinctions of Western civilization. Equality, again like freedom, stems in much larger measure than is generally realized from the industrial revolution.

Equality means the absence of artificial and arbitrary barriers. It does not, and of course cannot, mean the absence of individual differences, physical, mental, or even social. It is necessary to emphasize this point (which ought to be self-evident) because vastly increased knowledge of individual differences has seemed to convince some scientists that the writers of our Declaration of Independence were wrong in supposing that all men are created equal. Some men are large and some are small; some are strong and some are weak; some are bright and some are stupid; and formidable evidence can now be adduced to show that these differences were present at birth. They signalize differences of biological heredity which we deny or disregard at our peril. Furthermore, as scientists are establishing more fully every day, hereditary differences are prodigiously numerous and subtle. They affect the size, shape, and functioning of every organ of the body, and even the types of molecules that are present, or absent, in the various fluids of the body; and the most subtle of these differences may spell out the difference between genius and idiocy. To some scientists, therefore, the assertion that all men are created equal is tantamount to a denial of scientific truth itself.

But quite obviously such is not the case. Certainly we know a great deal more about genetics and biochemistry than was known in 1776. Indeed, these branches of knowledge are virtually children of the twentieth century. Nevertheless, it must have been sufficiently apparent to the authors and signers of the Declaration that men come in different sizes and shapes and colors. Even physical heredity has been known, in its grosser aspects at least, for rather a long time. When, for example, was it first noticed that children often resemble their parents and even earlier progenitors? Whatever equality may have meant to the founders of our nation, or to the French revolutionists, it could not have meant physical identity.

Nor does equality have that meaning now. Perhaps the most effective way to resolve the apparent confusion of equality with identity is by posing the question: Do biologically inherited physical differences coincide with distinctions of rank, class, nationality, or "racial superiority"? The answer which modern science gives to such a question is a resounding No! In recent years a great many studies have been addressed to just this question, and the results all run to substantially the same effect. In any considerable group of people wide differences are found among various individuals; but between one large group and another no such difference has ever been demonstrated. Such group differences as do appear are well within the margin of possible error of the measurements employed, and in any case are minute in comparison with the individual variations that appear in every group.

In this sense, indeed, group equality is just as definitely a fact of nature as individual difference. The truth is that some rich people are smart and some are stupid; some poor people are stupid and some are smart; and the same goes for Americans, Englishmen, and Hottentots. With regard to the "Aryan" and other "races" very determined efforts have been made to ascertain the truth, for obvious reasons; and the results have all been negative.

The pioneer equalitarians of earlier centuries were not in possession of these data. But they were sufficiently acute to recognize the arbitrariness and artificiality of the social barriers of their feudal heritage, and sufficiently stout-hearted to denounce them. In both respects, and indeed in existing at all, they were true agents of the industrial revolution.

2

In all ages such inequalities as those of feudalism are not only embedded in the social structure of a highly organized community. They are also sustained by an intricate fabric of tribal myths that is coextensive with that entire structure, so that every feature of the structure is made to seem to the human constituents of the system natural and inevitable. At the same time both the myths and the social structure they idealize necessarily coincide with a way of life with which they have been historically associated. Because such historical association is commonly of long duration, often persisting for centuries or even millennia, hindsight suggests that the social system in question is peculiarly, or even uniquely, appropriate to such a way of life. But this does not follow by any means. All that we can infer from the actual coexistence of such a system and such a way of life is that such a way of life is demonstrably possible under such a system.

Throughout modern times the industrial revolution has been eroding all three of these foundations of the feudal system: its myths, its social structure, and its way of life. Indeed, the process began well back in the Middle Ages. It has been a cumulative process not only because such is the character of the industrial revolution itself but also because the foundations of feudalism are so closely related that whatever weakens one weakens the entire structure, thus hastening the erosion of the other foundations of the system.

The most obvious changes have been in the social structure itself. Ours is now a middle-class society in the original meaning of that phrase. As all students of history know, this "class" was so identified originally because its members belonged neither to the aristocracy nor to the villeinage. I put the word *class* in quotation marks because a class which embraces the entire population is no longer a class at all. With the abolition of serfdom and the virtual disappearance of a feudal aristocracy, everybody has now joined what was originally a minority group having no distinguishing characteristics save negative ones: nonaristocratic and unbonded to a feudal lord. In this sense ours is now a classless society.

I do not mean to imply that this process of transformation of the whole social structure of Western society has been a passive one, or that no significant eruptions from below have occurred. Unquestionably the various peasants' revolts which history records did shake the entire structure of society, loosening all its joints, and hastening the entire process. It is also true that organized labor has been a potent force in recent generations. But it has been the middle class that has taken over all along the line. Trade union organization itself is a middle-class movement in style and method, as many commentators have long since pointed out. Some one has defined the spirit of the middle class as that of getting ahead; and in this sense, too, ours is now a middle-class society. Everybody in it is on the make. Higher wages plus fringe benefits is a middle-class objective.

The point is that is was the vigorous, shrewd, and persistent efforts of the historical middle class to get ahead that broke down the feudal system. But without in the least belittling those efforts we must note that the very existence of the middle class was a consequence of incipient industrial revolution. It was the development of the technology of transportation that made trade possible, and it was the development of handicraft that brought into existence the articles of trade. It was the occupations which this process brought into existence that provided a means of livelihood for escapees from feudal serfdom; and it was the towns which sprang up in the interstices, so to speak, of the feudal pattern that provided a *locum tenens* for the outliers of feudalism. Historically, therefore, the middle class is identical with the "bourgeoisie." It is the industrial revolution that has brought about the urbanization of Western society, and an urban society is a bourgeois society by definition.

Again, I do not mean to imply that town men have prevailed over country gentry without a struggle. On the contrary, modern history is largely the history of the struggle from which the "bourgeoisie" has emerged triumphant over feudalism. The point is rather that industrial revolution created the bourgeoisie in the first place and laid down the conditions under which they triumphed.

Even so it would be a mistake to attribute the attrition of feudal inequalities to the defeat of the feudal aristocracy in a simple class struggle. Even more important than the participants was their institutional alignment. In this sense the process of equalization was the result not of struggle but of the evolution of the institutions by which the human participants in the process were aligned; and in this sense also the evolutionary process was the one that has come to be known as industrial revolution.

As the phrase "industrial revolution" implies, the dynamic force that is at work in such an evolutionary process is technological. But it is a serious mistake to suppose that the institutional structure plays no important part in such a process. In order for technological development to come about the institutional framework of society must be susceptible to change and thus permissive of changes which a more rigid structure would have prevented. This is not the place for an extended discussion of the reasons why the institutional structure of Western society, even in medieval times, was (for that day) uniquely flexible. But it is important to note that such was the case.

3

The erosion of the feudal structure is most clearly exhibited in the development of the institution of property. In no other institution is that flexibility more clearly manifest, and no other institution played a more important part in the liquidation of feudal inequalities. Indeed, some writers have attributed the entire process to that one institution. The reason for this is that property is an instrumentality by which feudal privileges, originally, the exclusive prerogative of a small minority (as the word *privilege* suggests), might conceivably be distributed among the entire population. This is what was meant by the economist who, suspected of radicalism and challenged to say whether he believed in property, replied that he believed in it so strongly that he would like to see every member of the community participate in its benefits.

As I have tried to show in an earlier chapter, all social structures present two aspects and perform two sets of functions. One of these is ceremonial and static, and the other is technological or instrumental, and dynamic. Even feudal fief performed certain instrumental functions. It did organize the medieval community after a fashion. But as compared with later arrangements that organization was so thickly overlaid with superstition and ritual as to be relatively rigid. Land, the most important property of the time, was so encased in feudal entail as to be conveyable only to feudal heirs, sometimes only to the eldest male heir.

The institution of property inherits the exclusive rights and privileges of feudal fief. But property differs from fief in being freely exchangeable. It is in this fashion that property functions as an equalizer. On one hand, property stands as a bulwark against arbitrary seizure not only by individual marauders but even by the sovereign power of the state. It is in the sense, of course, that a man's house is his castle. But on the other hand, the institution of property makes it possible for anybody to own his home, and thereby to obtain a share of the *mana* of a lord of the manor. Indeed, even a renter may close his door against intruders and even against the police.

Since property is very unequally distributed, and always has been, equalitarians have long made this institution their principal object of attack. In this sense their attacks have of course been justified. But the institution of property also constitutes the instrumentality of equalization. To correct the evils of plutocracy we have only to bring about a less uneven distribution of property. Thus however great an evil plutocracy may be, we are bound to recognize that it is far less of an evil than hereditary caste. In particular, acquisition of property is not believed to endow the possessor with mystic powers, as legitimate noble descent was once supposed to do. True, people do defer to the rich in a fashion that often suggests that they are possessed of supernatural powers —of intellectual insight, artistic sensibility, and the like. But we also ridicule such toadying and laugh at the pretentions of the men in the gray flannel suits. No one really believes that wealth conveys clairvoyance.

4

In another respect the incidence of ownership stands in even sharper contrast to the rigidity of caste. In contrast to feudal rank, property can be lost as well as gained; and when it is lost, the power it confers is lost with it. Every generation produces a new crop of the newly rich and a much larger crop of the newly comfortable; and there is also the common saying that ascent and descent from shirt-sleeves to shirt-sleeves takes three generations. The expression "vertical mobility" has come into general use in recent years to designate the situation in which class differences remain more or less constant while individuals migrate more or less freely from one class to another.

As such discussion indicates, social scientists (lately and rather tardily) have become greatly preoccupied with the phenomena of social stratification; and as though to make up for previous neglect they now tend to exaggerate class differences. But the very rubrics they employ—such as *upper, middle,* and *lower*—contain no indication of scale. One could speak of higher, middle, and lower numbers without giving any indication whether the range was from one to ten or from one to a million.

The fact that such vague designations are employed is sufficient indication of the absence of any clear and definite stigmata by which to recognize actual existing classes, and this impression is heightened by the phenomenon of vertical mobility. The concept of mobility is itself the opposite of the concept of class. Insofar as streams of people are flowing into and out of "classes," those "classes" are not classes at all. It is true, as one sociologist has recently demonstrated, that the rich have more money than the poor; and this is regrettable. But as a matter of social structure it constitutes a situation very different from the class structure of feudal society or the caste system of India.

5

Meantime the institution of property continues to evolve; and its current developments, like earlier ones, are a direct reflection of continuing industrial revolution. As the scale of industry has steadily increased, industrial property has come to assume more and more generally the form of corporate stock. So different is a share of stock from ownership in fee simple of a specific physical property that some writers have gone so far as to assert that the institution of property has been replaced by the modern corporation. But this too is an exaggeration. The owner of a single share of stock is still an owner even though he is not the proprietor of any particular physical property but rather of a minute fraction of all the property of the corporation, tangible and intangible. Indeed, the corporation has no other claim to being a private enterprise. Nevertheless it is obvious that such a fusion of proprietorship, and in particular the wide distribution of shares (sometimes among millions of shareholders) is a process of socialization. Such property is not private in any meaningful sense.

As many writers have pointed out, the great corporations of our time have long since assumed the form of governments, at least in the bureaucratic sense. Theoretically, the "owners" still exercise all the rights of proprietorship. But actually the myriad of "owners" have long since forfeited all rights except the right to receive dividends, while to a steadily increasing degree the control and operation of the "property" has passed into the hands of a self-perpetuating group of functionaries known as "management." Here indeed we do find a new sort of social structure. Not only do these men exercise tremendous power, affecting the lives of vast numbers of people (employees, suppliers, and consumers) and even affecting the balance of inflationary and deflationary forces in the economy; they also enjoy all the perquisites which throughout the ages have always accompanied the exercise of power. All the resources of the corporation are at their disposal not only for business purposes in the more explicit sense but also for whatever "entertainment" they may judge to be in the corporate interest and whatever "rest and recreation" may be required to maintain themselves at the highest peak of efficiency, or piratical prowess.

At first glance all this would seem to reveal a trend toward grandiosity that bodes ill for the ideal of equality. Certainly the trend is a dangerous one. But the danger is mitigated by two sets of circumstances. For one thing, it has not gone unnoticed; and for another, *ex officio* grandiosity is by definition even more limited than that of ownership.

In recent years there has been much discussion of the "expense-account racket," the system by which corporate executives manage to live like millionaires (or billionaires) without paying personal income taxes on any such income as would be necessary to support their extravagances, which in fact are charged to their corporations as "business expenses." Doubtless this is very naughty, and

I do not wish to be understood as defending the system. But there is another side to the picture. The incomes on which such men do not pay taxes do not exist. Thus men whose cash incomes do not correspond to the swathe they are cutting will not be in a position to bequeath their swathe-cutting powers to their heirs and assigns. They are temporary grandees, like generals and admirals and Presidents of the United States, whose cash incomes are trifling, but who can and do live like oriental potentates during their period of command, and within the limits of reasonable prudence.

At first thought it may seem ridiculous to cite such persons as evidence of the trend toward equality. But retired admirals and generals, and even former presidents of the United States, often live quite modestly; and we have the word of Benjamin F. Fairless, former head of the United States Steel Corporation, that "Many of the top executives in some of our largest corporations"— and he specifically included himself—"have spent a lifetime in the field of industrial management without ever having been able to accumulate as much as a million dollars." My point is that insofar as magnificence is job-related, it does not have even that degree of perpetuity which property derives from its feudal origins. If plutocracy, however extreme, constitutes a long step away from caste, jobocracy represents a longer step in the same direction.

6

In attributing to industrial revolution far-reaching changes in social structure, such as those just indicated, I have minimized the importance of class warfare. What is important, as I have tried to suggest, is not the determination of the middle class—and ultimately the entire population—to get ahead, but rather the circumstances which have enabled these feudal dissidents to do so. Among these circumstances the gradual but progressive erosion of the mythology of feudalism is so important as to deserve special recognition.

All students of the social sciences now recognize the mutual dependence of the social structures of various peoples with the systems of tribal beliefs and ceremonial practices that prevail among those peoples. Indeed, so close is this relationship that some scholars declare the functions performed by magic and superstition to be indispensable and necessary, and so they are *for those particular power systems*. As I have tried to show in previous chapters, the powers exercised by various tribal functionaries are tolerated by the subject populations only because those peoples have been ideologically indoctrinated and emotionally conditioned, often for many generations, so that the prevailing structure of the community seems to them natural and inevitable, expressive of the purposes of Higher Powers, to question which is mortal sin.

It used to be thought that "simple" peoples invent myths because of their ignorance of the natural forces at work in the physical universe. But ignorance is a negative quantity. As all students now realize, and as I have therefore suggested in earlier chapters, the creation of myths and all the related ceremonialism can be understood only in terms of the operation of strong positive forces. The symbolic process by virtue of which man is able to use tools and speak words also has impelled mankind toward occultism. Nevertheless it is obvious that ignorance—lack of knowledge of the natural universe—has indeed exposed mankind to temptation, so to speak. Certainly the more we know the less accessible we are to mystic nonsense. Mankind is just as emotional as ever, and in a sense just as credulous—as witness the case of the "flying saucers." For that matter, astrology, numerology, and séance communication with the spirits of the dead are still widely practised. But today all such matters are subject to detailed scientific investigation, with the result that none enjoys general acceptance. Certainly the present structure of Western society does not depend for its acceptance and continuance upon any sort of occultism, as even medieval feudalism did.

Some people find it misleading and offensive to attribute this great cultural change to industrial revolution, but that is only because they take a limited view of the meaning of "industrial revolution." The more fully we explore the circumstances by which additions to scientific knowledge have been made, the clearer it becomes that the invention of instruments and the discovery of truths are inseparable aspects of a single process. Thus, for example, no set of circumstances has been of greater effect for the advancement of knowledge than the invention of printing from movable types, and this is true not only because printing vastly accelerated communication among inquiring minds but even more because it extended literacy to the entire population, so that the entire community became witnesses to the process of discovery and even potential participants in that process.

Moreover, the acquisition of literacy once and for all rent the veil behind which for thousands of years priestly castes had worked their ostensible miracles. For to the illiterate, written communication is itself a potent form of magic. A social anthropologist has recently given a detailed account of her extended study of a certain African tribe who had had no previous contact with any European. These people were unshakably convinced that her ability to write and to read what she had written (and what was printed in her books) was a manifestation of occult power acquired by magic. Such, in varying degree, has been the state of mind of illiterate masses throughout the ages. Thus in bringing literacy to the people the printing press at one stroke nullified the advantage which priestly scribes had always enjoyed over the subject populations.

It also opened sacred writings to the inspection of the laity. There has been much discussion in recent years of the possible effects of the discovery of the Dead Sea Scrolls. But as time passes it is becoming more and more evident that the scrolls are having no effect whatever. The truth is that educated people, who are the only ones likely to be influenced by such a discovery, have long since adjusted their thinking to the realization that the Biblical chronicles represent the age-old traditions, aspirations, and inspirations of the Hebrew people, and not a scientifically accurate record of actual events. Obviously it would be an outrageous exaggeration to attribute the changed attitude of the modern world exclusively to textual scrutiny of the sacred literature. A whole series of intellectual revolutions have contributed to this outcome. But the printing of the Bible, and especially the publication of translations into the languages spoken and read by common people, did play an important part in the Protestant Reformation, as it also subsequently opened the doors to "higher criticism," and so led eventually to the secularization even of the sacred literature of the Western peoples.

Doubtless the rise of the middle class and the abolition of serfdom and disestablishment of feudal aristocracies all contributed to the discrediting of the ideology by which the structure of feudal society was supported. But the direct impact of industrial revolution on that ideology was no less important. The Copernican revolution with the consequent realization that the earth is not the center of the universe but only a minor planet, the Lyellian revolution with the consequent realization that the world was not created in six days but is something over two billion years old, and the Darwinian revolution with the consequent realization that mankind is an animal species biologically continuous with the whole "animal kingdom," all served to induce a state of mind in which it seems increasingly evident that all men are created equal. Ancient delusions still linger in the far corners of the community, and demagogues still seek power by appealing to them, as perhaps they always will. But all such fantasies are now confronted by a body of knowledge so extensive, so solidly established, and so widely known as to make any permanent ideological retreat impossible.

7

Meantime industrial revolution has also been bringing into existence a way of life which, for the first time in human experience, makes inequality unnecessary.

To appreciate the vast significance of this revolutionary change we must first face the facts of life. The fact is that being waited on is very agreeable, and the more primitive the physical arrangements are, the more agreeable it is. In *The Theory of the Leisure Class* Veblen argued that menial labor came to be so considered only at a relatively late date in human experience. After a long period of peaceful, cooperative, and equalitarian savagery, barbarians who conquered and enslaved the savages appeared. Useful work thus fell into the disrepute it has suffered ever since in consequence of its association with the inferior rank of conquered and exploited menials. In short, the stigma that attaches to menial labor is secondary to and derivative from the stigma that attaches to menial persons. But this theory overlooks a very important consideration, and is more or less directly contradicted by another theory of Veblen's, that women constituted the first slave class. Of these two theories, the latter seems far more probable, for the following reasons.

We know virtually nothing of the structure of Old Stone Age society. But we do know that even under the most primitive conditions a favored individual can enjoy a considerable degree of comfort if he is waited on by a sufficient number of people. If he is hungry, he can require that food be provided and prepared and served; and if he is thirsty he can have water, or other potions, similarly provided. If he is cold, he can require that wood be fetched and a fire built; and if he is hot, he can require that he be fanned and that bothersome flies be whisked away. Moreover, the more onerous and irksome these activities may be, the greater is the advantage enjoyed by the favored individual. Let us suppose, for example, that the technology of the people concerned is so primitive that no vessels exist in which water might be stored. Nevertheless it can be fetched in small quantities in plantain leaves, or something of the sort; and the more inefficient the equipment is, the more important service is to the comfort of the favored individual.

Clearly this has always been true, and this circumstance alone makes it extremely difficult to imagine a "savage state" in which all shared equally in the performance of the necessary chores. Indeed, the sheer physical advantages of superior status are so obvious that dissidents have quite generally been misled into supposing that the myths by which status differences are supported have been deliberately invented by the beneficiaries of the system and foisted upon a docile and gullible populace. This is nonsense, of course, and I mention it only by way of emphasizing the reality of the perquisites of rank—a reality which even Veblen tended to overlook.

It is this reality which is being progressively altered by the industrial way of life. Denizens of industrial communities no longer require the services of hewers of wood and drawers of water. They live in steam-heated apartments to which water is piped. They no longer require slaves to flick away the flies. There are no flies in screened apartments. They no longer require slaves to fan them when they are hot. Electric fans are infinitely more efficient, and air conditioning is an even higher order of infinity.

It is true that the number of people who are employed in "services" has increased vastly and continuously. But this also is significant of the industrial way of life. The relationship of employees in a laundry to the company's customers is very different from the relationship of a "washer-woman" to her employer. The washerwoman is a servant; but laundry workers are not. Their connection with customers is remote and impersonal. They are industrial employees and union members, and as such are quite as self-respecting as the customers, and in many cases actually better off.

The impersonality of the relationships that prevail under the industrial system has been widely deprecated. But clearly there is another side to the picture. Impersonal relationships spell equality. It is of course true that the more intimate personal service is, the more degrading it is; whereas the more impersonal the occupation is, the less degrading it is. The collector of human excrement in an oriental city is inevitably a person of low estate. But the designer of an industrial sewage disposal system is an engineer, a member of a learned profession, and perhaps wealthy. Even the plumber is a practitioner of a skilled trade, a respected and self-respecting citizen. By taking personal service out of the home and relegating it to the impersonality of an industrial operation, the industrial revolution has been laying the physical foundations of social equality.

Personal service has been taken out of the home in more than one sense. Not only have domestic operations become industrialized, the general process of industrialization has reduced the "servant class" to the vanishing point. In times gone by, domestic service offered quite definite attractions. The work was far less onerous than that of working in the fields; and though the hours were long, they were no longer than those of serfs or slaves. Moreover, when workers generally were slaves or serfs, the social inferiority of house servants was no greater by virtue of their service. In medieval times and in the days of slavery, household service was a preferred occupation the advantages of which were passed on from generation to generation, so that household servants formed a more or less distinct class, a notch higher in the social scale than field workers. But as industrial occupations opened up, from the earliest days of the industrial revolution, the situation of craftsmen, and industrial workers generally, contrasted favorably with that of both field workers and household servants; with the result that in the end the "servant class" has been largely absorbed by industry.

8

Not only has the "servant problem" created a market for industrialized services such as that provided by laundries and ready-to-serve foods of all kinds, and likewise created a market for household appliances from vacuum cleaners and electric floor polishers to cake mixers, electrically controlled ovens, and deep freezers; it has also revolutionized the design for living. Veblen made much of "conspicuous waste" and "vicarious leisure," pointing out with ironic glee the immense amount of wasted motion that went into the polishing of unnecessary brass and the dusting of redundant bric-a-brac. It would be an exaggeration to say that the revolution in taste which has swept away the archaic clutter of the old-fashioned home has been due altogether to the disappearance of servants. Doubtless the ridicule of social philosophers like Veblen has had something to do with the change. But it is a fact that the elimination of unnecessary upkeep has been a driving force.

The effects of this force are by no means limited to the household. The laces and flounces and furbelows that once characterized the dress of the "quality" of both sexes are extremely ill-adapted to life in the modern industrial community—to the use of automobiles and airplanes and elevators; and they have therefore disappeared. Only a few years ago an American Cabinet member created something of a stir by complaining that it was impossible for him to wear a tall silk hat in the limousine which had been assigned to his official use and by insisting that a roomier vehicle be provided. No such vehicle is now manufactured. Even the most expensive of the present models are so low that it is virtually impossible to get in or out of them with any kind of hat. In these circumstances the more conspicuous contrasts of dress between the "upper" and "lower" classes have largely disappeared. Walking sticks, for example, have all but disappeared. Once the sole survivor of the noble's sword, and the constant companion of a gentleman who otherwise "wouldn't know what to do with his hands," the stick has become such a nuisance under modern conditions that it is to be seen only on the most special (and archaic) conditions, such as "the Easter parade." It may be as Veblen said, that the creases in men's clothes and a profusion of pleats in ladies' dresses were originally devised because of the wastefulness of the upkeep they required. But at the present time the magazines are full of expensive advertisements of quality clothes made of fabrics that will hold their creases through the heaviest shower and of "drip-dry" dresses to which an iron never need be applied.

As a social leveller the automobile has been more effective than the exhortations of any reformer. This is true for a variety of reasons. Most important, perhaps, is its incidence. At one time a gentleman was one who rode, a commoner one who walked. So significant was this distinction that in several languages the word for gentleman is "horseman." It was this distinction which Oscar Wilde evoked in his celebrated snobbism, "I never walk!" But the use of automobiles has brought it to pass that nobody walks any more. In American cities the provision of sidewalks has been generally abandoned. And with the disappearance of walking an immemorial social distinction has largely disappeared. It is also true that in times past only the quality travelled. Today everybody travels, and so another social distinction has gone by the board.

I do not mean to suggest that the automobile alone is the sufficient cause of all these changes. Obviously the automobile is but one of many appurtenances of the industrial way of life. The point is that in consequence of industrial revolution a way of life has been evolving in which it is possible for the entire community to enjoy comforts and even luxuries (as they used to be reckoned) such as have been accessible hitherto only to a small minority. This is not a mere matter of wealth, in the pecuniary sense. It is a matter of gadgets, if you will.

Those who decry the gadgetry of the industrial way of life should bear in mind that gadgets make it possible for people to live in comfort *without being waited on*, and in doing so they make a mighty contribution to the equalizing process. As an item of property a horse represents only a small fraction of the cost of an automobile. But a horse requires constant and expensive care—far more than an automobile. In order for an owner's horse to be ready for instant use, as an automobile is, that owner must employ a groom; and the same is true of bathtubs. People who decry what they consider the overemphasis of industrial society upon gadgets should remember that bathtubs make it possible for everybody to enjoy that sort of gentility which in former times could be had only through the employment of body servants; and that in doing so they virtually do away with body servants, thereby putting the whole community on the same footing.

I do not mean to imply that personal service has been entirely eliminated. Obviously it has not, and doubtless never will be. But its importance has been greatly reduced. In particular, the gadgetry of the industrial way of life for the first time in history provides an alternative to personal service, and in doing so it eliminates what has always been a powerful incentive to the perpetuation of social hierarchies.

Again, that incentive is not, and never has been, the sufficient cause of institutionalized inequality. All social inequalities presuppose mythical group differences, and doubtless had their origin in the process by which supernaturalism itself originated; and in all subsequent experience those inequalities have been embedded in the social structures of ancient societies. So potent are these considerations that it would be difficult to imagine the emergence of an equalitarian society resulting from gadgetry alone. But the industrial way of life did not develop alone, and could not have done so. This aspect of the industrial revolution is indissociable from its intellectual aspect, of which the decline of superstition is an outcome; and it is likewise indissociable from the structural changes Western society has experienced in consequence of the division of labor. But it is none the less significant that those ideological and structural changes which Western society has experienced in recent centuries have been accompanied by the development of an industrial way of life.

9

The identification of the ideal of equality with scientific enlightenment and the identification of its progressive attainment with industrial revolution do not mean that either the conception or the realization comes about automatically and effortlessly. Neither scientific enlightenment nor technological progress comes about automatically and effortlessly. Both are activities of men, and like all human activities both involve a considerable amount of fumbling. Moreover, both occur, when they occur at all, in the face of the cultural inertia of immemorial tradition and the organized opposition of vested interests.

But if progress is not inevitable and effortless, it is also true that fumbling and backsliding likewise are not inevitable. I have already referred to the disposition of certain scientists to find support in the scientific evidence of individual differences for the dictum that inequality is a fact of nature. Obviously those scientists have been led to that conclusion by confusing the biological differences between individuals with the social distinctions between classes and races. But the latter are not supported by scientific evidence. Those scientists could never have become involved in such a confusion if they had not as members of a community already been involved in a class-structured society and its tutelary myths. We do not extricate ourselves from such confusions without effort. But the fact that we know anything at all goes to show that we are not condemned to inextricable wallowing in error. The point is that the way out of all such error is the way by which we have learned to recognize and pinpoint biological differences.

The same is true of industrial revolution. Since the great technological breakthrough which hitherto we have identified by the phrase "industrial revolution" did occur in what we call the Western world, the Western peoples have for a time enjoyed a tremendous advantage over all other peoples; and in their exploitation of that advantage they have incontinently lorded it over all the rest of the world. Thus it might seem that science and technology have bred not equality but inequality, and seemingly such a conclusion derives further support from the fact that the scale of modern weapons seems to have left the populace more completely at the mercy of those who control those weapons than ever before in history.

But there are two important qualifications to these developments. One is that technology is no respecter of persons. What one can do, others can do. The advantage enjoyed by the pioneers of industrialization is bound to be short-lived as other peoples learn to use machines; and in the case of modern weapons, the greater the scale the larger the number of persons who must be trained not only to the use but also to the fabrication of the instruments of power.

In both instances, as always, this means exposing a constantly increasing number of people to the intellectual incidence of machine technology. This is the other qualification. Learning to use machines requires education, and education can be achieved only at the expense of myths—even the myths in the service of which, perhaps, people have sought to master the machines. Colonialism is disappearing not only because Kipling's "lesser breeds" are becoming industrialized but also because the Western peoples are learning that they are not the Lord's anointed, as the others also are bound to learn in their turn; and the dictatorships which modern technology has seemed to favor also are bound to collapse by the same process. These processes are not automatic and painless. But for all the blood, sweat, and tears they may occasion, they also are not hopeless.

So conceived, is equality worth fighting for? The answer to this question is Yes. It is worth fighting for because it is a valid ideal, and it is a valid ideal because the pretentions of inequality are false pretentions. They are false because they do not arise from individual merits. On the contrary, they originate in the traditional social structures of the communities in which they prevail, and they are sustained by systems of tribal superstition by which caste distinctions are hedged about with taboos. Through the ages wise men have denounced all such artificial and arbitrary barriers and have exposed the falsity of the superstitions upon which they have been based. Is it any derogation of their wisdom that we now know them to have been right? Or is equality any less ideal for being generally recognized as such?

Should we regret that circumstances have contributed to our

intellectual and social progress? But those circumstances are themselves the vehicle of our ideals. Truth is not merely that which works. Only what works is true, and it works only because it is true. Technology persists and advances because technical processes are the same for everybody. Only insofar as all men are free and equal can their works persist and advance. Equality before the law is a direct reflection of equality before the tool.

CHAPTER XIII

SECURITY

I

LIKE FREEDOM, SECURITY HAS A PRIMITIVE MEANING, and for obvious reasons. Until quite recently human life has been highly precarious, for communities as well as for individuals, so that experience of all other values has been conditioned by anxiety. Thus both for individuals and for communities, assurance of continued existence and continued enjoyment of the existing system of values has seemed to be one of the supreme values of life.

From the earliest times mankind has sought relief from anxiety and reassurance against the manifold hazards of existence by appeal to supernatural Powers. This is the "quest for certainty" of which John Dewey wrote. As he pointed out in the opening paragraphs of the book that bears that title (his Gifford Lectures, and one of the greatest books of the present century), throughout the ages man has sought to cope with the oppressive uncertainties of life in two ways: by problem-solving and the pursuit of clear and certain knowledge; and also by projecting himself into an imaginary world in which his security has seemed to be assured by some tutelary deity.

As already explained, the intellectual means—the power of mind—by virtue of which mankind was able to pursue both these courses was that of the symbolic process. By use of symbols man was enabled to communicate, to use tools, and to organize his activities; while at the same time the mysterious potency of symbols made it not only possible but perhaps inevitable that man should create for himself an imaginary world of Higher Powers by which his security was ultimately guaranteed.

The same process that provided the means to the quest for certainty by creation of myths and elaboration of mystic rites, also provided the motive. The sense of insecurity is a direct consequence of the power of "time-binding," as Korzybski called it. By virtue of the symbolic process man alone of all the animals lives in the past and future as well as the present. Man's anxiety likewise signalizes the supreme importance of group life. The supreme object of the whole ceremonial system of all cultures is security, not only of the group, but of each individual member of it. No greater misfortune has befallen any human being throughout the ages than that of being a displaced person. The fate of the individual is indissociable from the fate of the group. Even the lowliest untouchable has some assurance of continued existence so long as the social system of which he is the lowliest member is preserved—this, as compared with the situation of the outlier, the man-without-a-country, who has no assurance for the morrow, or even for the next moment.

It was the dawning realization of these truths that inspired Emile Durkheim, a generation before Dewey, to identify the imaginings of primeval man as "collective representations." In view of the seeming precariousness of human existence—the total dependence of every man, woman, and child upon group membership—no assurance of security could be too great; and man achieved the most vivid sense of security when the way of life of his community was identified with the purposes of Higher Powers. That all systems of mythology have this significance and serve this purpose is now recognized by all students of these matters, and many have therefore drawn the conclusion that man cannot live without the emotional support of such beliefs—that mythology is a *sine qua non* of all organized society.

On this showing, Western civilization is headed for disaster. For scientific knowledge and superstition are mutually exclusive. The more we know about the natural universe, the less credence can be given to any of the beliefs from which alone, according to this view, other peoples have derived that sense of security without which life is insupportable; and the more widely scientific knowledge is disseminated, the greater is the danger—on this showing—that the whole community will lose its bearings. Many writers point to the wide incidence of anxiety neuroses, and to the prevalence of such nugatory cults as "Existentialism," as evidence that the malady is already far advanced.

2

By way of refutation of these fears we might first of all take note of a serious flaw in the reasoning that ostensibly supports them. Which came first, tribes or tribal beliefs? It is all very well to argue that all mythologies are projections of the collectivity of the peoples whose myths they are. But does this proposition support the conclusion that all collectivities are derivatives of myths? Surely there is something wrong with such a supposition!

Doubtless the truth of the matter is that neither tribes nor tribal mythologies came first—that the dawning of human social life included both. If we are right in thinking that the instrumental and the imaginary aspects of symbolic behavior developed together, then the actual security which primeval man achieved by cooperative use of tools must have existed no less early in human experience than the imagined security of myth. Surely even the earliest humanoid creatures must have been aware of the advantage they enjoyed not only by the use of tools but also through efficiently concerted action. Even though the very earliest group action—such as that of driving wild horses over the brink of a precipice—may have been accompanied by the utterance of cries of a vaguely magical or invocational nature, the purpose of the invocation could only have been to magnify the effect of what we ourselves must now recognize to have been operationally efficient organization.

In short, the imagined security for which men have invoked Higher Powers derives its germinal meaning from the actual security men have achieved by use of tools and through efficient organization. Indeed, this proposition is a corollary of the relation of bogus to actual causality. Even though all systems of mythology deal with cause and effect, attributing to greater-than-nautral causes various greater-than-natural effects, these effects are in all cases exaggerations of natural occurrences—incredibly large crops or catches of fish, victory in the face of apparently overwhelming odds; and the causes likewise are exaggerations of natural agents —gods who are supermen, demons that are superanimals. So it is also with security. What the heart craves is the continuance in perpetuity of some actual and known security. Notwithstanding the quest for the absolute certainty of an imaginary world, man has always known that the gods help those who help themselves.

This is the truth which the authors of the theory of social contract sought to express. That eighteenth-century doctrine has long been in eclipse, partly because later events have clouded the optimism of that day, but even more because of our recent preoccupation with the irrational elements in culture. Moreover, the writers of the seventeenth and eighteenth centuries were of course anthropologically naive. They sometimes wrote as though primitive communities consisted exclusively of philosophers and professors of jurisprudence for whom the drafting of constitutions was a natural vocation. Obviously the "grisly brutes" (as H. G. Wells once called them) who peopled the later Pleistocene did not hold constitutional conventions. But we must not make the opposite mistake of supposing them to have been unaware of the real advantages of concerted action. However much they may have mysticized the potency of their primeval tools and their rudimentary organization, it is axiomatic that they had something real to mysticize.

It was that reality which social philosophers such as Hobbes and Rousseau sought to emphasize, and they were right in doing so. As modern knowledge dispelled the fogs of superstition, the real necessities and advantages of concerted action became more and more evident. The idea of mutual advantage progressively supplanted that of civil and ecclesiastical rule by divine right in Western civilization and in the modern conception of the nature of society. Applying the criterion of actual, as distinguished from imaginary, security, the philosophers judged that mankind had done well to form societies, and would do better to form better ones.

This judgment is virtually irrefutable. Judged by the standard of actual security, mankind has done well, and never better than in modern industrial society. This, at least, is attested by the statistics of population growth and life expectancy. As a summation of the values of life such a biological standard is not altogether satisfactory, as I have already noted. But we are here concerned not with a summation of all values, but only with the actualities of security; and these, in large measure at least, are physical.

3

The chief hazards to which mankind has always been exposed are those of famine, disease, and war. With regard to food-getting, at least, it is quite evident that from the earliest times actual security has been won by use of tools and by efficient organization. The crudest tools of primeval man reduced by so much the hazards of food-getting; and all the technological development that has followed, in consequence of which the threat of famine has completely disappeared from industrially organized communities, has been a continuation of that process. Obviously such development has been accompanied by the growth of large populations, and also by progressively higher degrees of specialization not only between individuals but even between large areas. But it has been accompanied also by the growth of large-scale organization through the functioning of which the hazards of regional failures affecting particular products can be (and largely are) spread over very large communities, and the advantages of localized abundance are likewise widely distributed. With regard to the hazard of famine, at least, the security afforded by civilization is quite actual, and never more so than in modern industrial society.

Even as recently as a few generations ago the situation with regard to disease would have seemed quite different. Not only did plagues, which have now almost completely disappeared from industrial communities, still rage, but the whole subject of health and disease was still clouded with superstition, as it had been since the earliest times. Notoriously there is no aspect of human existence in which superstition has been more rife. Nevertheless we must always bear in mind the vantage point from which we judge. The horror with which we now view the medical barbarities of the past assumes present knowledge and practice as a basis of comparison. If we compare the health measures of earlier cultures, not with our own, but with those of animals, we see at once that notwithstanding all the incantational nonsense of earlier times even the crude surgery and medication of primeval man represented a tremendous advance over animal existence, like the most primitive techniques of food-getting, such as driving wild horses over a cliff. For an animal to break a bone means virtually certain death. Even the crudest technique of bone-setting represents a tremendous forward step, and the same is true of even the crudest "sick-room" care.

But whatever may have been true in the past, there is certainly nothing imaginary about the security from disease that is enjoyed by the denizens of modern industrial society. Moreover, as everyone knows, the security we enjoy in this regard is a direct consequence of the scientific-technological revolution of modern times. I couple *technological* with *scientific* for reasons which I hope are now quite obvious. The triumphs of modern medicine result from the general growth of scientific knowledge, and that is a process which depends at every point upon the whole range of arts and crafts out of which the instruments of all the sciences arise. This is also true of the production and distribution of therapeutics for use in general practice. Everyone recognizes the strategic part played by the pharmaceutical industry in making such things as penicillin and Salk vaccine' generally available, and it is equally evident that the operations of that industry are dependent upon the operation of the whole industrial complex.

Not so apparent but no less significant is the part played by efficient organization. In very significant measure the security we now enjoy from the scourge of disease has been won by the expedients of public sanitation, vaccination, and the systematic supervision of the life of the community by public health authorities. I call them "authorities" because that is the word that is in common use in this connection. But the crux of the matter is that the kind of organization through which security from plagues has been achieved is not authoritarian. People do not submit to public health measures because they are forced to do so by the exercise of coercive authority. To an amazing extent the whole community cooperates voluntarily in matters of sanitation, vaccination, quarantine, and the like. Such cooperation requires organization. But what is required is efficient organization directed by competent persons, the situation being one in which efficiency is defined by skill and competency by knowledge. It is because the same skills and the same knowledge are shared in some degree by the whole community that compliance in public health measures is so general. In a very real sense, such skill, such knowledge, and such organization are functions of each other.

4

When we turn to the hazard of war, the whole picture seems to be reversed. We seem now to be living in the shadow of more horribly destructive weapons than mankind has ever known, and the passions which become manifest in wars seem to give the lie to all man's hopes for security through efficient organization. It would be foolish to minimize the dangers of our present situation. No one can truthfully deny the existence of antagonisms such as might lead to a death struggle between opposing forces of greater magnitude and extent than mankind has ever known before, or the possibility that such a struggle might result in greater havoc than has been done by any previous war. The very complexity of the modern industrial system may render it liable to total destruction. It is not inconceivable that all the great cities of the Western world might be totally destroyed, with the result that the whole remaining apparatus of the industrial system might be brought to a standstill, and the remaining fraction of the population thrown back upon preindustrial expedients for scratching out a living.

It is also possible that the earth might encounter an asteroid with results even more disastrous to humankind (and perhaps all other living things) than those of any holocaust man is yet capable of setting off. Only a few years ago such an asteroid whizzed past, the existence of which was unknown to scientists until after the near miss had been scored. My point is that all such conjectures are only conjectures. We cannot know what the future will bring; but we can distinguish between the possible and the probable.

We arrive at the possible by arbitrarily selecting any particular aspect of an actual situation and projecting it in imagination into the center of the stage. Thus we know that asteroids exist, and we can calculate with some nicety what the geophysical effects of a collision with an asteroid of a given size might be. Similarly, we know the complexity of the industrial system and the delicate interdependence of all its parts, and so we can calculate what the effect of the destruction of, say, a hundred major industrial centers might be—perhaps progressive and irreversible deterioration of all that remained.

But we arrive at the probable by projecting into the future not one but all the aspects of the actual situation; and the degree of probability we thus achieve depends entirely upon how completely we are able to take into account not any one possibility but all aspects of the actual situation. Thus in the case of the asteroids our knowledge is sufficient to sustain a statistical calculation which establishes with considerable certainty the extreme unlikelihood of any such collision. Considered similarly, what is the likelihood of the total destruction of industrial society?

In such a calculation history must be taken into account. Surely it is not without significance that throughout the whole of not only recorded history, but also the archeological record of prehistory, no great civilization has ever disappeared. Centers of culture have shifted to and fro, but no major retrogression has ever occurred. Mankind has never had to start over again. Throughout the ages cultural development has been cumulative. True, there has to be a first time for everything. This is the first time mankind has essayed to build an industrial system, and conceivably it may be the last. But what is conceivable is not therefore probable. If we take the whole record into account, it would seem that total collapse is highly improbable. At all events, it has never happened before.

Is the present period nevertheless one of extreme insecurity? Certainly we do not enjoy absolute security. The hazards of war are with us still. But are they greater than they have been in other times? This does not seem to be clearly established either by population figures or by production figures. Notwithstanding the devastation wrought by World War II, the devastated countries seem to have effected a truly remarkable recovery. It is at least an open question whether the total amount of suffering inflicted by earlier wars—say the Thirty Years' War or the American Civil War—was not considerably greater for the areas affected than that of World War II. Let me repeat: past experience constitutes no absolute guarantee of anything. But against the dire predictions which are now being made we should place the similarly dire predictions which were being made a decade or so before the outbreak of World War II. Even then predictions were being made by those who claimed to be "in the know" that the next war would be one of "push-button warfare" in which destruction so cataclysmic would be rained from the air that the issue would be decided in a matter of hours.

5

But more important than the question, How much? is the question, How? Granted that all warfare is a menace to the security of the people involved, how do such hazards come about, and how (if at all) can they be prevented? Are the forces that make for war somehow magnified by the evil genius of industrial society? Or is there any ground for supposing that even as regards the hazard of war the genius of industrial society is not evil but good?

It is very commonly assumed at the present time that the development of the industrial system has somehow magnified the hazard of war. But this assumption involves a very elementary confusion: the confusion of instrumentalities with motivating forces. Unquestionably the advance of science and technology, at any given stage, is reflected in the greater lethal potency of weapons. It is this obvious fact that has preyed upon the consciences of so many nuclear physicists in recent years. But is the existence of a lethal weapon the sufficient cause of any outbreak of violence?

In the so-called warfare of the sexes, husbands not infrequently murder wives, and vice versa. Do they do so primarily, or to any significant degree, because of the availability of any particular weapon? Would anybody say, "It seems likely that a murder will occur in such-and-such a family, inasmuch as they are now using arsenic to rid their garden of insects; and, as we know, arsenic is often used to poison people"? After all, as we also know, the commonest instrumentality of violence is "a blunt weapon," of which nature has always provided an inexhaustible supply. If the occurrence of violence were to be explained in terms of the availability of means, the human race would have exterminated itself as soon as human hands learned to grasp stones.

Violence is a product of antagonism, and organized violence is the product of organized antagonism. It is true that human culture

215

does organize and codify antagonisms. War is a cultural phenomenon. Animals kill each other for food, but only human beings kill each other on principle. Such principles are ceremonial, as I have called them, after Veblen. That is, they give expression to a traditional power system that is sustained by tribal beliefs of which the tribal ceremonies are an expression and an enhancement. Wars are fought for honor and glory, so defined, and in obedience to a purportedly divine command. It is true that actual material interests are always present in the background of every conflict. They are always present in the background of all ceremonial imaginings. One tribe believes that the Great Ancestor Bear has dedicated a given hunting ground to them, and another that their Great Ancestor Beaver has directed them to seize this area and will assure the success of their effort to do so. What is at stake is an actual material interest; but what prompts men to organized violence is "the ashes of their fathers and the temples of their gods."

So we come again, as we must throughout any discussion of the values of industrial society, to the central issue. Are ceremonial principles such as these the necessary foundation of all organized society? If they are, as many competent scholars now suppose, then indeed the hazard to which industrial society is exposed is incalculably great. For if we are savages at heart, and can never be anything else, we are savages into whose hands the development of science and technology has thrust the most lethal weapons ever known.

That we have the blood of savages in our cultural veins no one can deny. Let me reiterate what I have already said repeatedly before: ceremonial principles have pervaded all cultures since the very dawn of culture, and they persist even today. As the psychiatrists keep dinning into us, we are all subjected from infancy onward to the constraints of affection and antagonism. The question is whether this is the whole truth. I have argued consistently that it is not, and I still do so.

Even the hazard of war is being progressively reduced by the same sort of efficient organization that has been the decisive factor in reducing the hazard of disease. That such is the case is clearly indicated by three distinct, though related, bodies of evidence.

6

One of these—the most obvious and undeniable—is that of the scale of organization. Throughout modern times the scale of political organization has been increasing on a curve which points unmistakably toward world organization as the consummation of the process. The day of tiny principalities is long past, and not only because of the growth of omnivorous national giants. Alliances, ententes, and leagues are the order of the day, and not only as a matter of military might. With the growth of the industrial system, no small area can possibly remain economically self-contained. The logic of industrial organization has superimposed itself upon the sentiments and traditions of tribal separatism. The necessities of coal and steel disregard frontiers, and oil links remote and seminomadic tribes to the industrial centers of the world.

Moreover, industrial technology links necessity to possibility. Modern facilities of transportation and communication have made long-range organization easy and inevitable. In this sense Saudi Arabia is in closer touch with New York than Philadelphia was when the Declaration of Independence was being written. But all this is too obvious to require exposition.

A second consideration is less obvious because it is, so to speak, internal. But on that account it is the more significant. Organized violence is the prerogative of sovereign powers, and the growth in scale of sovereign powers therefore means a corresponding growth in the scale of violence. But the same circumstances that have brought about the increase in scale of organization are also effecting an internal change of vast significance.

Modern governments are still sovereign powers in the traditional sense. But to an extent that would astound and perplex the sovereigns of earlier days, and even their most astute counselors, the governments of industrial society have become vast administrative machines. This is true not only of the apparatus of organization but also of the objects of governmental concern. As Don K. Price pointed out in *Government and Science*, no single fact is more indicative of the changing character of the sovereign power than the institution of the decennial census by the newly formed government of the United States of America. At the present time government has become in effect a vast statistical organization, and this means that to a steadily increasing degree the decisions of "the sovereign"—the vast administrative apparatus which now functions as a sovereign—are made on the basis of facts.

This development does not constitute a total change, as it were from black to white, or vice versa. Behind even the murkiest superstition certain obdurate facts always lurk. To secure the well-being of the community has always been the responsibility of chiefs and princes; and however much the notion of well-being may have been surcharged with ceremonial considerations, it always must have contained a nucleus of physical fact. To the chief, his sacred honor may seem paramount; but it can be so only so long as he continues to be a chief, and he can continue to be a chief only so long as the tribe continues to exist.

What has changed with the evolution of industrial society is the vast complexity of the physical conditions of existence. Significant as it is, the change in the character of national establishments does not signalize any overt decision. It has come about—or is coming about—through a gradual shift of the focus of attention from ceremonial objectives of power and glory to technological processes of sound economic growth: five-year plans, inflation control, export-import balance, and the availability of essential raw materials.

Underlying and conditioning this change is a third, still more general and still more significant, since it affects the whole of the day-to-day life of the whole community. Life itself is becoming less ceremonial, less a matter of authority and obedience, more responsive to demonstrable facts—in a word—more rational. I am well aware that this judgment is contrary to prevailing opinion. In recent years, as I have noted repeatedly, psychiatrists have been emphasizing the emotional aspect of the basic domestication which all human beings undergo. The idea is that infants become socialized by the approval and disapproval of their elders, and that this discipline colors their whole lives. It is true, of course, that all human beings are more or less sensitive to the approval and disapproval of others, and infants most of all. At all events, infants are aware of such attitudes, as animals are, and are able to respond to them, as animals do, long before it is possible to communicate to them the reasons for these attitudes. But this does not mean that no reasons exist.

A very good example of the confusion of emotional and rational considerations is that of toilet training. It is a favorite of present-day social theorists precisely because the toilet training of infants commonly begins before the infant in question can possibly be expected to understand the rationale of the procedure, and therefore it is conducted at the outset altogether on an attitudinal basis. Taking this stage of the socializing process as though it epitomized the whole of social organization, many theorists talk and write as though there were no reason for continence of urine and feces on anybody's part except the emotional pressure of social attitudes. But surely it is a fact that the wearing of clothes—not to mention all sorts of occupational necessities—contraindicates incontinence. This is so patently the fact that even small children can be expected to see it long before they have become letter perfect in the control of their animal impulses.

My point is, first, that it is the logic of socially organized activity that imposes sanitary measures upon us all; second, that this necessity is so obvious as to be well within the intellectual compass of small children; and third, that as civilization has advanced in the direction of industrial society the logic of efficient organization has become more and more important and, coincidentally, more and more apparent. It is general understanding of the logic of sanitation, and not mere emotional subservience to authority or to community attitudes, that has brought us the high measure of security from the hazard of disease we now enjoy. The same is true of the hazard of war. More fully than ever before the whole community now understands that war is incompatible with the industrial way of life.

We still live under the threat of war. But that does not mean that civilization has been marching in the wrong direction—that organized violence is inherent in social organization itself—that the more highly organized the world becomes the greater is the hazard of mutual extermination. On the contrary, the increase in the scale of social organization has brought us already within hailing distance of world organization, while the same process signalizes a profound internal change in the character of "sovereign power" which coincides with an even more pervasive and significant spread of rationality throughout the whole of the day-to-day life of the community. If we are prone to exaggerate the horrors of modern warfare and the risk of such an outbreak, that circumstance itself is evidence that the world is growing up.

7

In the foregoing paragraphs I have contrasted emotional response to social attitudes with understanding of the logic of social organization. The significance of this contrast of course goes far beyond the hazard of war. Indeed, it is a rephrasing of the contrast between the two quests for certainty of which Dewey wrote, and between the primitive meaning of security and the technological actualities that define genuine security. On one hand is the emotional dependency upon immediate, primary-group contacts which all human beings seem to feel; and on the other is the fact of large-scale organization. Early in the present chapter I noted that the increase of scientific knowledge has the inevitable effect of weakening the beliefs upon which, in earlier ages, the emotional sense of security has rested. Does the increasing prevalence and importance of large-scale organization and of long-distance relationships likewise involve a fatal weakening of the foundations of society?

To put the same question in another way, How stupid is the human race? I repeat: no one doubts the importance of emotions or the emotional importance of immediate social contacts. The relations of parents and children, and of husbands and wives, are of course of profound significance for the personality development and emotional "balance" or "adjustment" of every human being. This has always been so, and it remains so notwithstanding modern industrial organization. Indeed, it seems unlikely that world-wide economic interdependence or even world government will abolish these relationships or reduce their importance in the lives of all individuals. True, they are now undergoing a process of rationalization. The processes of personality adjustment which used to be conceived in terms of the interplay of occult forces are now coming to be understood as natural processes. Moreover, we seem to be well on the way to coping with this problem. But the question still remains whether such intimacies are the essence of all social relationships—whether the fact that a man no longer knows his neighbors and now owes his employment to decisions of unknown corporate officials in a far distant city means that the foundations of society are insecure.

It seems to me ridiculous—an insult to human intelligence—to suppose that such is the case. The reason we no longer know our neighbors today is that we no longer need to know them. In earlier days, with no means of communication but word of mouth and no means of transportation but "Old Dobbin" or "shanks' mare," neighbors, however distant, were quite literally dependent on each other in every emergency. But today, even though we may live in rabbit warrens with neighbors just on the other side of a tenement partition, the telephone is even nearer, and we can call the doctor, or the police or fire department, or the plumber, as occasion arises, even more quickly and more surely than we could call the neighbors. Our immediate relatives and closest friends may live across the city or across the country, and yet we can, and commonly do, keep in closer touch with them than our grandparents did with the closest neighbors.

The truth is that secondary- as well as primary-group relationships have always existed, and the distinction has always been one of kind as well as of degree of intimacy. Anthropologists declare that even the simplest peoples are aware of the contrast between their ceremonial activities, including relationships such as are fraught with emotion, and their proto-industrial operations and relationships in which considerations of efficiency are paramount. "Impersonal" relationships, as we call them (by something of an Irish bull, since no relationship between persons can be really impersonal), are no new thing. What industrial society has brought about is only a very great increase in the number, importance, and remoteness of the relationships we now maintain by "remote control."

That a development of such magnitude as that of modern industrial society has created problems should go without saying. The industrial-relations counselors who insist that people need to be informed about the organizations of which they are a part are of course right. People need to know what is the bearing of the operations they perform upon the perfection of the ultimate finished product, and they need to know what is the pattern of the "chain of command" of which they are a part.

My insistence that human intelligence is quite capable of comprehending all such matters does not assume clairvoyance. It is quite true that, in order for people to understand their situation, the essential information must be made available; that insofar as they are treated like cattle, whether through stupidity or brutality, they will feel dehumanized and will behave accordingly. I am not trying to argue that under the industrial dispensation all is necessarily and inevitably for the best. Obviously blunders of appalling proportions have been made and are still being made. Whether we shall succeed in realizing the possibilities of the industrial system still remains to be seen. My point is only that the large-scale operations which the industrial system does necessitate do not necessarily involve a loss of security and need not necessarily induce in people generally a sense of insecurity. The possibilities of genuine security, and of a common appreciation of it, are there.

8

For the realization of these possibilities social apparatus is necessary, some of it of a very general character and some quite specific. General education is one of these, as it is also a prerequisite to the operation of the industrial system and a *sine qua non* to the realization of all the values for which men strive. I have argued that no loss of orientation necessarily results from the scale of modern social organization, since the process of which this increase in scale is one aspect also necessarily includes the apparatus of travel and communication by which intimacies can be, and are maintained. The same is true of general education. One must be able to read in order to use the telephone directory. But also one must be able to read in order to obtain industrial employment. The educational level upon which our security depends is continually rising; but so are the occupational requirements of industry, and so are the educational opportunities which industrial society affords.

Of the social mechanisms specifically devised to secure us against specific hazards no better illustration could be given than the apparatus of public health, which has already been discussed with reference to the perennial hazard of disease. There are many such, big and little. One in particular calls for special notice not only because the hazard it combats is of great and growing importance but also because the apparatus in question—that of "social security"—has therefore come to typify the whole problem of security.

One of the principal features of industrial society is the wage system. This system has many advantages. It facilitates movement from one occupation to another and so makes possible the mobility which is a prerequisite to industrial development. It also provides the machinery by which the whole community has been able to share the advantages of industrial development. I do not mean to be complacent about this. Such sharing has not come to pass without a struggle. But if wage earners have had to organize and fight for higher wages, at least the wage system has provided the social mechanism by which it has been possible for them to better themselves without tearing the whole social structure to pieces.

However, the wage system has certain obvious disadvantages. Though it may not be true, as Marxists claim, that the wage system reduces human beings to the status of commodities to be bought and sold, it is true that the system makes no provision for those who are not employed. In this regard it stands in sharp contrast to the feudal system and even to the family system. Under the feudal system no one was ever unemployed, and the family farm always offers useful occupation not only for robust adults but for small children and their aged grandparents. But neither the very young nor the very old, nor the ailing and the handicapped, have any place in the wage system. Moreover—and as we have come to learn in recent decades this is the greatest disaster of all—there are times when jobs are not available even to robust adults.

As everyone knows, it is these circumstances which have led to the development of various systems of "social security," the object of which is to make special provision against the hazards that are inherent in the wage system. This is not the place to discuss the details of the apparatus of social security, or the comparative merits and disadvantages of various systems. But for anyone who is concerned about the values of industrial society the social-security system raises an insistent question. Is security a good thing?

9

It may seem a little late, not only in the present chapter but in the history of mankind, to be raising such a question. Throughout the foregoing discussion I have assumed that security is good, since in one way or another men have always sought it. Indeed, it could be argued that security is the primary object of all social organization. Conceived as the conservation of all that is good, it might even be regarded as the summation of all human values— a synonym for the *summum bonum*. But there is an important difference between retention and creation, and there is more than a verbal relation between conservation and conservatism.

Safeguards against hazards do not necessarily lead to achievement. They may even inhibit achievement. Precisely that is the penalty mankind has paid throughout the ages for seeking the fictitious security of supernatural agencies. The beliefs from which various peoples have derived their sense of security, being contrary to fact, have invariably impeded the pursuit of truth; and the social systems, to which those beliefs have given supernatural sanction, have therefore resisted adaptation to changing circumstances. What is feared by people who view with alarm the seemingly excessive concern of the present generation with economic security is that a community whose safety and comfort are guaranteed from the cradle to the grave may lose all interest in greater achievement.

Theoretically, this fear is justified. Security is not the sum of all human values. It is not an absolute. Indeed whenever it is treated as an absolute, the consequences are likely to be disastrous. Thus, for example, any individual who becomes obsessed with security from the hazard of disease to the point of surrounding himself with sanitary barriers runs the risk of reducing himself to complete impotence. Since anything he might do involves some risk of contamination, absolute security dictates that he do nothing.

Making an absolute of national security entails the same risk. The circumstances which dictate security measures are of course real and imperative. We are confronted by the manifest hostility of a great power. The technology of warfare is undergoing unprecedentedly rapid development. In our midst exists an organization of our own people who are nevertheless loyal to the enemy, bound together by secret ties, and subject to rigid discipline in the interest of that enemy. In these circumstances complete security might seem to dictate that all scientific research be conducted in strict secrecy, and that all persons to whom the slightest tinge of suspicion may attach be arrested and sequestered.

But to treat security as an absolute is to sacrifice all other values —including, in this case, not only the civil liberties we are striving to secure but even the scientific and technological progress on which our safety may depend. For the development of science and technology is a cultural process, and as such it is facilitated by close and general contact not only among all scientists but among all tool-users, unimpeded by any sort of barrier or isolation. Moreover, scientists, and intellectuals generally, are frequently eccentrics—just the sort of people to whom suspicion is likely to attach. In short, the pursuit of security at the expense of all other considerations is virtually certain to result not only in the sacrifice of freedom and justice but also in decimation of the ranks of scientists and the retardation of the efforts of all those who remain in service.

10

Such being the case, our problem is that of achieving a balance between what we have and what we hope to gain. This is true of all forms of security. Quite commonly the people who are most fearful of the effect social security may have in eroding the initiative of its recipients are themselves the beneficiaries of a much older form of social security—that of property. As a device for securing the rights of common citizens against the exactions of arbitrary sovereigns, property has played a leading role in the development of industrial society. But insofar as property rights are institutionalized—insofar as they are regarded as absolute and eternal—they are so clearly an impediment to further development that it is doubtful if the industrial system could have been achieved at all under such a dispensation. Could railways or highways have been built, if it had not been possible for public authority to

225

exercise the right of eminent domain? Not infrequently the construction of a dam, even by a "private" utility, involves the flooding of a whole town site, including a cemetery where perhaps several generations of villagers have been buried. If it were not possible to require these people to move, even with reasonable compensation—if the "final" resting place of their forebears were taken to be consecrated in perpetuity—the interests of a much larger number of people in the generation of electricity would be permanently thwarted. Indeed, it is this public interest, before which even the rights of private property must give way, that causes such enterprises to be designated as "public utilities," even though they too may be privately owned.

The public interest likewise underlies and sustains the modern device of social security. What is at issue is not only the fate of individuals for whom the wage system of industrial society makes inadequate provision. In recent decades economists have learned that the fate of the whole industrial economy is profoundly affected by the community's aggregate ability to consume the product of industry. Obviously the consumption that bulks largest in this situation is that of the great mass of wage earners. But for reasons too complex for recapitulation here the wage system by itself fails to keep pace with burgeoning production. Thus social security is a device for sustaining aggregate consumption, just as property is a device for sustaining industrial enterprise.

Both systems have some unfortunate effects which might be serious if either were to be treated as an absolute. In certain circumstances both may have the effect of robbing their beneficiaries of initiative and "gumption." Property is sometimes bequeathed in such a fashion as to insure the idleness of its recipients, and social-security benefits have sometimes been circumscribed in such a way as to discourage recipients from developing their talents or from striking out for themselves as independent enterprisers. But in both cases provision can be made, and is being made, to eliminate such undesirable effects.

Theoretically, property is eternal. But if it were really so, it would set up a feudal class of hereditary owners. We prevent this by inheritance taxation. Social-security benefits could be so restricted as to impede movement from one occupation to another, and even from one employer to another. In some instances this has actually been the case. But this can be prevented by broadening the coverage to include all possible employers and employments—even self-employment; and that is what we have been doing. Many critics have made the mistake of supposing that the broader social-security coverage becomes, the more deadening is the effect. But in fact precisely the opposite is the case.

Efficient organization is the keynote of all such devices. Traces of primitive sentiment and ceremonial tradition inevitably persist, and as always they stand in the way of constructive change. This is conspicuously the case in the area of national security. The chief obstacle to the development of efficient organization for collective security is nationalism. We citizens of the United States should never forget that our own representatives, supported by overwhelming national sentiment, were chiefly responsible for hobbling the Security Council of the United Nations with the veto power. But the world moves forward nevertheless. The actual security of mankind now, as always, is a function of technically efficient organization for mutual advantage.

The great technological revolution of modern times has brought to man greater security from all the hazards to which humanity is subject than he has ever known. To be sure, it has also brought new risks. The magnitude of the natural forces men have learned to harness, and the vast scale and complexity of modern organization, spell out the possibility of a greater catastrophe than mankind has ever experienced. But catastrophe is not the inevitable fate of industrial society. The process of efficient organization for mutual advantage, by which dawn men first learned to secure themselves against the rigors of the winter season, is still going on, and may still secure us against the hazard of mutual destruction.

CHAPTER XIV

ABUNDANCE

I

THAT THE INDUSTRIAL ECONOMY PRODUCES all kinds of goods and services in far greater profusion than mankind has ever known before is obvious and incontestable. Not only is abundance a fact; it is one of the most conspicuous facts of modern life. Moreover, in the apprehension of the community at large it is the proudest boast of Western civilization, and especially of the United States. The standard of living of the Western peoples is far higher than that of any other people, present or past, and that of the United States is by far the highest. Poverty and want have not been entirely banished; but that is not because the resources of the community are inadequate. It is a statistical fact that our resources are sufficient to afford a substantial degree of comfort to all members of the community.

Nevertheless there are certain respects in which this situation has been a source of embarrassment throughout modern times. In other respects it has been fraught with doubts, and in still others it has been, and still is, a source of shame. Many conscientious and thoughtful people have been deeply concerned lest in achieving quantity we have forfeited quality. To some of them ours seems to be a brummagem abundance, redolent of the pig sty. This is indeed a genuine problem. Certainly quality is no less important than quantity. But, as a value, excellence is sufficiently distinct to be treated by itself, and sufficiently important to merit a separate chapter. The present chapter will therefore be devoted to a discussion of the paradox of plenty.

The truth is that Western society both welcomes abundance and resists it. We welcome it as the successful consummation of all the community's efforts. Adam Smith declared that consumption is the end for which all other economic activity is undertaken, and almost without exception later economists have echoed this dictum.

On this view there can never be too much of a good thing. But recent experience has seemed to show the contrary. Thus we have been plagued by crop "surpluses" ever since the end of the war. On the assumption that there can never be too much of a good thing, we should have been welcoming our bumper crops. But instead of doing so we have been hiding them away and doing our best to pretend that they do not exist. We have even been trying to curtail production, lest we should suffer an embarrassment of riches.

Our greatest embarrassment occurred, of course, during the great depression of the 1930's. As subsequent investigation showed, even at the height of the prosperity of the preceding decade we were producing at a rate that was 19 per cent short of capacity. Even then, it seems, we were shying away from the terrifying prospect of unrestrained abundance. But in the years that followed, what had been mere hesitation became a panic. Production was cut back to less than half that of the days when it had been a fifth short of capacity—all in order to avoid the abundance which would have resulted from full-time operation.

Such is the paradox of plenty. When Adam Smith declared that consumption is the end for which all other economic activities are carried on he overlooked the established order of society. Consumption is not an end in itself. The consumption patterns of society are determined by a higher end: the social structure itself. When industrial efficiency produces an abundance that threatens to upset the established order of society, then tribal values require that it be resisted.

2

The classic method of dealing with "surpluses"—that is, the margin of difference between scarcity and abundance—is by "dumping" them on foreign markets. The struggle for markets in which all the leading industrial nations have been engaged from the earliest days of modern nationhood has been prompted by this resistance to abundance. Such dumping is a concealed giveaway. Because it is concealed, the impression still prevails quite generally that the economic struggle between nations has been, and is, primarily a matter of access to raw materials. In certain specific instances, usually highly publicized, such has been the case. Present concern over supplies of oil is such an instance. But more important, continuous, and general has been the apparent necessity under which the leading industrial nations have labored to find relief from the threat of abundance. Foreigners are the only possible recipients of such give-aways, since gifts to fellow citizens would decrease the volume of sales and hence would not reduce the surplus; and at the same time the giving must be concealed, since the community would hardly stomach such altruism.

Indeed, it must be concealed even from the givers. This has been accomplished in a variety of ways. In the first place, dumping, to all intents and purposes, is a sound business proposition. Properly speaking, dumping is the sale of goods below cost. This is not an act of folly. When the entire overhead cost of production of a given line of goods has been covered by domestic sales, an additional volume can be sold at prices just sufficient to cover the additional costs of producing that particular volume, plus a reasonable profit, providing those goods are sold in a market in which they will not compete with the goods that are priced to cover overhead costs. Foreign markets ideally fill this bill. That is why travellers often find home products offered for sale in foreign countries at prices lower than those which prevail at home. Producers in other countries naturally object to this sort of thing, even though they may be doing it themselves. Thus dumping has been a perennial cause of international friction. But it is as persistent as the threat of abundance which gives rise to it.

However, by far the most effective disguise of give-aways, and by far the greatest nuisance, has always been foreign investment. Properly speaking, trade is the exchange of goods for goods. But in order to avert the threat of abundance a country must export more than it imports. This can be done, and the illusion of a sound business proposition can be maintained, only if the party of the first part extends credit to the party of the second part. Such a transaction may involve numerous participants. Thus the seller of the goods in question may be paid in cash. But the cash may be that of his own fellow citizens who are concurrently subscribing to the bonds of foreign companies (or countries), or buying shares in those (or similar) companies.

This, of course, is colonialism. As such it is deeply resented by patriotic citizens of the debtor countries. What they resent is that the resources of their country should be owned by foreigners. This is a condition which they can correct by the simple expedient of expropriating the properties in question. Such a maneuver may require a revolution for its consummation, but that also is by no means impossible. The investors of the creditor country are of course fully aware of this possibility, and they usually require the government of the debtor country to give solemn guarantees against expropriation and any other discriminatory measures. But no government can guarantee that it will not be supplanted.

It is when this happens that foreign investments turn out to have been give-aways. This is the case notwithstanding the fact that the givers are almost always not the original sellers of surplus goods. Thus all the parties to the transaction are able to conceal not only from the general public but even from themselves the fact that such disposition of a surplus is a give-away.

Military programs also constitute a concealed method of disposing of industrial surplus. Goods consigned to military use are disposed of in the sense of being removed from the ordinary channels of trade; and such disposal is concealed by virtue of appearing to be a national necessity rather than a subterfuge for avoiding abundance. Indeed, at any given moment it may actually be a national necessity. But throughout the colonial period the circumstances which have given rise to that necessity have been those of which colonialism itself has been the product. It has been the armed might of the colonial powers that has enabled them to "open the markets" of the rest of the world; and it has been the struggle for dominance among the colonial powers themselves that has found expression in a whole series of wars and so in the necessity of continuous "preparedness." Such preparedness —not to mention the actual conflicts—is a veritable sinkhole of industrial substance. There is no limit to its capacity to absorb the product of industry, and to do so with the unstinted approval of the community.

3

This does not mean that the community rejoices at the spectacle of destruction, in this or any other instance. In resisting abundance society does not undervalue it. If such were the case, there would be no problem and no paradox, for surpluses could be destroyed outright without compunction or regret. We actually do this sometimes, but only in desperate crises such as the harvesting of unexpectedly and disastrously large crops, or when the sudden termination of a war leaves us with vast stocks of unused goods on our hands. But burning mountains of potatoes, or dumping clothes, watches, and automobiles into the ocean, is definitely offensive to the Puritan conscience, which still deplores the waste of valuable goods of any sort. It is this conflict of conscience and apparent necessity that constitutes the paradox. We still value abundance; but we sacrifice it to what seems to be a higher value.

This value is the established order of society. In the case of modern Western society it takes the form of economic order. In all the maneuvers by which we seek to dispose of surpluses what we are trying to prevent is the disorganization of the market, and in this sense a surplus should be defined as "any quantity of any goods which cannot be sold at prevailing prices." The immediate alternative to disposing of the surplus would be a catastrophic drop in prices and the consequent bankruptcy of many dealers and producers. At the moment such a decline in prices would of course be to the advantage of the consuming public. But its remoter effects would be widespread and progressive disemployment and general distress such as might threaten the whole economic system. In effect, therefore, preservation of the existing balance of forces in the market is preservation of the existing social order.

In the broader sense this necessity is no new thing. Since the technological process is inherently developmental, while the institutional structure of all societies is inherently static and change-resistant, this contrast should lead us to expect a more or less continuous resistance to such an enlargement of consumption patterns as would be required if consumption were to keep pace with perpetually increasing abundance. It is true that over most of the history of mankind the advancement of technology has been extremely slow, and it is also true that over a correspondingly long period—measured in hundreds of thousands of years—the fruit of human toil has not been what we would now call abundance. But we must bear constantly in mind that technological expedients which appear to us superlatively clumsy and inefficient are nevertheless astonishingly productive in comparison with the best efforts of man's nearest evolutionary relatives.

Viewed in that perspective even the crudest tools are so effective as to seem, at least occasionally, to be endowed with supernatural powers. In short, the effects of a technological revolution may continue to be felt even over periods that are to us almost unimaginably long. Such in fact is the testimony of the anthropologists. According to them the first great technological revolution occurred at the dawn of human culture, to which indeed it actually gave rise. That revolution included the origin of articulate speech, the use of fire, and the creation of the first tools. These achievements (made possible, of course, by zoological evolution) were so prodigious as to have given rise simultaneously to the sense of mystic forces by which our species has been haunted ever since.

In these circumstances it is not surprising that simple peoples should have been shocked by the abundance that occasionally crowned their efforts, an abundance so far out of line with their ordinary experience as to cause them to hesitate to accept their good fortune. According to the anthropologists, even among the most primitive societies now known to us there are none who do not practice systematic ceremonial waste. They do this in various ways. Unable to credit their good fortune to their own technical expedients, they offer the first and best fruits of their efforts to the Higher Powers. They also press upon their leaders, of whose *mana* their coup is clear evidence, a heaping share of the spoils; and they themselves also indulge in orgies of ceremonial consumption in frantic efforts to reduce their surplus.

4

All of these resistances to crediting the actuality of abundance are with us still, even in advanced industrial society, and are now deeply ingrained in the social structure and the ceremonial value system of modern Western society. As Veblen showed in *The Theory of the Leisure Class*, the philosophy of waste is one of the foundation principles of our society. Indeed, it is indissociable from the principle of status. We do not abhor the waste of our social superiors but tolerate it because of their superiority. In literal truth we regard abundance as a heavenly illusion. On the same principle we accept poverty as the appointed lot of mankind. This is evidenced by our "finders-keepers" conception of profits. Good fortune is not the common lot, and by implication cannot be. Samuel Butler's Erewhonians regarded it as evidence of genius, and so do we. Precisely that was Samuel Butler's point. This, too, is the essence of the "brummagem" argument, as I shall try to point out in the next chapter—the argument that whatever is possessed by many people is therefore necessarily mean, poor, tawdry, and vulgar. We simply refuse to credit the possibility that really good things may be abundantly available to all.

Moreover, during the last few centuries the Western peoples have been confirmed in this attitude by an articulate philosophy of scarcity. A great many ideas converged to form this theory, and this is not the place to trace them all. But one is of sufficient importance to require mention. This is the idea that the decisive factor in economic growth is the accumulation of capital.

At the present time we know a great deal more about the process of economic growth than was known in the seventeenth and eighteenth centuries, when the philosophy of scarcity was being formulated, or even in the nineteenth century, when that body of ideas was being elaborated into a formidable logical system. Even the business community is now well aware of the importance of research not only for the development of new products but for the achievement of major economics such as make large-scale production possible. On the physical side, the apparatus of modern industry has been brought into existence by the industrial revolution, not by economizing. For example, the copper which is now consumed by the electrical industry could not conceivably have been accumulated by early generations economizing in the use of copper pots and pans. And, on the financial side, it is now obvious that industrial expansion is self-financing. We create credit based on the assets which the credit brings into existence.

But to earlier generations it seemed self-evident that new industry requires capital and that capital is accumulated only by abstinence and saving. As Edwin Cannan pointed out a quarter of a century ago, this notion owes its plausibility to the fact that it is true of individual participation in the ownership of growing industry. Individuals commonly (though not invariably) acquire shares in growing industries by purchase. Their purchases commonly (though not invariably) are made possible by the prior ownership of liquid funds, and these in turn commonly (though not invariably) result from saving. Thus if what is true of individuals is true in the aggregate, it appears that industrial growth is a function of economizing.

This seems to mean that scarcity rather than abundance is the keynote of modern life. As a matter of fact many economists find the popular notion that ours is now an economy of abundance extremely irritating. To them it seems a product of ignorance and folly. Notwithstanding the vast outpouring of modern industry and the unprecedentedly high standard of living that Americans now enjoy, they insist that the whole function of the economy is to economize in the allocation of scarce resouces among alternative uses not all of which can possibly be pursued at the same time.

Curiously enough, this highly articulate and intellectually formidable refusal to accept the fact of abundance is not put out of countenance by the extravagances of great wealth. Indeed, the "Mandeville effect," as it might be called, has all along been an integral part of the philosophy of scarcity. This is the doctrine that luxury spending is a good thing, since it gives employment and provides a market for goods which would otherwise have no market. Early in the eighteenth century the celebrated (or rather, notorious) author of *The Fable of the Bees* had argued along just such lines that "private vices [are] public virtues." Scarcely any writer has ever been more generally and vigorously condemned. Nevertheless, the central idea, somewhat more decorously expressed, has become a part of the dominant philosophy of scarcity; and in doing so it has established a clear line of connection between the philosophy of scarcity and our immemorial concern lest abundance upset the established order of society.

Abundance

Higher wages are upsetting; but bigger profits are not. At the present moment, for example, wage raises (especially those which result from the "escalator clauses" of union contracts) are being blamed, generally and insistently, for continued inflation—and this notwithstanding the obvious fact that the escalator clauses, which tie wage rates to the cost of living (as measured by the Bureau of Labor Statistics), cannot possibly do more than prevent real wages from being cut by price rises that have their origin elsewhere. The reason high wages provoke such an outcry, whereas big profits (such as are now being made) do not, is not simply the rapacity of the businessmen concerned. Except for the spokesmen of organized labor, the whole community shares such sentiments; and it does so because for several generations its intellectual leaders have been representing by one argument after another but always in terms consonant with the basic philosophy of scarcity that high wages are bad and big profits good.

5

This is the "religion of the cake," as John Maynard Keynes once called it. In one of the most vivid passages in the whole literature of economics he drew a thumbnail sketch of the institutional background of *The Economic Consequences of the Peace* (of Versailles). The successive generations of men who have built the cloudcapped towers of modern industry—so Keynes then declared —have no more been free to consume the abundance that industry has made possible than were the men who built the pyramids of Egypt, but for a different reason. Whereas the slaves of Egypt labored under the lash, the free citizens of modern Western society have been persuaded or, as Keynes said, "cajoled" into putting up with their immemorial scarcity by an extraordinary argument. This was the classical philosophy of scarcity. Its central idea was, and is, that all the energies of industrial society must go to the creation of a cake which of necessity must grow and grow and never be cut. Thus the growth of the cake has been, he said, "the object of true religion."

What keeps us going is the growth of a cake which by definition can never be eaten. Strangely enough, years later Keynes himself was the principal author of the investment subterfuge. Investment

—that is, the enlargement of the physical plant of industry; in short, the growth of the cake—gives employment and through the wages of those who are so employed provides a powerful stimulant to the entire economy. When investment slackens, men previously engaged in construction are laid off, and their distress is transmitted to all the trades of which they have been customers and so becomes a downward spiral of depression. Consequently, Keynes argued, the first essential of continuing high-level employment is the continuation of investment, which must therefore be encouraged by whatever means, and especially by low interest rates such as will encourage businessmen to borrow.

It is this argument that has provided contemporary economists with their favorite paradox. We have learned, they now say, that the sovereign cure for too much investment is more investment. I call this a subterfuge for the same reason that Keynes, in 1920, called it "true religion." Surely cake has no other reason for existence than to be eaten! As a subterfuge to avoid cutting the cake investment is vastly superior to give-aways or throw-aways. But why not cut the cake and be done with the bugaboo of scarcity?

Clearly, the more we invest, the more we are eventually going to have to consume. The crowning paradox of the religion of the cake, or the "philosophy of scarcity" as I have called it, is its idealization of eventual abundance. It is easy to be cynical about "pie in the sky by and by," in the words of the Wobbly song. But the fact remains that pie, like cake, is a tasty comestible. It is sometimes said that there are but two forces by which people, like animals, are moved: the carrot and the stick. In this sense, ours has been a carrot society. As I have already noted, from the earliest days of the industrial revolution the primary motive force of Western society has been the prospect of improvement. For all its emphasis upon the economical use of scarce resources, the philosophy of scarcity has kept alive the dream of future abundance. It has owed its hold on the mind of Western man to the actual and progressive realization of that dream. Marx predicted that under capitalism the condition of the masses would steadily worsen. But it has not done so. On the contrary, it was steadily and greatly improved —was doing so long before Marx's time and has continued to do so down to the present day. However, this is not altogether a tribute to the institutions of capitalism or to its philosophy of scarcity. There is also the industrial revolution.

As the fruits of industrial revolution have become more and more abundant, the actuality of abundance and the potentiality of still greater and more widely spread abundance have been more and more generally and clearly realized. The role of high wages and of the mass market in the growth of the American economy are now widely recognized, even by the same people who deplore further wage increases as inflationary. Many economists now declare that consumption is "the controlling factor" in economic growth, and in this spirit statisticians and businessmen keep careful watch on the indices of mass consumption. As a matter of ideology we still adhere to the philosophy of scarcity. As J. K. Galbraith has said, in *The Affluent Society,* it is the "conventional wisdom" of our society. But abundance is now generally accepted as a fact and as an ideal. Whatever the conditions may have been that have prompted past generations to resist abundance, they have proved insufficient. We are now fully committed to an economy of abundance.

6

Even so, as an idea and as a condition abundance has definite limits. It may be possible for every family in the United States to be reasonably well fed, well clothed, and well housed—far better, at all events, than they have ever been in the past. But it is not possible for every family to be better off than its neighbors. In short, abundance ends where snobbery begins. Is snobbery likely to increase as fast as our capacity to produce, or even faster? If so, all hope of future abundance might as well be abandoned. However large, the product of industry is always a finite quantity, whereas the capacity to waste has no limit. What Veblen described as "conspicuous waste" might conceivably become more and more conspicuous, with the result that all our abundance, however vast in quantity, might become as meaningless qualitatively as a sounding bell and a tinkling cymbal.

To many people this dreadful prospect seems very real. They see in such things as the forest of television antennas that rises over every American town clear evidence both of compulsive emulation and cultural bankruptcy. It is true, of course, that the value of abundance is indissociable from those of excellence and of equality. Both of these values are discussed in other chapters. But because they are indissociable from abundance, I cannot avoid repeating here my basic denial of such cynicism.

The presumption that what is mass-produced must therefore be inferior is itself a form of snobbery; for it assumes as a major premise that whatever is enjoyed by many people, and is perhaps accessible to all, thereby necessarily loses its distinctive excellence. This identification of excellence with exclusiveness is reminiscent of the definition of wealth propounded by Lancelot Hogben as an ironic comment on the philosophy of scarcity: wealth is what I have and you lack; if you had it too, mine would not be it. To deny the possibility that excellence could be abundant is to deny the objective reality of excellence. True, rejection of such snobbery does not prove that excellence is real, let alone abundant. But it does leave that possibility open. Granted that quantity alone is an unsatisfactory ideal: still there is nothing about the quantitative potency of the industrial economy that is necessarily debasing.

Nor does it necessarily lead to endless emulation. The Smiths may get television sets because the Joneses have them; but they may just as plausibly get them because they are worth having. Moreover, as we approach the saturation point—the point at which virtually everybody has access to a television screen—possession of a set ceases to be a basing point of emulation. The story used to be told of the trench warfare of World War I that the soldiers in a front-line German trench raised a sign reading "Gott mit uns!"; whereupon the American boys opposite them raised a stick on which they had placed a mitten, together with a sign reading "We got mittens too!" When all God's chillun got mittens, the possession of such wealth ceases to be a class distinction.

The inevitable consequence of increasing abundance is a steady reduction of the distance from one extreme of the social scale to the other. Thus abundance is not only consistent with the ideal of equality; it is itself an equalizing agent. Doubtless this is a process which, like human life itself, may go on forever without being complete. But the half-life of snobbery, like that of a radioactive isotope, may be a finite quantity. Even though the Smiths

may continue struggling to keep up with the Joneses to the end
of time, the importance of the struggle to both of them may be
progressively diminished.

There are many signs that such is already the case. For example,
bathtubs are now in use by virtually the entire population. Veblen ridiculed the "ceremonial cleanliness" of the upper classes,
which the lower classes so sedulously copy, and back-to-nature en-
thusiasts have often decried the fetishism of the daily tub. But
all this overlooks significant facts. For one thing, the universality
of the bath means that social classes can no longer be distinguished
by their stench. Time was when the rich carried their bathtubs with
them at all times, inasmuch as they were conspicuous for their
sweetness. The disappearance of this class distinction has now
been replaced by the snobbery of the dirty shirt. This is based on
the presumption that only the highly placed can now afford to be
dirty in public. But even they do not go verminous. After all, the
cult of the tub is not altogether ceremonial. Squalor breeds vermin, and vermin breed disease. The abundance which has raised
cleanliness from a luxury to a necessity has also become a major
safeguard against plague, an achievement which the Joneses necessarily share with all the Smiths.

The mutual enhancement of abundance and equality is not peculiar. On the contrary, it is a basic characteristic of all real values
and as such is the central theme of this entire discussion. We cannot reiterate too often that equality—the progressively wider participation of all in all good things—is good because it contributes
to the progressive multiplication of all good things; and that
abundance—the progressive multiplication of all good things—
is good because it contributes to progressively wider participation,
and likewise to greater freedom and security. Such is the nature
of real values.

7

The last and perhaps most fateful limitation upon abundance
is that of population. It is of course true and obvious that the very
idea of abundance, as well as that of scarcity, assumes and implies
a ratio between production and population. The volume of production alone tells us nothing. It makes no difference how much

production may be increasing in any given community at any given time; if the population of that community is increasing faster, the net result is increasing scarcity. Genuine abundance is achieved only by an increase of *per capita* production.

Historically, marked increase in production has invariably been accompanied by marked increase in population. This circumstance therefore raises a fateful question. Does population increase faster than production? Must it inevitably do so? These questions have been raised many times in many forms in many ages, but most dramatically by Thomas Richard Malthus in 1798.

Two sets of circumstances set the stage for Malthus' dramatic announcement of "the principle of population": the industrial revolution of the eighteenth century, and the French Revolution, late in the same century. The harnessing of steam power seemed to give promise of a tremendous increase in the absolute volume of production, and to many idealists in all lands Western civilization seemed to have taken a giant stride toward liberty, equality, and fraternity. These circumstances inspired such idealists as Condorcet in France and Godwin in England to proclaim the "perfectibility" of mankind. But the excesses of the later days of the French Revolution (in which even Condorcet lost his life) turned many thoughtful Englishmen, such as Edmund Burke, not only against the revolutionary government of France but against the whole roster of ideas of which it seemed to be the fulfillment. One of these skeptics was Malthus. It was in these circumstances that this young man, only recently ordained by the Church of England, wrote *An Essay on the Principle of Population as it Affects the Future Improvement of Society, with Remarks on the Speculations of Mr. Godwin, M. Condorcet, and other Writers.*

I recall these circumstances because I think it is significant that the specter of Malthusianism seems always to be conjured up by extreme anxiety and general pessimism, such for example as has followed World War II. But what is at issue, of course, is not the circumstances which may have prompted the writings of Malthus and his later disciples, but only the answer they have given to our questions.

Malthus' original argument was very simple. It was that human fecundity is such that population continually threatens to exceed the available food supply. This threat brings into play the "positive checks": war, famine, and disease, by which in fact the balance is maintained.

Whatever may be said of Malthusianism, the *Essay* was a very remarkable production—indeed, by any reckoning one of the world's "Great Books." In its imaginative grasp of the operation of natural forces in the "struggle for existence" it anticipated Darwinian evolution. At certain points it even foreshadowed the principle of "natural selection"; and it was in fact one of the influences by which Darwin was guided to the formulation of the principle of organic evolution. But as a proof of the impossibility of abundance it is far from being conclusive.

In particular, the ratios according to which Malthus represented population as doubling every twenty-five years, whereas food supply increases only by arithmetical ratio, are wholly conjectural. There is no "law" either of zoology or of society that supports any such "principle." Human fecundity is indeed potentially far in excess of actual population growth; but so is that of virtually all creatures, both animal and vegetable. As a matter of zoological fecundity there is no reason to suppose that the increase of the human population should be greater than that of the plants and animals by which human beings live. Moreover, the increase of agricultural (and industrial) production has virtually nothing to do with zoological fecundity. It is a function of human knowledge and skill—in short, technology; and there is no basis for setting any absolute limit to the rate or magnitude of technological advance. Indeed, many scientists have pointed out, especially in recent decades, that the potential food resources of the earth are far in excess of its present human population.

However, it is true that in some parts of the world where population is already dense the immediate effect of alleviation of famine and disease has been an alarming increase in population. Does this mean that the rate of increase of population is absolutely uncontrollable? Present-day Malthusians frequently talk and write as though such were the case. In their alarm they seem to represent the population problem as uniquely insoluble. Other problems may yield to scientific knowledge and organizational skill, but seemingly population growth defies solution and in the end nullifies all other achievements.

But does the population problem defy solution? It is interesting to note that Malthus himself was not a Malthusian in this sense. In the second edition of his celebrated *Essay* he added a "preventive check" which completely alters the picture. The "moral restraint" which Malthus then invoked may be a rather slender reed. But it is a tool that is capable of improvement. Doubtless we have not yet found the perfect means of solving the population problem. But what tool is perfect? This only means that the population problem is like all other problems.

Luis Muñoz Marin, the distinguished governor of Puerto Rico, has remarked of his own island that its problem arises from the fact that it has an industrial death rate and a preindustrial birth rate. There is a reason for this. The causes of death are much more accessible to control by presently available tools than are the causes of birth. The area in which procreation occurs is still, as it always has been, peculiarly susceptible of the influence of sentiment, tradition, mores, and religious belief. Malthus counseled late marriage. But public policy with regard to the rate of population growth is not the only consideration in terms of which people make their decisions with regard to marriage; and the same is true in varying degree of present means of achieving "planned parenthood." But this may not always be the case. We have no reason whatever for supposing that it will always be the case. On the contrary, all our experience of problem-solving points toward the probability that the population problem can and will be solved. Scientists are already engaged in perfecting a method of controlling human fecundity in which one simply swallows a pill, a means that would involve no invasion of privacy and would give no affront to any moral principle or religious belief.

Granted that the achievement of abundance is contingent in the end upon the solution of the population problem—this contingency does not mean that universal abundance is forever unattainable. Even if it did carry this pessimistic implication, however, it still would not mean that abundance is not a genuine and noble value. On the contrary, the despair of Malthusian pessimists is itself an acknowledgment of the real value of abundance. Otherwise, why should they despair?

8

Indeed, as I have tried to show throughout the present discussion, the real value of abundance is a corollary of man's use of tools, the technological way of life to which mankind has been committed since the dawn of civilization. Does this mean that abundance is good because it is a product of technology? Or is technology good, as Adam Smith implied, because it produces abundance? Smith's dictum, that consumption is the end for the sake of which all other economic activities are carried on, seems to imply, first, that a clear distinction can be drawn between consumption and "other" activities, and second, that consumption is the intrinsically agreeable "end" to which those other activities are the intrinsically disagreeable "means." But in fact neither one of these implications is valid.

Do we eat to live, or live to eat? Clearly neither is the case. Eating is a part of living, and like all other parts it is both consequent and antecedent. Like other social philosophers of his day, Adam Smith was a hedonist. As such, he thought of human behavior as being guided by sensations of pleasure and pain. Thus he thought of production as "work," and as such disagreeable, in contrast to consumption, which is agreeable and therefore not work. But these distinctions, which seem so simple and obvious in particular cases, break down completely when the attempt is made to extend them to human activity, or economic organization, as a whole. Some men enjoy their work and gulp their meals hastily in order to get back to it. Which, then, is the end, and which the means? Wages are generally accounted a cost of production, and a necessary one since—as economists saw even before the time of Adam Smith— the maintenance of a labor force is a necessary part of the effort society must make in order to carry on the economy. When wage earners then spend their wages, are they consuming? Or are they participating in the general effort of production by maintaining their health and strength?

The truth is that all such distinctions are arbitrary. As such they may serve important purposes in definitely limited situations.

In tracing moneyflows it may be important to make a distinction between the disbursements of business firms and the budgeting of household incomes, and no crime is committed if we call one of these situations production and the other consumption—provided we do not make the mistake of supposing the two activities to be inherently and generically different—of supposing, for example, that we can tell whether a person is producing or consuming "by inspection," as the mathematicians say—or of supposing that we ourselves can differentiate these activities by our sensations of agreeableness or the reverse.

Abundance is not good in any secondary or derivative sense, "merely" because it derives from the technological process. Nor is the technological process inherently disagreeable in itself but good in consequence of producing abundance. Both are good because they are inseparable—from each other, and from all other real goods. In a sense abundance is the aggregate of all goods and derives its goodness from all that is good. But in an equally valid sense all other goods derive their meaning from that of abundance, since a good is anything we would be better off for having more of. Thus abundance carries us back to the interrelatedness of all human experience, from which the meaning "good" derives, and it is that interrelatedness which is likewise manifest in the technological process from which abundance flows.

CHAPTER XV

EXCELLENCE

I

HAS INDUSTRIAL SOCIETY SACRIFICED QUALITY for quantity? In view of the obvious facts it seems strange that such a question should ever have been raised, and strangest of all that it should continue to be raised even in the middle of the twentieth century. The development of all the arts and crafts throughout the ages has been a cumulative process. Each successive step has been taken solely because it represented an improvement on what was being done before or the achievement of something that could not have been done at all before. No art and no knowledge has ever been permanently lost. Anything that any earlier people ever did can be done much better and more easily today, whereas much the greater part of what is done today could not have been done at all by any earlier people.

Why then should anyone suppose the contrary? In the light of present knowledge of the bipolarity of technological and cere-monial processes, the answer to this question is no less obvious than are the facts of industrial technology. Judged by the criterion of the tribal fictions of any other culture, industrial society and all its works are unqualifiedly and irremediably bad, since they explode ancient myths and subvert ancient authority. Moreover, as we know, these ceremonial values are amazingly pervasive and persistent. To devout Catholics it may well seem that Western society has been backsliding ever since the Protestant Reformation. But it is not necessary to believe that feudal society was ordained by God in order to feel a vague uneasiness with regard to the vul-gar hurly-burly of the twentieth century. All that is necessary is a correspondingly vague nostalgia for some past era, or even a fix-ation on some particular feature of some earlier culture.

The effect of such nostalgia is greatly magnified and intensified by a methodological error to which all mankind is unhappily prone: that of comparing what is common in one situation with what is best in another. So even Henry Adams was able to regard the cathedral of Chartres and the abbey of Mont St. Michel as typical of medieval culture, and our own as contrasting sadly, notwithstanding the obvious fact that those great architectural monuments had no equals even in their own day and are far more widely known and admired today (thanks in part to Henry Adams) than they were in the thirteenth century. So also the glories of the Elizabethan Age—Shakespeare and Ben Jonson—are contrasted with the "comics" and television "spectaculars" of our time, and the music of Bach or Haydn or Mozart or Beethoven with present-day calypso or "rock and roll."

In putting the matter thus baldly I also may be guilty of exaggeration. But is there any other basis for the wholesale condemnation of our present culture? One of the commonest indictments of our age is that it mistakes bigness for excellence. It is true of course that a big building is not necessarily more beautiful or more useful than a small one, and also that Americans in particular have often been guilty of silly boasting. But it is also true that a small building is not necessarily more beautiful or more useful than a large one. Moreover, the vulgar moderns who boast of the size of their buildings, their bridges, and their hydro-electric dams can take this much comfort: it was not the superior taste of earlier generations that saved them from building such "monstrosities"; in literal fact they were utterly unable to build anything of the kind, good, bad, or indifferent.

2

A more serious defect of modern taste is perhaps revealed by the very general effort to make everything look like something other than what it is, especially something antique. Thus modern skyscrapers sometimes have been made to look as much like medieval cathedrals as has been possible under the circumstances, and the approaches to suspension bridges have sometimes been made to look as much as possible like Greek temples. Let us concede at once that this sort of thing is silly and tasteless. It is silly and tasteless to try to make electric light fixtures look like candles or telephone instruments like vases. But what standard of taste is responsible for such cultural aberrations?

Why has it been so widely and persistently supposed that anything made of steel, or even more particularly anything made of concrete, must therefore and by definition as it were, be ugly? There can be but one answer to this question: because earlier generations did not employ these materials. The criterion of beauty (and of excellence generally) on which such judgments have been based is not one of "significant form," of "unity in diversity," or anything else of the sort. It is one of association with past achievements. The Greeks built with stone. The Romans built with stone. The medievals built with stone. All the great monuments of antiquity are of stone. Therefore to share the excellence of those great works, anything man builds must at least seem to have been built with stone. Hence we have built vast steel structures, and hung stone upon them, reinforcing the steel frames to carry the weight of the stone facing, in the hope that they might resemble the accredited triumphs of the past. It is not the logic or esthetics of machine technology that has produced these monstrosities; it is ancestor worship, pure and simple.

No feature of the machine age has been more generally, or more justly, ridiculed than the early products of the power lathe and scroll saw. But why? Obviously these machines made it possible for their users to do quickly, easily, and cheaply what earlier craftsmen had been obliged to do with hand tools. Hence these machines effected a *reductio ad absurdum* of the art of decoration. But the absurdity was implicit not in the machine but in the principle of fanciness. There is no imperative that compels us to use such machines to imitate the handicraft of the past. If we do use them so, that is only because the dead hand of the past is guiding our machines. The cast-iron stands of the first sewing machines were covered with floral decorations. But a sewing machine does not require to be supported by flowers. The requirement to which those early products of the machine age responded was that of a still earlier generation.

In justice to the designers of all such imitative monstrosities we should note the limitations under which they worked. Where present-day designers would employ the flat surfaces and clean and simple lines of steel stampings, the early modern designers used cast iron, in part because steel was not available to them; and they employed floral decorations in their molds, in part to conceal the irregularities to which cast iron is peculiarly subject. So also early builders covered their steel frames with stone and brick, in part because sheet aluminum and stainless steel, as well as rock-wool insulation, were not available even a half-century ago. Cultural bastardy is still a crime; but these are extenuating circumstances.

It is only within the last few decades that bold estheticians have made the revolutionary discovery that some of the concrete structures which modern engineers have designed with no thought of decorating the landscape are in fact comparable with the finest work of the ancients. Like the tapered pillars of the Greeks and the flying buttresses of the medievals, their significant forms have been dictated by the functions they perform—of spanning the East River or the Golden Gate, or of holding back a vast body of water or even carrying away the smoke of a great mill. In their single-minded execution of the purpose for which they were designed, even smokestacks have come to be recognized as manifestations of that unity-in-diversity which is the true criterion of excellence. The absence of decoration, or avoidance of fanciness, far from being an assertion of vulgarity, is in fact a manifestation of good taste.

Crudeness and vulgarity still abound. People still stick a few imitation Greek pillars on the front of otherwise undistinguished structures under the impression that they will signalize distinction. It is still possible to find a Greek temple perched on the top of a structural steel tower. But it is not true that steel and concrete are inherently ugly, or that bigness is inherently vulgar. After all, the seven wonders of the ancient world were so identified primarily because of their size.

3

Mass production is commonly accounted one of the greatest crimes against good taste that industrial society commits. This charge is particularly interesting because it puts quantity and quality in direct opposition. Apparently good can become bad if only it be multiplied sufficiently. Let us admit at once that bad can be multiplied quite as readily as good, and that the manufacturers of wall paper often employ extremely poor designers. Does it therefore follow that whatever is produced in quantity is necessarily shoddy or tawdry?

When they talk in this vein critics of industrial culture often make a great point of the almost incredible fineness of the handwork of the skilled craftsmen of other times, and of the prodigious care they have lavished on their work. But does anybody really suppose that in point of fineness any handicraftsmen of any age ever exceeded what is common practice in every present-day machine shop? It is standard operating procedure in every shop for bearings to be ground to tolerances measured by one- or two-thousandths of an inch. This is of course done with machine tools. No craftsman of any age could ever even approach such tolerances with hand tools. For many years the machine most widely used throughout the world has been the common sewing machine. Sewing machines are in use in Thibet and Timbuctoo. Compared even with an automobile engine the sewing machine is a relatively crude affair. But no craftsman of any age could possibly fabricate such a thing. This is not to say that the sewing machine is an object of great beauty. What is at issue here is not beauty or even usefulness but only tolerances: the fineness of workmanship that is manifest in the delicate adjustment of part to part. The marble traceries of the Taj Mahal may be more beautiful, but they are not finer.

Granted, then, that machines can do a very good job of mass production, and even that what they mass-produce may conceivably have been excellent in the first place, does mass production necessarily debase? Is the artistry of Van Gogh somehow dissipated, or even vitiated, by the wide distribution of prints of his once-striking canvases? Has Van Gogh been vulgarized by being mass-produced?

Is excellence synonymous with rarity? People often talk as if it were. But such an identification reduces the very meaning of excellence to absurdity, since it implies that there is no criterion of excellence but that of quantity. To be sure, an escape hatch from this vicious circle seems to be provided by the theory of the elite.

According to this theory excellence is rare because it is detectable only by especially gifted persons. It is rare because such persons are by definition few. Others know of it only by grace of its prior identification by the elite, and prize it only in imitation of their superiors.

Strangely enough, this theory enjoys wide currency at the present time, even among people who would indignantly repudiate the suggestion that they are subscribing to a superstition. Yet the theory has no other basis or significance. If we suppose that excellence is sacramental in character, so that it can be achieved and even apprehended only by a ceremonially chosen few, then the theory makes sense, though only ceremonial sense. In this sense, of course, industrial society is vulgar and "common" (in the deprecatory sense) as a direct consequence of having dispensed with kings by divine right and aristocracies by divine appointment and ecclesiastical consecration, and all characteristic features of modern Western culture are likewise "common" and vulgar for the same reason. Thus the wide distribution of prints (however faithful) of masterworks (however great) is evidence only of the suffocating conformity which industrial mass production has induced.

4

I have said that the elite theory of excellence has none but a mystical basis, and I shall not recede from that position. But those who hold, as many leading intellectuals do, that all the great achievements of every age have been the work of a very small number of very unusually gifted individuals, and that all the rest of mankind trails along so to speak in the wake of the intellectual elite, can at least plead extenuating circumstances. They have been misled by what might be called the statistical illusion. In a certain statistical sense their basic proposition is true. But taken in that sense, as of course it should be, it does not have the significance either for their supposed elite or for the meaning of excellence which they seem to suppose it has.

It is true of course that in any given period only a few names will become sufficiently well known to find their way into the school books, and it is also true that some of these will be associated in the public mind with great events. The trouble is that we have no independent assessment either of the individuals or of the events. Given a great event, and given also the universal (and ceremonial) craving for a hero, it is inevitable that some particular name will be associated in the public mind with each supposedly great event. If we had some accurate way of measuring the potentiality for greatness of all infants, and if all were so measured in infancy; and if we had some independent measure of the greatness of events; and if it then developed that all the Class-A events were being brought about by Class-A individuals, with no Class-A individuals or events left over; then we could regard it as established that all great achievements are the work of unusually gifted persons. But actually we know none of these things. The supposed gifts of the individuals concerned are attested only by their supposed authorship of the supposedly great achievements.

This is the statistical illusion. If a dozen hundred-carat diamonds were to be scattered over the length and breadth of the United States, no more than a dozen hunters could become diamond finders, however numerous were the assiduous and skillful hunters; and no doubt the finders would get their pictures in the papers and be invited to appear on television and in the movies, on the principle "To him that hath shall be given." Perhaps this analogy is a slight exaggeration. But it does not miss the mark altogether. For all the great achievements of mankind are manifestations of slow and general processes. The greater the event, the larger is the number of people who are more or less directly concerned in it, and the greater is the difficulty of assigning responsibility to any particular one.

Works of art seem to be an exception to this rule, even more so than scientific discoveries, since a given discovery is often made simultaneously by two or more scientists, whereas no more than one artist can possibly be the creator of any one work of art. It is on this basis that such an authority as Sir Donald Tovey has judged Beethoven to have been "the greatest musician, perhaps the greatest artist, that ever lived." But suppose that Beethoven had died just short of thirty-six, as Mozart did; and suppose that Mozart had lived to be seventy-seven, as Haydn did; and suppose that his powers had continued to develop throughout his life, as those of both Haydn and Beethoven did: who would then be judged the greatest artist? My point is not that Sir Donald Tovey erred in his estimate of Beethoven's greatness but only that his judgment was made after the event. The finding of a diamond would be largely a matter of luck, and so was Mozart's dying of typhoid fever. Meantime Tovey himself remarks of "the immense changes which [Beethoven] brought about in the range of music [and so] in the possibilities of emotional expression. . . ." that they "would . . . almost certainly to some extent have arisen, from sheer necessity of finding expression for the new experience of humanity, if Beethoven had never existed." In short, even in the case of artists it is the event that identifies the individual, not the other way around.

As I have already remarked in a similar connection, this does not mean that our admiration of great men is always and altogether misplaced. Obviously some of us are brighter, and some are stupider, than others; and no less obviously the men whose achievements shine the brightest have been men of unusual powers. But admirable men are not as rare as "great events." There is a logic that is inherent in the cultural process itself by which great events are defined and identified. Their rarity—or apparent rarity—is a function of that process, and their excellence derives not from their rarity but from the process of which they are the periodic consummation.

By the same token amenability to diffusion is an essential determinant of true excellence. Things which can be "appreciated" only by the few are not excellent; they are taboo. The supposition that only the elite can appreciate true excellence is not merely snobbery; it is ceremonialism, pure and simple. Not everyone appreciates the contrapuntal intricacies and subtleties—the amazing fertility of imagination—of Bach's Goldberg Variations. But this is true only because not everybody has studied counterpoint. The significant fact is that virtually anybody could, if he wished, and if his circumstances were such as to make such a wish practicable. Such accessibility is the distinguishing mark of all true values, as it is of the technological process generally.

254

5

So great are the potentialities of mass production that in con-templating the present situation people's minds are liable to be numbed. It is their stupefaction at the scale of modern operations that has raised the bogey of conformity. The inevitable conse-quence, so it is said, of our mass exposure to television, radio broadcasting, colored prints, recorded discs and tapes, and all the rest of our modern apparatus of communication, is bound to be a sort of mass brain-washing by which we are all being reduced to dull conformity.

In recent years conformity has come to be a dirty word. But is conformity inherently bad? Is it bad that we should all conform to the multiplication table? Is it bad that hundreds of millions of people should hear the same language spoken? Let us admit at once that present conditions are unfavorable to the development of local dialects, and even to the preservation of such dialectical peculiarities as have developed in the past. Is this bad? Would it be better if the people of Texas were "free" to develop a language of their own, in consequence of which they might eventually be-come unintelligible to the people of California, and vice versa? If so, the whole course of modern civilization has been bad.

Let us concede at once that the mass-communication industries do assail us with egregious mispronunciations, outrageous sole-cisms, and assorted illiteracies and vulgarities. Nevertheless, the decisive question is, What is the trend? No one could argue that any of these evils had its origin only recently, and that they were all spawned on the premises of RCA and CBS. But do they thrive there? Are they on the increase? Or, to view the problem from another angle, is it true that, what with comics and television, the ability to read is dying out?

Before giving our final answer to such questions, we might do well to inquire whether just such objections as these might not have been brought against printing, and even writing. Might not the bards of Homer's day have taken bitter exception to having the verses, to the memorization of which they had devoted their lives, written down, so that any fool could recite them? It was perhaps the glory of their profession that each vied with all the others in decorating the familiar tales with his own unique figures of speech and other verbal cadenzas, all of which would be lost once the standard text was written down and so reduced to dull conformity. We might also inquire whether the people who now spend their time gazing at television screens were assiduous readers of the classics before they bought their sets, or whether the people who now devour comics ever did read anything more taxing than baseball scores. In the case of the children, who after all constitute the comics' largest public, we know that they did not; and I suspect that such is the case with adult *aficionados*.

All these instrumentalities are vehicles of education. In making this assertion I would not claim that everybody who goes in for comics or pin-ups or hill-billy "music" is thereby undergoing unintended improvement. As we all know, there are a great many elderly children among us. Not all children grow up. But this would be true quite irrespective of the instrumentalities of mass communication. The important point is that for those who are capable of improvement, any exercise of any skill—such as reading, or trying to carry a tune—is improving. Practice may not always make perfect, but it does always make better. Nor do I mean to deprecate criticism. The community should be constantly reminded of how tawdry and jejune is most of the stuff that pours from our mass-production industries. That too is educational, especially when the criticism points the way to better things. But we must not be overborne by our own educational efforts into supposing that all but we are nasty children. There is no evidence of a decline at the top of the scale—that good books find no readers, that good pictures gather dust in empty museums, or that symphony orchestras dwindle away for lack of audiences. In every field precisely the opposite is true.

Moreover, mass communication unquestionably constitutes a powerful stimulus to the highest achievement. For many years music critics have been castigating virtuosi and orchestra conductors for constantly repeating a small repertory of the best-known classics. It is not true that even constant repetition debases. Beethoven's Fifth Symphony is just as glorious today as ever. But it is true that constant repetition whets the appetite for novelty. A half-century ago only the critics, who were paid to attend concerts every night, were subject to that influence. But by grace of radio broadcasting and recordings the whole community is now weary of the "standard repertory" and eager to hear something new. This means that contemporary composers enjoy a sellers' market such as never existed before throughout the entire history of music; and something of the same sort is the case with all the arts. Let us by all means deplore the low level of mass culture; but let us not make the mistake of supposing that the masses have been reduced to this low estate by industrial technology, or that mass production has none but debasing effects.

6

Excellence, of course, is not altogether a matter of beauty or craftsmanship. There is also truth. Throughout all the foregoing chapters I have emphasized the indissociability of technology and science. They are indissociable because each is an aspect of the other. Science is the knowing aspect of technology, and technology is the doing aspect of science. The technological revolution has brought with it, or has been brought about by, an intellectual revolution of which modern science is the outcome. That we know a great deal more than mankind has ever known before is too obvious and incontrovertible to be subject to challenge. Nevertheless, this aspect of modern culture is still subject to disparagement. Thus it is often said today, and by people who have every reason to know better, that for all our modern knowledge industrial society lacks the wisdom of the ancients.

Such disparagement arises from the same sort of cultural nostalgia and outright ancestor worship that motivates all disparagement of the explicitly secular character of modern Western culture. Moreover, the same methodological error of comparing what is commonest in one culture with what is best in another, which I have already cited with reference to things of beauty, is equally prevalent in the realm of truth. Thus an eminent classicist has recently been quoted as declaring that in ancient Greece "the great spiritual forces that war in men's minds flowed along together

in peace; law and freedom, truth and religion, beauty and goodness, the objective and the subjective—there was a truce to their
eternal warfare, and the result was balance and clarity. . . . a
reconciling power, something of calm and serenity, the world
has yet to see again." A comparison of the Hearst press and the
dialogues of Plato would indeed point such a contrast. But if
such a figure as Albert Einstein, or John Dewey, be selected for
purposes of comparison, the contrast is not quite so obvious. Not
all of their contemporaries manifest the calm and serenity, the
balance and clarity, of a Dewey or an Einstein. But the same was
unquestionably true of Plato. The Dialogues properly rank as
one of the Great Books of all time; but they were less widely
read in his day than in ours.

What is wisdom? Is it wholly separate from knowledge? One
of the peculiarities of modern science by which we are liable to
be misled is its seeming fragmentation. Although creative work of
the highest order calls for broad understanding of the nature and
meaning of science as such and of the interrelatedness and interdependence of all branches of science, nevertheless valuable and
significant discoveries can be made, and often have been made,
by scientific journeymen who do not look beyond the confines of
the particular area in which they are working. Moreover, in the
present age of specialization a vast amount of scientific spade
work is done by men who have little thought and less concern for
the cumulative significance of all their digging. Granted that not
everybody who dons a white coat is a master mind: does this
mean that scientific knowledge as such is inchoate, inconsecutive,
and insignificant?

Correctly defined, knowledge and wisdom are the same thing.
When we speak of wisdom, what we have in mind is significant
knowledge, knowledge of all those matters which are relevant to
the question at issue, a view of that question in its broadest possible setting; and when we contrast such "wisdom" with "mere"
knowledge, what we have in mind is an assortment of unrelated
factual information such as may enable a headwaiter or a taxi-
driver to win sixty-four thousand dollars on a television show.
But to take bits and scraps of information, however numerous, as
representative of the accumulated knowledge of Western civiliza-

tion is just as egregious an error as to compare a reader of comic books to Plato. The supposition that Western civilization has won knowledge by the sacrifice of wisdom is sheer nonsense.

In particular, the notion is widely held today, even by people who ought to know better, that our present knowledge of nuclear physics and microbiology has been gained at the expense of neglect of man and society. But the evidence of this supposed neglect is not proof that no efforts in this direction have been, or are being, made. It is rather the fact that men still abuse and persecute each other. By the same reasoning one might argue that the medical sciences have been neglected, since people still die of cancer. If it appears that we know less than we could wish about man and society, there are two very important reasons for this deficiency which should be noted in any sensible discussion of the matter.

One reason is the contingency of our knowledge of man (and all his works) upon other areas of knowledge, some of which have undergone revolutionary change only quite recently. What is man? Up to barely a century ago we had no alternative to supposing that our species is a special creation, endowed by its Creator with semidivine faculties and attributes. It was not until the publication of Darwin's *Origin of Species* that the evolutionary orientation of the human species was possible, and it was not for another generation or two that a cultural explanation of man's amazing capacities and perversities was possible.

Meantime the efforts of self-understanding which have been made by wise and curious men throughout the ages have been blocked, opposed, distorted, and misled by the dense fog banks and glimmering *ignes fatui* of superstition by which their societies have always surrounded such errant inquirers. Indeed, such is still the case. It is not from lack of knowledge that men still abuse and persecute each other; it is from their stubborn retention of beliefs that are demonstrably false. Certainly we need to know a great deal more than we do about man as a species and about the subtleties of culture and the structural intricacies of society. But our trouble is not a unique deficiency of knowledge but the crushing weight of the dead hand of the past and the extraordinary difficulty of extricating ourselves from under it.

There is no basis whatever for the indictment of industrial society on a charge of lack of wisdom. Such a charge can of course be brought against particular individuals today as in all previous ages. But the vast increase in knowledge which industrial society has achieved has not been won at the expense of wisdom, any more than has abundance been achieved at the expense of any other sort of excellence, including individual skill and pride of craft.

7

One of the commonest clichés of modern intellectual snobbery is a lament over the common man's loss of ancient skills and so of ego-sustaining pride of craft. As the lament goes, machinery has robbed the worker of one of the essential ingredients of the good life. One would suppose that superior intelligence, of which this lament is presumably a manifestation, would put people on their guard against such a common chorus of despair. But instead each new lamentation seems to draw its inspiration from the number and apparent distinction of its predecessors. Indeed, it must; for in fact there is no other basis for any such lament.

Just what has been lost? In our nostalgia for the olden days it is easy to fall into the habit of supposing that only a few centuries ago virtually everybody practised the arts of Benvenuto Cellini. But we know quite well that most of Cellini's contemporaries were plodding serfs. Moreover, Cellini is celebrated precisely because he far surpassed the skill of his competitors in the luxury trade. When we think of ordinary tailors and shoemakers as skilled craftsmen whose pride of craft was their dominating passion, we are supposing that virtually all "hand-made" coats and shoes fit better and look better than any machine-made product does today. Otherwise we make the craftsman out to be a fool whose pride was fatuous. But it is quite impossible that such could have been the case. All that we know of human kind points in the opposite direction. The probability is strong that most craftsmen were bunglers whose pride in their work, if any, was indeed fatuous.

Meantime, the supposition that industrial society has suffered a fatal loss assumes a present dearth of skills. But what is the basis for that supposition? Such a proposition can be sustained only if the skills under consideration be limited to those of medieval craftsmen. Few people make shoes today; ergo there has been a net loss of skill. But if we define skills as present-day employers do, it is a statistical fact that throughout modern times unskilled labor has been steadily decreasing relatively to the volume of skilled labor.

The point is that different skills now practised—a very great number and variety of different skills—were unknown and undreamed of only a few decades ago. People who lament the passing of skill sometimes speak of the modern worker as doing nothing but throwing a switch, thereby revealing that they know nothing about switch-throwing. It may be true that the principal skill exercised by a given operative is that of throwing a certain switch; but in that case it is also quite likely that the throwing of that switch is so important, and that knowing when and how to throw it involves such a complete understanding of a whole industrial complex that no one is ever allowed to touch the thing who has not had years of experience in that plant.

Are we then to suppose that the man who throws that switch has no pride of achievement? But that would be not only contrary to human nature as we all know it but contrary to common observation. Much more characteristic of the modern age is the attitude of the hod-carrier who looks up at the towering skyscraper and says. "I built that building!" Doubtless there are industrial workers who have no sense of the significance of what they are doing and so take no pride in it. But that has always been the case. Indeed, it is a carry-over from serfdom rather than a logical consequence of industrial operations. Doubtless the children who were employed to pick the slag out of coal in the early days of modern industry had no pride of achievement. But was their condition a manifestation of past social conditions or an augury of the future?

The more alert managers of modern industrial establishments are well aware of the need of all their employees to understand how their operations mesh with those of the entire plant and affect the whole industrial picture. Pride in the efficiency of the whole establishment, and particularly in the performance of their own particular section of it is by no means unknown today. Obviously not all establishments are conspicuously efficient, and not all managers are alert and progressive. But the significant point is that the operation of large-scale mechanical assemblies does not of itself inhibit natural human feelings or wholesome self-expression.

In this regard, indeed, the complaints of humanitarians have served a useful purpose in making alert managers more aware than ever before of the emotional needs of their employees. The human side of industry has become the subject of a voluminous literature, the ideas of which are sedulously circulated by schools of business and professional industrial counsellors throughout the land. All this may of course be taken as indicative of need; but it must also be credited with meeting the need.

Meantime the steadily lengthening hours of leisure which modern industry has made possible offer to virtually every denizen of industrial society the opportunity to cultivate a hobby, and as everybody knows vast numbers of people are making full use of that opportunity. The do-it-yourself craze is ample evidence of this. So numerous and so widely varied are the alternatives with which modern industrial society presents the potential hobbyist that, as John Maurice Clark has said in *Economic and Human Welfare*, the most enlightened discussion of human welfare yet to come from the pen of an economist, there is no reason why every single member of the community should not be able to excel at something. He may not become world-celebrated. But he can enjoy the satisfaction of accomplishing what he set out to do, and in a world in which such striving is general the chances are good that some of the results will be of superlative excellence.

8

To sum up: none of the features of our present industrial culture justifies complacency. If no other age has ever had a monopoly of excellence, it is equally true that we enjoy no such monopoly today. Each new phase of the industrial revolution brings new problems, and at any given moment it always remains to be seen whether they will be solved. But there is no ground for assuming that failure is inevitable save that of ceremonial commitment to some particular tribal pattern. On the contrary, we have every reason to suppose that we have a better chance than any previous generation has ever had of continuing to improve on the achievements of the past. For guidance we have the accumulated wisdom of the past, and for inspiration whatever of excellence mankind has ever managed to achieve.

If the contemplative life is the highest manifestation of human genius, it must be noted that we have more to contemplate than any previous generation has had at its command. There are some who seem to think that this is bad—that the scale of the industrial culture threatens to exceed our human powers of assimilation. But that is an objection which might just as well have been raised at any previous point in human development, and quite probably was. The story is told that one of the oldest clay tablets unearthed in Mesopotamia records the lament that things were not so in the olden days. What we are now doing is an extrapolation of what mankind has always struggled to achieve. Those who say that it is still not good enough are of course right. Now, as always, greater achievements lie still in the future. But it is also true that we are nearer to the future than any previous generation or culture has ever been.

CHAPTER XVI

THE "MORAL" VALUES

I

THE PRECEDING CHAPTERS HAVE BEEN CONCERNED with what might be called public values. In discussing them I have tried to keep three principal objects in view: (1) to show that all such values are closely interrelated and interdependent; (2) to show that such values derive their common meanings from what I have called, after Veblen, the life process of mankind, in consequence of which their meanings are the same for all peoples; and (3) to show that real values, which (in contrast to the fancies of particular tribal cultures) are common to all mankind, have been more fully realized by industrial society than by any of its predecessors because industrial society manifests the highest development to date of the life process of mankind. In the present chapter I propose to argue briefly that the same is true of the "private" values of "personal" morality.

As I noted at the outset, many well-informed people seem to doubt this, and for obvious reasons. What we call "personal morality" is the medium in which conventional "mores" flourish. The feelings of guilt and shame, by which in varying degree everyone is haunted, almost invariably have their origin in violations of the code of personal behavior. Stealing a silver spoon is a shameful act in a sense that seems not to be true of stealing a railroad. Poisoning one's wife is a mortal sin, whereas poisoning thousands of people by selling adulterated foods or drugs is a mere business misadventure.

So we are apt to think; and yet no one would deny that large-scale rascality is deplorable. Moreover, it is deplorable for the same reason that personal immorality is to be deplored; or rather, the same case can be made for condemning acts of personal immorality that we do in fact make in our condemnation of large-scale rascality: namely, that such acts violate the basic principles of all organized society.

The truth is that ceremonial and technological considerations are mingled in all human affairs. The shame we feel at soiling our clothes of course has its origin in the emotional conditioning to which we were all subjected in childhood; but there are sound hygienic reasons for personal cleanliness. Obviously there are some areas in which ceremonial considerations predominate to the almost total exclusion of technological considerations. Thus Veblen used the phrase "ceremonial cleanliness" to designate situations in which no considerations such as those of hygiene are present. But we must remember that, to the people who practise them, all ceremonial acts have a putative efficiency. Even when the act in question has only the significance of placating evil spirits, the presumption is that the crops may suffer an all-too-actual blight in the event such evil spirits are not placated. Thus for values generally the problem is to distinguish genuine from putative operational efficiency, and the same is true of personal morality. Granted that our notions—and especially our feelings—of personal cleanliness, and of personal decency generally, are still to some extent suffused with superstition: the question is to what extent they do nevertheless reflect the facts of hygiene, medical and social.

2

Lying is sinful. It is a violation of the Commandment: Thou shalt not bear false witness. But veracity is also a foundation principle of all organized society. The vast organizational significance of human speech, to which I have had occasion to refer repeatedly, is entirely contingent upon truthfulness. Moreover, even the mores of primitive peoples reflect this fact. So does the common parental injunction that, whatever they may do otherwise, children must under no circumstances ever lie to their parents. Primitive mores commonly stipulate that truth must be told among the members of the tribe, though deception of non-members is not only tolerated but expected. Obviously such a stipulation not only recognizes the tribe as a working team among whom organizational efficiency must be maintained but also insures the continued exclusion of all others from that team. The common parental injunction is not quite so exclusive, but it does have as its basis the realization that the members of a family must be able to work together in concert, or in effect cease to be a family.

This does not mean that morality is a simple matter. Social organization is not a simple matter. As children grow older they find themselves involved to a steadily increasing degree in situations which imperatively require concealment of the truth and even outright deception. They learn never to contradict a teacher and always to assure a hostess that they have enjoyed her party. In much the same fashion societies grow in size and complexity, and their communicational necessities grow accordingly. Thus the exigencies of mass production for mass markets make it necessary that all drugs shall be plainly and truly labelled. At the same time tribal limits still persist. Thus a punning aphorism defines an ambassador as "one who is sent to lie abroad for his country." In short, the simple personal morality of truth-telling is a projection of the technical necessities of organized societies, and hence no clear line can be drawn between the values of individual character and those of society at large.

This is true of all virtues and vices. Sobriety is such a virtue. But it is so, as I have already noted in an earlier chapter, for the reason that is most succinctly stated in the categorical imperative of the motor age: If you drink, don't drive; if you drive, don't drink. Here is the truth that is so ill-defined in the age-old maxim, moderation in all things. What defines moderation? The answer is, the other activities in which men engage. Should a cook use prussic acid in moderation? There is nothing inherently immoral in either prussic acid or alcohol, nor is there any absolute measure of moderation. Is knowledge desirable in moderation? If so, then Alexander Pope was wrong.

3

In every case the simple virtues prove on examination to be simplifications of the technical necessities of organization. This is even true of sexual continence. I venture into this area because more than any other it is commonly held to be synonymous with personal morality. Whenever anyone is described as immoral without further qualifications, everybody understands that reference is made to his sexual behavior. The reasons for this are obvious: sex is a more or less continuous preoccupation of all members of the human race throughout life; more than any other aspect of life sex is a focal point of mores, myth, and magic; while at the same time the smooth operation of all the complex activities by performance of which human beings live in organized communities is continually threatened by perpetually incipient sexual interests.

So obsessive are sexual mores that in dealing with this topic even modern scholarship has been able to think of very little else. The reasons for this, too, are obvious. Sexual activity is fraught with violent emotions both of attraction and repulsion—virtual seizures which strongly suggest the influence of mysterious forces. This is true of the exercise of "will power," by which "self-control" is thought to be achieved, no less than of the mysteries of "affinity." At the same time sex is a phase of that greatest of all mysteries, the creation of life. Given the power to imagine any mystery or to make any magic, it surely was inevitable that mankind should have made a mystery of sex, and should have surrounded it with the sternest of taboos. Moreover, as a consequence of this it is inevitable that the most obsessive feelings of guilt and shame should therefore result, and should provide psychiatry with its principal field of operations.

But if we could somehow manage to view the phenomena of sex without emotion as manifestations of natural processes, it would still be true that in the absence of some sort of control or organization these processes would intrude upon, interrupt, confuse, and nullify all the other organized activities by which we live. It is not only Mrs. Grundy who makes war on sex. Modern industrial management does so, but in a totally different spirit. Wherever men and women work together, and especially wherever men have supervisory control over work forces of women, it is the standard policy of management to forbid such male supervisors to make free with the women under their working control, and again for obvious reasons. These reasons do not include the "morals" of either the men or the women. Management is usually quite candid in disavowing any interest in the chastity or continence of either. All they are concerned about is the operating efficiency of the plant.

But what is true of any plant is likewise true of industrial society as a whole. The preoccupations of sex work at cross purposes with all other activities; and the more highly organized those other activities are, the more serious the problem becomes. A great deal of nonsense has been written about the idyllic sex life of various simple peoples—Pacific islanders and the like—by writers who seem never to have considered that what can happen under a palm tree might not be entirely appropriate to the New York subway. It is all very well to cry out against routine in "matters of the heart." The fact remains that routine—that is to say, organization—is what has made modern civilization possible. One might even say it is what distinguishes mankind from the lower animals. Their sex life too is idyllic in the sense of being free from all sense of guilt or shame, since it conflicts with nothing, neither mores nor workmanship.

Given a way of life that is as highly organized as that of industrial society, some sort of regularization of sex relations is absolutely essential, for reasons that have only an indirect relation to the mythology that sustains taboos. (I say indirect by way of noting, as always, that all taboos are putatively operational.) It may be that, if a commission of efficiency experts were given the task of devising a system of sex behavior that would comport with the organizational necessities of industrial society, what they would come up with would differ from the prevailing "system" in various respects. But it would almost certainly not be entirely different. Almost certainly its guiding principle would be a regularization of sexual relations.

4

Would such a regularization be "moral"? Doubtless many would say No. They would do so in the same spirit in which moralists sometimes declare that being honest because honesty is the best policy is mere expediency, and as such a travesty of righteousness. Such a rejection of "mere expediency" can mean only one of two things. It can mean that in the opinion of those who hold this view only the mores can be the basis of true morality. But this position is only one of words. We can, of course, agree to restrict the use of the word "morality" to irrational conformity to tradition. But in doing so we cannot deny that considerations of expediency (as we have agreed to call them) play a very important part in life—far more important, indeed, than those we have agreed to call morality.

The only other ground on which it is possible to condemn being honest because honesty is the best policy involves a misunderstanding with regard to the meaning of "best policy." If that maxim is taken to mean only that a reputation for honesty will be advantageous to the exemplar, perhaps as a preliminary to some climactic dishonesty like that of the villain in *Toilers of the Sea*, such a meaning of course deserves our scorn. But is that the only sense, or the really important sense, in which honesty is the best policy? Is it not just as true of honesty as it is of veracity that efficient organization is impossible on any other basis? Honesty is the best policy for individuals—not intermittent, but continuous, reliable honesty—because it is the best policy for societies. This is not "mere" expediency; it is the expediency which is synonymous with effective organization; and if that is not morality, then morality is less important than we had supposed.

The same things are true of the intimate, personal values of "private" life that are true of the ideals to which societies dedicate themselves. All values are fraught with emotion, and all values have their traditional, tribal aspects; and since the "personal" virtues and vices are those which are so identified for us in childhood, that being why we think of them as personal, they are the values we identify most insistently with our tribal mores by reason of the emotional conditioning through which tribal mores are transmitted. But it is also true that the effective working relationships which constitute the life process of mankind spell out values which thus derive not from our sentiments but from our necessities, and this likewise is just as true of the values that prevail in intimate personal relationships as of those which pertain to whole societies. The truth is that honesty, decency, and veracity are not only the best policy but the only policy in terms of which human beings can work together to live better than the animals.

PART FIVE

CHAPTER XVII

THE INDUSTRIAL WAY OF LIFE

I

WITHIN THE LAST FEW DECADES an extraordinary development has occurred in Western civilization, and especially in the United States. It has become common practice for people of all cultural levels to identify all they hold most dear as a "way of life."

In the United States, where this expression is in commonest use, it usually takes the form of "the American way of life"; and yet, notwithstanding the apparent egotism of that expression, it is never intended to imply exclusiveness. On the contrary, the presumption is that what we have others might have; and not only would they be better off for having, or achieving, such a way of life as ours, but we too would be better off if others throughout the world were to share our way of life. We call it "ours" only because it is ours, but we claim no monopoly. What other peoples find most disagreeable in our national character is not exclusiveness but rather the brashness of our missionary zeal. To all the rest of the world we seem always to be saying, "Do as we do, and you will be healthy, wealthy, and wise!"

One of the most significant features of this development is its anonymity. Who originated this expression? I have been quite unable to find out, and in any case it makes no difference. Whoever it was who first spoke of Western civilization, or its American variant, as a way of life, it has not been his authority that has brought this expression into general circulation. That has been a matter of common usage—the spontaneous and general adoption of a phrase which has only to be heard to be recognized as pat. Ours is indeed a way of life. We call it that simply because that is what it is. That is, we have somehow come to recognize our civilization (and by implication, all civilization) as a process, a doing, an operating procedure—a way of life.

273

This is perhaps the most extraordinary development of modern times. For if we look back upon the history of mankind we see that throughout the past men have always idealized not processes but states of being, commonly personified as Beings. We even know why that has been the case. Although the knowledge is fairly recent, we know that cultural egotism is an inevitable accompaniment of the process of indoctrination by which all cultures are perpetuated. It is impossible for any people to bring up their young in the way they should go without imbuing them with the conviction that the prescribed ways of doing things are right, and all others are wrong; and this necessarily means that in their own esteem the people in question are in some sense or other the Chosen People. This sense of their uniqueness is objectified in a tribal totem or tutelary deity. Thus the dedication of the present Western community to a way of life represents a break with traditions by which mankind has been bound throughout the past.

2

This break is all the more significant for having been largely unconscious. It does not represent any deliberate decision, but is rather a consequence of forces or circumstances the effects of which have been felt and gradually realized by the entire community. These circumstances range over the entire cultural spectrum. A complete account of them would necessarily involve all aspects of Western life. But viewed in terms of the consequences, two features stand out in bold relief.

One is the fact of change. As we now realize, all cultures are subject to change. But in the past change has always been so slow that the peoples affected have been almost completely unaware of it. Even the vast cultural mutation, as one American anthropologist has called it, which resulted from the discovery or invention of agriculture and was consummated in the great city civilizations of the ancient world, occupied some thousands of years. In the perspective of the hundreds of thousands of years of human experience—the perspective in which we now view it—this mutation appears as a sudden break. But such change as occurred within the life-span of any one generation of people was so slight that in their apprehension it was virtually imperceptible. Indeed, even in the earlier centuries of the modern period, when as we now realize changes of unprecedented magnitude were occurring at an unprecedented rate, the people who actually experienced those changes could still regard them as matters of detail in what on the whole still seemed to be a stable and unchanging world. Even as recently as "The Industrial Revolution of the Eighteenth Century in England" the wisest and best-informed living witnesses of what we now recognize as earth-shaking events—such, for example, as Adam Smith—were entirely unaware of the significance of what was going on before their eyes. Indeed, I have capitalized and quoted the name of this now-familiar event because these phrases formed the title of the celebrated lectures in which the elder Arnold Toynbee first expounded the significance of the industrial revolution, in the early 1880's—roughly a century after the event.

Our present situation is quite different. The changes which have occurred at a constantly accelerating rate during the past half-century have been so general that every literate member of the present Western community (not to mention the rest of the world) is now well aware that he lives in a rapidly and profoundly changing society. This does not mean that the processes which make for change are fully understood. On the contrary various false notions prevail, for reasons to which I will return shortly. But in spite of all limitations the general awareness of past, current, and probable future change does induce a vivid sense of process. Sir Henry Maine described the evolution of modern institutions in a celebrated aphorism as a shift "from status to contract." In the same spirit the idealization of our way of life might be said to represent a shift from status to process.

3

Another set of circumstances has had even more significant effects. The difference between status and process is not only a matter of fluidity. To pursue this figure, our whole conception of the nature of the universe is altered when we come to realize that the solid earth beneath our feet is not solid in any absolute and eternal sense, that with a change in temperature the solidest rock may be liquefied or even vaporized. A fluid society is not a static one that has been set in motion. It is utterly different, as different as the modern conception of the universe is different from that of bygone ages.

The fact is that the whole outlook of the modern mind has undergone a qualitative change. A way of life is a secular conception, and its occurrence gives expression to the process of secularization that has been going on at a steadily accelerating rate in all aspects of modern culture. Earlier generations and earlier societies all conceived their way of life to have been decreed by Higher Powers. They did so not only because their arrangements were relatively durable but most especially because they seemed to share the seemingly ineffable and mysterious durability of the universe itself. It was this conjunction—the oneness of man and nature, if you like—to which earlier peoples gave expression by personifying their way of life, which was thus conceived to owe its stable character to the steadfastness of the Higher Power in whom it was personified.

All this has changed, so much so that it is difficult for the modern mind to assume the posture of animism. We commonly say that animism is the imputation of animate qualities to inanimate nature. But primitive animism misconceives man just as completely as it does inanimate nature. Both are conceived by the superstitious mind as being the playground of supernatural forces, the starry heavens above no less than the moral law within—but, by the same token, the moral law within no less than the starry heavens above. Whatever may be the causes of the mysticizing to which mankind has been so conspicuously prone throughout the ages, it must be taken for granted that so long as that state of mind persists human society itself will be so conceived. So conceived, the way of life of any given people is not merely static; it is conceived to be fixed in the familiar pattern by the will of some tutelary deity.

In contrast to all this, the way of life is a naturalistic conception. Not only does it register the fact of change as a recognized feature of human affairs; it also signalizes the secularization of Western culture as a whole, and in doing so it focuses directly upon the central feature and most distinctive characteristic of Western civilization. That the true spirit of modern Western civilization should thus have been caught by an anonymous phrase that owes its general acceptance to nothing but common usage is itself highly significant. For the process itself has come about in precisely that fashion.

In considering this process our thoughts turn naturally to science. But in thinking of science as the torchbearer of secular culture we are liable to overlook the intimate relationship between the intellectual discipline we call "science" and the skills and operations, materials and apparatus, of what we now call "industry." These two are indissociable. Indeed, it is a great misfortune that common usage provides us with no word that covers both aspects of this single process. There are words which are capable of being stretched so as to serve this purpose. But so strong are the associations of common usage that any such word is liable to misinterpretation by the vast majority to whom it has only the common meaning. For many years John Dewey used the word *instrumental* in this broad sense, seeking thereby to identify the intellectual procedures of science with the use of instruments and at the same time to identify the instruments of scientists with the tools which are in still wider use by artisans and craftsmen. But many scientists and nearly all of those who philosophize about science like to think of science as the exercise of pure reason, to which the instrumental procedures of laboratories and observatories play a secondary part, that of verifying flights of "pure, creative imagination." Meantime, neither scientists nor craftsmen think of ordinary tools as being "instruments" in the scientific sense. Thus Dewey's instrumental logic fell between two stools.

Following Veblen, I have used the word *technology* in the attempt to bridge this extraordinary linguistic gap; and in one of his last articles Dewey remarked that he had become convinced that it is the better term, one that is not subject to the misconceptions which have so tragically dogged his *instrumentalism*. But he was wrong. The word *technology* is so widely used in a deprecatory sense, to refer to the commonest and meanest skills, that most people can see no connection between what they identify as "mere" technology and the higher achievements of the human spirit. To them the word *technology* has reference only to such physical apparatus as has become so common that it seems to them a part of the natural environment of modern man, external to his culture. I have done my best to state explicitly and repeatedly that I am using the word in the broadest possible sense to refer to that whole aspect of human experience and activity which some logicians call operational, and to the entire complement of artifacts with which mankind operates. So defined, technology includes mathematical journals and symphonic scores no less than skyscrapers and assembly lines, since all these are equally the product of human hands as well as brains.

In this broader sense it should be clear that the secularization which Western culture has undergone in modern times is a consequence, or expression, or reflection, not only of science but of the whole technological process of which science is the intellectual aspect. I realize, of course, that in identifying ours as the industrial way of life I am risking misunderstanding by people who read the title but not the text. Nevertheless I take this risk in order to throw the emphasis in the other direction. Most people are well aware today that modern industry could not have come into existence and would not continue to expand but for science. What is equally true but not so widely appreciated is the reverse. Modern science could not possibly have come into existence except in conjunction with what we call industrial technology. All the achievements of the creative scientific imagination have been projections of industrial skills, conceptualizations of the progressively cunning tools by use of which the everyday living of mankind has been revolutionized.

Moreover, it is the industrial way of life that validates science. The universal acceptance of the truths of science has sometimes been cited as evidence of the gullibility of modern man. According to this view, science is a cult which, no less than any other cult, must be accepted on faith. Farfetched as it is, there is an element of truth in this interpretation. All superstitions, as we have seen earlier, owe their acceptance ultimately to their apparent operational efficiency. No doubt rain did eventually fall in Thebes, thereby confirming the Thebans in their belief that the drought they had suffered was due to Oedipus' violation of the incest taboo. The decisive difference between science and superstition is that the operational efficiency of scientific "beliefs" is rather more apparent than that of other "cults." It is in industry that the substantial truth of science is made manifest, today as throughout human history. To doubt the validity of science is virtually to doubt the existence of industry. Obviously the common man does not understand all the subtleties of science. Indeed, no one man understands them all. But everybody can see what comes of acting on such "beliefs."

For these reasons it does not seem amiss to think of our way of life as the industrial way. As we are beginning to understand, it came about through the agency of a vast technological revolution, the effects of which have been felt in all aspects of modern life. Consequently it should go without saying that all these changes are related. In all, the progression has been from the sacred to the secular, from authority to efficiency, from status to process.

4

That process is manifest in every aspect of modern culture. But there are three—religious, economic, and political—in which related developments of major significance have been taking place.

For many years now scholars have been discussing the relation between church history and economic history. As everyone knows, striking changes occurred in each of these areas in early modern times, changes so striking and so nearly simultaneous that some sort of connection between them is strongly indicated. The question is, What was the connection? Did one of these changes bring about the other? Or were both manifestations of some deeper process? Unfortunately, the attempt to resolve this problem has been complicated by premature definitions. On one side, ecclesiastical change has seemed to be epitomized in what has been known for centuries as the Protestant Reformation. The characterization of the economic change has come about much more recently. It was only after Karl Marx had applied the epithet "capitalism" to the modern economy that scholars, accrediting this characterization, began to inquire into the origins of capitalism and so to raise the question whether what they now called capitalism did not owe its inception in important degree to the Protestant Reformation.

In a sense the answer must be, Of course it did. But the question is, In what sense? As I have already suggested (and as everybody knows) one of the principal features of the Protestant Reformation was greatly increased emphasis upon the individual conscience, and one of the principal features of what is called "capitalism" is likewise the greatly increased importance of private (that is, individual) ownership and individual enterprise. So far, what we seem to find is evidence of a common process running through both changes. Is the kinship any closer?

Some scholars have argued that it is. But their argument exaggerates the importance of money-making both for the economy and for the church. The most significant change which the Christian religion (in all its variant manifestations) has undergone throughout modern times is a shift of focus from salvation hereafter to good works here and now, good not merely in the ceremonial sense of prayer and fasting, but good in the here-and-now sense implied in the phrase "good work." Moreover, as industry and thrift came to be recognized as Christian virtues, inevitably the Christian conscience adjusted itself to the rewards of industry and thrift—to the accumulation of capital. In this sense Christianity and capitalism have proved not altogether incompatible.

But this does not mean that Christian doctrine gave rise to the ideology of capitalism, or even that the compatibility of the Christian church and the institutions of capitalism is particularly significant. What is presumed to lend significance to this relationship is the central dogma of capitalism, namely, the belief that money-making has been the prime mover of the vast technological revolution by which Western civilization has been transformed, the thesis that trade is primary, industry secondary and derivative. As Adam Smith put it, the division of labor is limited by the width of the market. This is the major premise of the whole classical theory of the economy. Even the elder Toynbee, though he was the first to sense the magnitude and the significance of the industrial revolution of the eighteenth century, attributed that whole development to the free market. It was this state of mind, objectified as it was in the institutions of his time, that prompted Karl Marx to identify the prevailing economy as capitalism; and it was of course this dogma that prompted scholars of the past half-century to trace the roots of capitalism to the subsoil of Christian doctrine.

To argue that industry is antecedent to trade, as I have done, is not to argue against trade. But that view of the matter does put the mutual relations of ecclesiastical and economic change in a different perspective. Doubtless it is true that the amenability of all Western institutions to change has been a necessary condition of the great transformation, and doubtless it is significant that such amenability has been manifest in ecclesiastical as well as economic institutions. But this does not establish either as the sufficient cause of the entire transformation. What it does suggest is a deeper process underlying both. Ours is an industrial economy, and it is so primarily because of a cumulative process of invention and discovery that has been going on actively in Western civilization for at least five centuries and incipiently for several centuries more. True, the process has been let go. Endemic in all cultures, it has become epidemic in ours, in significant part because of the institutional adolescence of the wandering barbarian tribes who were the ancestors of the European peoples.

It is that deeper process which now finds expression in the industrial way of life. Much has been written in recent decades of the making of the modern mind, and the significance of that intellectual process cannot be overestimated. But even more significant is the coincidence of the building of science and the building of industry. Both manifest a progressive abandonment of what might be called the life of fancy and a progressive commitment to the realities of a life of doing and making. It is that deeper and broader coincidence that was manifest in the coincidence of the Protestant Reformation and the rise of capitalism. For neither of those events was terminal. On the contrary, each gave dramatic evidence of what in each case was a continuing process—a single process of which we are only now becoming more fully aware.

5

Moreover, the same is true of the political development of the Western peoples. Ours is a democratic society. More than any other word, *democracy* has come to stand for the ideals and aspirations of the Western peoples, if not of all mankind. There are various reasons for this. One is the inclusiveness of the idea of democracy. In idealizing democracy we do not cherish freedom any the less, nor equality, nor human brotherhood. The point is rather that democracy embraces all of these, and more.

Secondly, democracy is a positive concept. Other values are haunted by a certain negativity. Freedom is freedom *from* domination by others; equality is *absence* of arbitrary distinctions; even abundance is "freedom *from* want." Granted that negative conceptions such as these fail to tell the whole story. Values such as freedom and equality are in the truest sense affirmative, and that is certainly the case with such values as abundance. Indeed, it is only when they are so conceived that they are fully understood. Nevertheless we have sought these values negatively, through the effort to escape contrary evils. But democracy is not merely an escape from tyranny. It is the enthronement, so to speak, of a new sovereign: the people.

Democracy is of the people, by the people, for the people. Its meaning is essentially that of an affirmation: "The People, Yes!" It is therefore the essence of humanism. Throughout the ages humanists have all agreed that the value and significance of human life are to be found in human life itself—that what is most precious in life is life itself. This is no mere zoological conception. What is precious is not protoplasm, nor the mere zoological proliferation of the species. It is in the life of the human species that values arise—all values, in a mutually intensifying system of concerted values. Thus the highest aspiration of mankind is for the fullest possible realization of all the potentialities of the human mind and character. All this democracy affirms.

But a third and consummatory reason for the store we set by democracy is its organizational significance. Democracy stands for the procedure by which alone all the other values can be achieved. In order to be free and equal a people must acknowledge no other sovereign, and the same is true of security and even abundance. Only people who know no master can be affluent and secure in the enjoyment of their affluence. Democracy is an operational concept. It is the technique of self-government, and therefore of self-realization. It is inconceivable except in terms of the apparatus of the ballot box and of parliamentary procedure. Thus it is in its very essence technological. That is why it is so all-inclusive and so affirmative. It is the mode of affirmation, so to speak, of all other values. Hence it is continually liable to the same misunderstanding that dogs the technological process itself.

Just as technology is commonly misconceived as "mere" apparatus, so democracy also is commonly misconceived as being "merely" the apparatus of majority rule. It is that, of course, just as technology is; but like technology itself, it is not "merely" that. If democracy were nothing more than the rule of the majority, and if its appurtenances were merely the apparatus by which majorities asserted their dominance, democracy might have been the cruelest and most oppressive tyranny ever concocted. There is nothing particularly admirable about a majority. Indeed, it is this misconception that has given rise to the bitterest cynicisms with regard to majority rule.

The essence of democracy is not the fact of majority rule, but rather the process by which majorities are formed. It is notorious that the highest degree of unanimity prevails in those societies which are most tightly gripped by tribal superstition. Voting has democratic significance only to the degree that it registers the free choices of an informed electorate. This means not only that the voters must be free on election day. Even more important is their freedom at all times from the bugaboos of prejudice and superstition and the paralysis of ignorance. Obviously this is a matter of degree. No community is ever wholly free from the dead hand of the past, and no human being is ever wholly free from prejudice—wholly unaffected by the sort of emotional conditioning that has characterized our tribal past. Modern civilization is cluttered with "residues," as Pareto called them, of past ceremonialism. Nevertheless a process of liberation and enlightenment has been going on with cumulative effect for several centuries, a process of which democracy is the political manifestation, as are all the manifestations of industrial-scientific culture. The self-government of peoples is a possibility only because it is possible for large numbers of people—in effect, whole communities—to arrive at common conclusions.

Short-sighted and cynical observers have often sought to dis-

283

parage the democratic process by pointing out the propensity of opposing political parties for adopting each other's programs. This
does actually happen in all genuinely democratic communities.
Thus, for example, in Great Britain the essential features of the
"welfare state," enacted by a Labor Government in the face of bitter Conservative opposition, are accepted and continued by a subsequent Conservative Government. Meantime the same thing happens in the United States with regard to the essential features of
the "New Deal." The history of democracies is full of such instances. The American Republican Party, once the sponsor of high
"protective" tariffs, now strongly advocates reciprocity in the low-
ering of tariffs. Meantime the Democratic Party, once the staunch
defender of "states' rights," now appears as the advocate of strong
central government, while a Republican administration proposes
"returning" to the states the "sovereignty" they are presumed to
have lost.

But is this sort of thing to be taken as evidence of the sense-
lessness of mob rule? Or is it a manifestation of the process by
which whole peoples arrive at virtual unanimity? And if the latter
is the case, wherein does such unanimity differ from that of super-
stition-ridden savages? In effect this entire book is an attempt to
answer these very questions; but let me repeat.

There are two kinds of unanimity. One is produced by emotional conditioning and is therefore limited to the particular community to whose beliefs and practices the members of the community have been emotionally conditioned. The other derives from
the uniformities of nature, as manifest in the uniform behavior
of the tools and materials with which all peoples operate, and is
therefore the same for all peoples and all ages. Democracy is not
merely a transfer of authority from a divinely-hedged king to a
"sovereign" people. The "sovereignty" of a people cannot possibly have the same meaning as that of a king. Whereas in the concept of kingship-by-divine-right considerations of tradition-grounded authenticity are paramount, in democracy considerations of
operational efficiency are paramount.

The confusion that is so often manifest in the democratic process is the confusion of learning. Conditions change, and it is not
immediately apparent to anybody—certainly not to all—in what

direction operational efficiency lies. In all such cases as those I have just mentioned, that is what is going on. It is useless to fulminate about "states' rights" and "local autonomy" where air traffic is concerned; and indeed nobody does, since everybody can see that local authority is utterly incapable of regulating air traffic. For a county sheriff to attempt to regulate the movements of transcontinental planes would be like trying to dig the Panama Canal with a spoon. Such a case is easy. The really troublesome cases are those in which we are gradually and painfully learning that long established practices, such as those of racial segregation, are based on ancient tribal beliefs (and all the emotional conditioning that goes with such beliefs) that are contrary to fact, and also that the practices in question run contrary to the major premise of operational efficiency. Nevertheless, in all such cases the democratic process is a process of learning the truth and operating accordingly, and the unanimity towards which the process aims is that of the universality of science and technology.

The democratic process is an aspect of that broader and more general cultural process which defines our way of life. In putting the matter in this way I do not mean to overlook the fact that dedicated men have fought and bled and given their very lives in defense of the democratic ideals to which they were dedicated, nor do I mean to depreciate such heroism. On the contrary, it is of the highest importance that such is the case, and I shall therefore return to this issue very shortly. But first it is necessary to emphasize the cultural significance of the democratic ideals for which men have fought and died.

6

In identifying the struggle for democracy with the progressive liberalization of Christianity and even with the emergence of an industrial economy as aspects of a vast process of secularization through which our whole culture has been passing, I have not meant to suggest that the consummation of this process is in any sense inevitable. Nothing is inevitable. That process may still be terminated and mankind may relapse into savagery, perhaps through self-destruction by nuclear warfare. Nevertheless, the process through which modern Western civilization has come into existence is a cultural process. As such it transcends the life and character—the mental compass, the ideals, and aspirations—not only of any individual but of any nation or any single generation of people.

I emphasize this point because men of great learning and intellectual influence seem recently to have been asserting the contrary. Thus Arnold Toynbee, the celebrated author of *A Study of History* (nephew of the historian of the industrial revolution), has declared that modern Western man has lost his religion and in its absence has taken to worshipping himself, and that the consequence of this travesty is bound to be the collapse of Western civilization unless a new religion can be found or created. This judgment is especially significant coming as it does from one who has devoted his life to the study of the historical processes by which, it seems, the great civilizations of the past have risen and fallen.

But what does it mean, to say that man worships himself? Such a pronouncement raises two major questions, one with regard to the meaning of worship, and one with regard to its object. As regards the former there seems to be little difficulty. Although we do use the word *worship* in metaphorical and even frivolous connotations, as when we say "He just worships her," or "He just worships that car," surely everybody is clearly aware that such "worship" is not literal. In using the word literally everybody always has reference to ceremonial acts such as prayer, sacrifice, hymn singing, and the like. In this sense it is ridiculously false and misleading to say that modern man worships himself. Nothing of the sort occurs, anywhere, or at any time.

The other question is more serious. There is such a thing as self-love, and it is quite generally recognized as a dangerous state of mind, for individuals and also for groups. "Mutual admiration societies" are not only far from admirable. Since by common understanding such closed-circle admiration is founded on fatuity rather than fact, it is also extremely dangerous to the participants, as is all behavior that is founded on fancy rather than fact. Is this the state of mind into which we have been betrayed by the secularization of Western culture?

At this point we should try to make a clear distinction between secularism and complacency. Complacency is one of the dangers that attend success. Certainly it is a danger to which by its very successes Western civilization is exposed. There is a common saying about the self-made man that he worships his creator, and this may be the state of mind which critics such as Toynbee impute to the whole Western community. But if so, we must be careful not to exaggerate. In the first place, as I have said, such complacency has nothing to do with real worship; and in the second place, what has betrayed us (insofar as anything has) into complacency is not our secularism but our success.

Fortunately for our mental health, our success is by no means complete. On the contrary, we are more keenly aware of its limitations than any previous society has ever been, and this is true in whatever direction we look. Though our knowledge of the natural universe and of ourselves as a part of it is far greater than any previous generation has possessed, we have learned that every answer raises a dozen questions the answers to which are still to be discovered. We have achieved a degree of abundance far in excess of anything that has ever been known before; but, as an eminent economist has only recently pointed out, we are just beginning to recognize ourselves as *The Affluent Society* and have yet to learn how to make the best of our affluence. Meantime the spread of industrialism to other parts of the world is creating a situation the outcome of which, for ourselves as well as for others, no one can foresee. Granted that complacency is the penalty of success, it is by no means certain that we are doomed to succumb to it.

But in any case that is not the issue. The warnings of critics such as Toynbee have to do not with the dangers of success but with the purported loss we have suffered in the process of secularization. These critics, including even Toynbee, are extraordinarily vague at this point. They talk much of loss of faith, but are extraordinarily vague as to what sort of faith it is that a society cannot live without. Granted that mankind must have faith in what the great Danish philosopher, Harald Höffding, called "the conservation of value"; granted also that inspiration comes only from faith in what Matthew Arnold called "some power, not ourselves, that makes for righteousness": the vital question is, Must that power transcend the natural universe? To be effective must faith be the schoolboy's belief "in things you know ain't so"? Our critics do not say so. Indeed, they imply the opposite; and in doing so they abandon the only ground on which it is possible to pronounce the doom of industrial society.

7

For the truth is that we do owe our way of life to a power not ourselves that makes for righteousness, as mankind has always done. That power is culture. It is not ourselves in a very real and definite sense. Not only is its existence independent of that of any particular individual; it is independent of his entire generation. For when any one of us lays down the torch, others pick it up and carry it on. Indeed, when a whole society lays down the torch—or has the torch snatched from its hands—another takes it over and carries it on. This is an aspect of the human way of life which Toynbee has underemphasized. In his concern to try to understand the rise and fall of particular societies—a perfectly legitimate concern, and one·of great importance to any particular society, such as our own—he has nevertheless de-emphasized the most conspicuous and significant fact of all: namely, that each successive community takes over and carries on from the point at which its predecessor faltered.

Note that I do not suggest that Arnold Toynbee, or anybody else, is unaware of this. Everybody is aware of it, and always has been, even the illiterate savages of the Old Stone Age. It is perfectly evident, even to the simplest primitive, that every human infant learns to talk from association with the older members of his community, and that all the skills and arts of his society are acquired in precisely the same way. So are all the taboos and superstitions of his people. Indeed, the flow of culture from generation to generation down the ages is the supreme mystery of human life. I call it a mystery because it has seemed so to countless generations. In an earlier chapter I have even ventured to suggest that this "mystery" may have been the *fons et origo* of all mystery-making. It was indeed the power of speech and the related power of organized and cooperative action that enabled mankind to rise above the animals; and to our ancestors who did not understand this power, it must have seemed to be a magic potency, one which set their minds, so to speak, on the channel of mystery-making. To us it is a mystery no longer. But the force of culture is no less, just as the force of gravitation is no less, for being a feature of the natural universe. In a very real sense culture, no less than gravitation, is a power not ourselves. It is an aspect of nature.

Nor is it therefore any less a force that makes for righteousness. This is true with regard to the fancied values to which each different culture conditions its community. But it is no less true of the genuine values which are common to all. The discovery that values are culture-borne—that men prize and abhor what they have been taught to prize and abhor—is one of the great intellectual achievements of modern times. Indeed, that discovery is so significant that we have been quite generally misled by it. Because the discovery was first made, or first won general acceptance, in the area of ceremonial values and emotional conditioning—or perhaps, as I have tried to indicate, because such value-preferences have always seemed most "natural" and in-born—the impression has been created and has gained general acceptance especially among intellectuals that such values are the only values: that that is what values are. I suspect that Arnold Toynbee and his compeers who fear that our society may be heading toward moral bankruptcy are suffering from this myopia. But surely clear and certain knowledge is culturally transmitted and culturally accumulated, no less than supernatural fancies; and surely all those philosophers who, throughout the ages, have tried to show us that truth and goodness are related have not been altogether wrong! If we have to thank a cultural power that transcends our little lives for the prejudices and illusions by which we are afflicted, we are no less indebted to that transcendent power for the clear and certain knowledge and the operational achievements by which we live; and we know them to be good since we judge them by a criterion which is inherent in that power itself.

All this is why men are willing to give their lives in defense of their way of life. It is quite true, now as always, that men can be aroused to the highest pitch of emotional dedication only by causes that transcend their individual interests and even their immediate community advantage. But this does not mean that the causes by which men are inspired to the highest efforts and greatest sacrifices are entirely irrelevant to their individual interests. Men have always fought for the gods of whom they have conceived themselves to be the chosen people. In this sense, dedication to a way of life is a manifestation of the same emotional dynamism by which men have been inspired throughout the ages. In all cases it is not merely the transcendence of the common cause that makes it effective. It would be ridiculous to suppose that men can be inspired by an anthropological theory of culture; but it would be equally ridiculous to suppose that men have been inspired in the past by cosmological theories of the origin of the earth. What has inspired them has been a vision that gave meaning to their own community existence and gave promise of an assured future not just for any one of them but for all, and for their children and their children's children.

8

Such is the significance of the industrial way of life for modern man. What is at issue is a matter of principle. Does that principle lack force by virtue of being true? Apparently there are some who think it does. At all events much talk today is to the effect that modern man has lost his way in consequence of having lost his sense of the meaning and purpose of life. Ours is said to be a "beat generation," just as that of the nineteen-twenties was a "lost generation," and its most significant manifestation is "existentialism"—a sort of know-nothingism the upshot of which is, "We're here, because we're here, because we're here, because we're here."

There are two answers to this line of thought, either one of which should be sufficient. One is empirical and obvious. Nothing could be more obvious than the fact that modern man is not lacking in spirit and devotion. In one sense it is very odd that people should suppose the contrary immediately after the conclusion of a war in which millions have made what we all call the supreme sacrifice; but in another sense it is quite natural. It is natural that a supreme effort should be followed by a letdown. It is also natural that a defeated people should feel that all civilization is collapsing. The French have taken up existentialism for the same reason that, in the nineteen-twenties, the Germans took up Spengler's theory of the collapse of Western civilization. (The Germans have rebounded from their recent defeat because for most of them it has meant an awakening from the nightmare of the nineteen-thirties.) Meantime the "beat generation" consists of a handful of "free spirits" who are so far from being lost that they are determined to lead the rest of us out of our spiritual no-man's-land, just as the "lost generation" consisted of a handful of cultural expatriates in Paris who went on to win Nobel prizes and found a "new school" of American culture. Are these people evidence of the bankruptcy of Western civilization, or of its vitality? Quite irrespective of their feelings at the moment, they will unquestionably go down in history as evidence of our cultural vitality.

The other answer to the supposition that modern man has lost his way is a matter of common knowledge. Modern man has more knowledge—clearer and more certain knowledge—of what his existence means than any previous generation has had, and for obvious reasons. Man has come a long way, far longer than any previous generation has realized, since his ancestors began tending "sacred" fires; and his achievements have been so great as to suggest the exercise of magical powers; and even so, we now stand only on the threshold of what one prophet has called the era of "neotechnics." In doing so, to be sure, we have left behind many of the fancies of our ancestors. It is those meanings, and only those, which we have "lost." Better than any previous generation we know what we are doing, and what is good for us.

9

Moreover, we have firmer ground for hope than any previous generation has ever had, precisely because of the technological threshold on which we now clearly see that we are standing. Men have always sought security, or, as Dewey called it, certainty. They have always dreamed of better things; and if they could see no hope of better things in this world—for themselves, but even more for their children and their children's children—they have dreamed of other worlds beyond pearl-studded gates, where the streets would be paved with gold, and milk and honey would flow in the gutters. It is only since the effects of the great technological revolution of modern times began to be apparent that boldly imaginative men began to catch sight of the possibility of general abundance here and now. Beginning only a little more than a century and a half ago a whole series of utopian prophecies and schemes began to appear, to the great alarm of the more sober-minded members of the community.

For it has always been quite apparent that in order for abundance to be generally shared substantial modification of the prevailing institutional patterns would be necessary. Indeed, the dreams and prophecies of the late eighteenth and early nineteenth centuries were inspired not only by the steam engine and power-driven machinery but also by the American and French revolutions. Thus long before the time of Karl Marx "the conventional wisdom" (as Professor J. K. Galbraith has called it, in *The Affluent Society*) turned its face firmly away from all such utopianism. Not that such reactionaries as Malthus and John Stuart Mill were hard-hearted characters: quite the contrary was the case. But such men reacted against the new utopianism because, far more than they realized, the conventional wisdom with which their minds were learnedly saturated was a reflection of the prevailing institutional order.

That is still the case. As Professor Galbraith points out, our conventional wisdom still assumes that scarcity is the natural condition of mankind, to which Adam was condemned on the occasion of his expulsion from the Garden of Eden. Indeed, not only that: present-day exponents of the conventional wisdom still maintain that economic growth is possible at all only by virtue of the "involuntary saving" of the poor—that such affluence as we can achieve necessarily rests on the foundation of poverty.

Nevertheless, times change. Marx argued that the condition of "the working class" must inevitably grow progressively worse until the time came for a cataclysmic upheaval to destroy "the capitalistic system"; and that might indeed have been the case if the institutional patterns of Western society had proved obdurately unamenable to change. But such has not proved to be the case. The institutional flexibility which had already made it possible for the institution of property to supplant that of feudal fief continued to manifest itself, with the result that the condition of the common people has steadily improved.

Indeed, the whole attitude of the community has changed in this regard. One of the most important discoveries of modern times is the discovery that mass production requires a mass market, and that the adequacy of the mass market depends on the ability of the masses to buy the products of mass production. This idea, so obvious that it now seems almost axiomatic, has crept into the thinking of the modern community as gradually and anonymously as the idea of scarcity did in earlier times. Many eminent thinkers have given expression to it, but none more effectively than Gilbert Seldes in a single sentence which I have been quoting ever since: "The one luxury the rich cannot afford is the poverty of the poor." In order for the economy to operate at capacity, the steel industry must operate at capacity; and in order for the steel industry to operate at capacity, its principal customer, the automobile industry, must operate at capacity; and in order for the automobile industry to sell five or six million cars a year there must be each year five or six million people who are willing and able to buy new cars; and in order for them to do so there must be millions more who are willing and able to buy used cars of various ages. In short, our affluence rests not on poverty but on participation by the whole community in the benefits of industrial production. The conventional wisdom still persists in official pronouncements and academic lucubrations. But the axiom on which we actually operate is that of general participation.

And what is true of abundance is true of all real values, which indeed are indissociable from abundance as they are indissociable from each other. Freedom is a necessary condition to the attainment of abundance, and abundance is a necessary condition to the attainment of freedom. Freedom is possible only among equals, and equality is possible only when men are free from arbitrary social distinctions. These values are attainable only when men have achieved a measure of security; and real security is possible only when men have achieved a measure of abundance and a reasonable prospect of its continuance. But it is also possible only for those who enjoy freedom among equals; for any other condition

293

implies a threat of insecurity. And the same is true of the highest achievements of the human spirit. The golden ages of mankind have invariably been periods of relative prosperity enjoyed by communities which had in some measure thrown off the shackles of their institutional past. Only free men can know excellence, and only affluent societies can afford to indulge in such pursuits. But only through excellence can societies become affluent.

Such is the industrial way of life. It is a way of life to which modern man has dedicated himself because it is the epitome of the real values which take their meaning from the life process of mankind. And its supreme value is hope—a hope, warranted by past achievements—of a far better life next year for ourselves, in the next century for our children's children, and in the next millennium for all mankind.

INDEX

"ceremonial adequacy": and technological efficiency, 130, 136

ceremonialism: Veblen on, 30 ff.; origin of, 31; defined, 77 ff., 132 ff.; obsession with, 81 ff.; and symbolic process, 93 ff.; as aspect of mores complex, 131 ff.; imitates technology, 131 ff.; arts originate in, 150 ff.; in personal morality, 265 ff.; and democracy, 283

Cézanne, Paul: 151, 153

Chaminade, Cécile: 153

change as feature of modern life: 274 ff.

chaplains, incident of: 141 ff.

Chartres, Cathedral of: 248

Chopin, Frédéric: 153

Christianity and capitalism: 280 ff.

Clark, J. M.: 262

classes in Western society, 192–193. *See also* status

coercion, freedom from: 171 ff.

colonialism: waning of, 205; as check on abundance, 232

Condorcet, Marquis de: 242

conformity, bogey of: 255 ff.

consumption: as "end," 66, 229, 245

consumption, aggregate: importance of, 226; as controlling factor, 239–293

continuum: of means and ends, 115–116; of science, 120; of moral values, 155 ff.

Copernicus, Nicholas: 44, 71, 198

corporation as form of property: 193 ff.

craftsmanship: supposed superiority of, 251; supposed decline of, 260 ff.

cultural relativism: theory of, 21 ff., 47 ff.; as cultural hedonism, 67 ff.; as product of ceremonialism, 82

culture: concept of, 74 ff., 91; and society, 76 ff.; material and nonmaterial, 78 ff.; polarization of, 49 ff., 76 ff., 89 ff.; contacts and conflicts, 165 ff.; and moral dedication, 288 ff.

Darwinism, 26, 44, 47, 60, 63, 67, 71 ff., 82, 87, 123, 134, 198, 243, 259

Dead Sea scrolls: 197

death, moral significance of: 34, 158

Declaration of Independence, and equality: 188

dedication: significance of, 141 ff.; and culture, 288 ff.

democracy: efficiency of, 8; and freedom, 184 ff.; meaning of, 281 ff.

"Descartes effect": exemplifies feedback, 58

destruction, world: probability of, 215 ff.

Dewey, John: influence of, 29 ff.; cited, 44, 98, 115, 116, 258; and "quest for certainty," 207, 208, 220, 291; instrumentalism of, 277

disease, security from: 211 ff.

divine right of kings: 173 ff.

dreams and superstition: 97–98

dualism of mind and body as feedback: 58

dumping to reduce abundance: 231

Durkheim, Emile: 208

economic individualism: and moral agnosticism, 24 ff., 45 ff.; classical theory of, 63 ff.; and freedom, 177 ff. *See also* individualism

economic planning: and moral agnosticism, 26

economics: and values, 6 ff., 27 ff.; classical theory of, 63 ff.; and doctrine of scarcity, 235 ff.; and industrial revolution, 280–281

education: and logic of social organization, 222; and democracy, 283 ff.

efficiency: and value, 8; and ceremonial adequacy, 130, 136; of democracy, 284. *See also* teamwork; technology; social organization

Einstein, Albert: 113, 258

Eliot, T. S.: 153

elite: theory of the, and excellence, 251 ff.; statistical theory of, 253 ff.

emotion: evidentiality of, 31, 53 ff.; evoked by mores, 129 ff.; in the life of reason, 139 ff.; in science and technology, 144 ff.; in the arts, 147 ff.; in moral values, 155 ff.; and need for myths, 208 ff.

emotional conditioning: as source of values, 18, 22 ff.; feedback effect of, 32, 53 ff., 83; and origin of emotion, 159; and war, 218 ff.

Index

ends: defined with *means*, 65 ff.; and consumption, 66, 229, 245; continuum and harmony of, 114 ff.

equality: defined: 187; and individual differences, 187 ff.; and feudalism, 189 ff.; and property, 191 ff.; and enlightenment, 195 ff.; and service industries, 199 ff.; and gadgetry, 202–203; and abundance, 240–241; and democracy, 282 ff.

Epictetus: 110, 175

esthetic values: 147 ff.

excellence: compatibility of, with abundance, 240, 247 ff.; fallacies of comparison of, 248, 257 ff.; and ancestor worship, 248 ff., 257 ff.; and mass production, 250 ff.; elite theory of, 251 ff.; and the statistical illusion, 252 ff.; and conformity, 255 ff.; and wisdom, 257 ff.; and supposed decline of craftsmanship, 260 ff.

existentialism: 208, 290 ff.

expediency, in personal morality: 269–270

expense-account racket: and equality, 194–195

expropriation of foreign investments: 232

false values. *See* mores; ceremonialism; myths; superstition; values, false

famine: security from, 211

fantasies: 18 ff.; and ceremonialism, 31; as fictitious causation, 50 ff. *See also* folklore, myths, superstition

fashions in ideas: 13 ff.

feedback effect: in emotional conditioning, 32, 53 ff., 83; and natural order, 60 ff.; in symbolic process, 94; in mores, 129

fetishes: distinguished from tools, 135

feudalism: and natural rights, 173 ff.; and industrial revolution, 179 ff.; and equality, 189 ff.

folklore: and mores, 127 ff. *See also* ceremonialism; fantasies; mores; myths; superstition

folkways: and mores, 126 ff.

food: as value, 32

foreign investment: and abundance, 231 ff.

France, Anatole: 99

Frazer, Sir James: 82

freedom: significance of; 33; of the will, 109 ff.; primitive conception of, 171 ff.; and individualism, 172 ff.; and natural rights, 173 ff.; and property, 174 ff.; as process, 176 ff.; and industrial revolution, 177 ff.; of the mind, 181 ff.; and abundance, 182; and the life process, 182; and democracy, 184 ff., 282 ff.

Freud, Sigmund: 19, 67, 83, 97

Fuller, Margaret: 18

functionalism in social theory: 20 ff., 47 ff., 64, 75, 125, 132–133

gadgetry: and equality, 202–203

Galbraith, J. K.: 239, 287, 292

Galileo: 44

Godwin, William: 242

Gordon-Childe, Verne: 15

Greece, wisdom of: 257–258

Grimm, J. L. C.: 82

Grimm, W. C.: 82

Guest, Edgar: 153

Gutenberg, Johann: 177, 180

Hamilton, Walton H.: influence of, 27 ff.

Haydn, F. J.: 248, 253, 254

Hearst press: 258

hedonism: 62 ff.

Helmholtz, H. L. F. von: 109

Henley, W. E.: 61

Hiroshima: 159

Hitler, Adolph: 24

Hobbes, Thomas: 76, 210

Höffding, Harald: 287

Homer: 178

human nature: and culture, 71 ff.

humanism: 118 ff.

humanist revival: 179

Hume, David: 109

Huxley, Thomas: 90, 92, 117, 128

incest: and moral values, 156 ff.

individualism: as manifestation of feedback effect, 59 ff.; and freedom, 172 ff. *See also* economic individualism

297

Index

Mont St. Michel, Abbey of: 248
moral agnosticism: 24, 39 ff.; prevalence of, 41 ff.
"moral" values: of "private" life, 155 ff., 265 ff.; continuum of, 155 ff.
mores: significance of, 125 ff.; aspects of, 126; based on myths, 126 ff.; in personal morality, 265 ff. *See also* ceremonialism; myths; status
Morgan, Lewis H.: 73
Morley, E. W.: 113
Mozart, W. S.: 147, 148, 248, 253, 254
mystery, sense of: 16 ff.; impedes technology, 95 n.; originates in symbolic process, 95 ff.; suffuses culture, 288
myths: as basis of mores, 125 ff.; imply causality, 129 ff.; inherently false, 130. *See also* ceremonialism; folklore; mores; superstition
Nagasaki: 159
Napoleon: 136
natural order and feedback effect: 60 ff. *See also* uniformities of nature
natural rights: and freedom, 173 ff.
nature, uniformities of: as determinant of truth and value, 51, 113 ff.; as basis of science and technology, 92, 93, 106 ff., 113; and human freedom, 109 ff.; implied in ceremonalism, 133; and democratic unanimity, 284
numerals, Hindu-Arabic: and industrial revolution, 179, 181
operational logic: 278. *See also* science; technology; social organization; reality; truth; value
operational theory of value. *See* value
Pareto, Vilfredo: 283
Parthenon: 151
Pavlov, I. P.: 89, 90
peace: factors making for, 217 ff.
personality: cult of, 118 ff.; adjustment of, to large-scale organization, 221
Phidias: 151
Pirenne, Henri: 59
"planned parenthood": and the population problem, 244
Plato: 33, 95, 96, 99, 178, 258, 259
plutocracy: and equality, 192 ff.

polarization of culture: 49 ff., 76 ff., 89 ff.
Polynesians: 95, 134
Pope, Alexander: 267
population growth: limits abundance, 241 ff.
Price, Don K.: 185, 217
pride of craft: supposed decline of, 260 ff.
printing: and industrial revolution, 177 ff.; and enlightenment, 196–197
probability: and total destruction, 215 ff.
property, institution of: as vehicle of freedom, 174 ff.; evolution of, 191 ff.; corporate form of, 193 ff.; as social security, 225 ff.
psychiatry: on emotional conditioning, 19; on importance of childhood, 67, 83; on esthetic catharsis, 153; concern of, with sex, 156; and warlike emotions, 218 ff.
purpose: meaning of, 109 ff.
Pythagoras: 151
Raphael: 151
RCA: 255
reality, operational theory of: 105 ff.
reasonable society: steps toward, 16; possibility of, 32; promise of, 290 ff.
Reformation, Protestant: and origin of capitalism, 279 ff.
reification: and superstition, 97 ff., 131
relativism, cultural. *See* cultural relativism
religion: as defined by anthropologists, 129; and capitalism, 280 ff.
Renaissance: 179
revolution, industrial. *See* industrial revolution
Ricardo, David: 6
Riemann, G. F. B.: 113
rites: as function of mores, 131 ff. *See also* ceremonialism
Robinson, Jackie: 136
Roman Empire: and the industrial revolution, 178 ff.
Rossini, G. A.: 57
Rousseau, J. J.: 76, 88, 89, 175, 210
Royal Society: 174
Salk, Jonas: 212

DATE DUE

GAYLORD			PRINTED IN U.S.A